D0265769

Competitive
and
Corporate Strategy

Cliff Bowman
Senior Lecturer in Strategic Management
Cranfield School of Management

David Oakley Faulkner
Tutorial Fellow in Management, Christ Church
Oxford University Lecturer in Management Studies
(Strategic Management)
Oxford

IRWIN

London Chicago Bogotá Boston Buenos Aires Caracas Madrid Mexico City Sydney Toronto

Publisher	Cathy Peck
Project Manager	Peter Harrison
Development Editor	Alison Taylor
Designer	Lara Last
Layout Artist	Jonathan Brenchley
Illustration	Lee Smith
Cover Illustration	Danny Pyne
Production	Susan Walby
Index	Cliff Bowman

Published in 1997 by Richard D. Irwin Books, an imprint of Times Mirror International Publishers Limited

Printed by Arrowsmith

ISBN 0 2562 1423 9

For full details of all Times Mirror International Publishers Limited titles, please write to Times Mirror International Publishers Limited, Lynton House, 7–12 Tavistock Square, London WC1H 9LB, England.

A CIP catalogue record for this book is available from the British Library.

Library of Congress Cataloging-in-Publication Data applied for.

Contents

External Analysis

External Analysis

v

vi

vii

Preface

Competitive and Corporate Strategy emerged out of discussions between the authors while they were teaching the MBA at Cranfield School of Management and conducting top management team strategy workshops with a variety of medium and large sized companies.

Following an impulse to record our developing thoughts as to how to conceptualize, plan and implement strategy we developed the two primary tools in this book, the customer matrix and producer matrix, as devices for capturing the strategic problem at the market level and clarifying the internal strengths of the competing companies.

We subsequently became interested in strategy at the corporate level, and developed an approach that involved seeing corporate problems through a lens focused at the competitive level. As our thinking developed, however, we came to address the corporate problems of selecting, resourcing and controlling businesses as discrete but interlinked areas of interest. All these processes have culminated in the writing of this book.

We are well aware that approaches to strategy in the mid 1990s have moved away from the apparent certainties of the early 1980s and that it is now fashionable to produce books comparing and contrasting the various strategic approaches. We have deliberately avoided doing this.

This book is intended to appeal to both students of strategy and practitioners, and to provide a set of approaches and tools that we have found valuable in our teaching and our consultancy to simplify the messy complexity of real life and give it a coherent framework. Whilst not entirely a textbook or a book intended to develop one single theme, it has some aspects of both. The tools we present are of the nature of frameworks which help to organize data, rather than models which purport to lead to accurate predictions of the future.

We know that these techniques help the strategy debate, but we accept that they can be improved and that they will ultimately evolve into something different. At present, however, we are happy to stand up and be counted using them.

We have used 'he' in the book. We tried other ways of tackling the problem of male bias (he/she; s/he; they; alternating 'he' and 'she') but we felt that, in the interests of readability, we should use 'he'.

We would like to thank Elaine Parocki and Véronique Ambrosini for their valuable help in preparing the manuscript.

Cliff Bowman/David Faulkner
1996

Introduction

Setting the strategic direction for a business is the most complex task facing any top management team. The complexity arises for a variety of reasons that are peculiar to strategy making:

- Strategy is about the future, which is unknown and unknowable.
- There are many paths that a firm could follow.
- Firms operate in dynamic competitive environments.

But because strategy making involves people, complexity is compounded:

- Each executive involved has his/her own views and motives, which may or may not be explicit.
- In deciding strategy, individuals are constrained by their past experiences, taken-for-granted assumptions, biases and prejudices.

There are ways of dealing with these layers of complexity. One is to avoid the problem of strategy altogether by running the business on an ad hoc, day-to-day basis. This can work as long as the things the firm is doing continue to be relevant to the markets it operates within. Another might be to engage in some form of longer-term planning, which can be a more or less elaborate process: at the simpler end of the spectrum, planning can be merely a form of extended budgeting. Elaborate planning systems would involve scenario building, extensive market, competitor and company analysis, option generation, evaluation and selection of strategy, and detailed action plans, budgets and control systems. Planning processes do not eliminate complexity, but they can provide a structured way of coping with an uncertain future.

Complexity can be dealt with by deciding on a broad view of what the organization should look like some time in the future; this can be captured in a mission, core values or other visionary statement of intent, and in allowing people to evolve strategies within these broad guidelines. This approach might be favoured in organizations facing turbulent environments.

We believe that a sense of strategy is an important component in the management of successful businesses. A shared understanding of where the firm is trying to go can be liberating and empowering. Some view of where and how the firm is trying to compete gives confidence to managers from the top downwards. It assists managers in making resourcing decisions, and it can instil a sense of purpose. Because the future is uncertain it is impossible to rationally analyse the firm's situation in a way that produces a single *correct* strategy for the business. However, we believe that, faced with uncertainty and complexity, *some* sense of direction is better than *no* sense of direction. However, we should take heart from the fact that a 'right answer' is not attainable. A well thought-through and well argued strategy will not necessarily be the *optimal* strategy for the business, and there may be several viable alternatives, each with their advantages and disadvantages. Nevertheless a shared and agreed view of where we are trying to take the firm is an essential ingredient for the successful management of *today's* activities.

Strategy making can be approached from a descriptive and theoretical perspective. Recently, a number of excellent academic textbooks have ably set out the issues involved, and have comprehensively reflected the ever widening range of theoretical perspectives that have been brought to bear on strategic management. Insights from economics have now been augmented and sometimes contradicted by contributions from cognitive psychology, anthropology, organization sociology and political theory. We are now far more aware of the problems of rational planning and why it often does not lead to successful change.

However, this book does not set out to be a comprehensive text. Although we recognize the complexities involved in strategy making, and that there are strong inertial forces constraining organizational change, we are also aware that, in spite of these problems, senior managers have to make strategic decisions. They are not in the comfortable position of an academic observer, who whilst being able to point out how complex everything is, can always walk away from the problem. The essence of senior management work is to wrestle with the problems of strategy. So, although we are aware of these important theoretical insights and developments – and we have incorporated some of these perspectives in our approach – at the end of the day this book is for people who have to strategize. The concepts, models and techniques we explain should be regarded as tools for thought. None of them gives the right answer to the strategy problem. They are designed to help executives *structure* a strategy debate; they do not take the place of the debate!

The tools and techniques we use have evolved over the last decade. Some are slight adaptations of existing methods; others have been newly created to address a particular problem encountered in facilitating strategy debates with top teams. All the tools have been used with, and developed with, top teams. We have found that the tools help focus and structure debates in helpful ways. Benefits are derived from the thinking and discussion involved in applying the tools, as well as from the insights generated through the analysis. None of the techniques is a substitute for the exercise of judgement. The techniques covered force important questions to be asked which are not routinely discussed. This prompts a search for better information, for example on customers' real needs, and it usually provokes a more critical evaluation of the firm's situation.

So, whilst we recognize the complexities of strategizing we also recognize that it has to be done. Rather than walk away from the problem, shaking our heads and marvelling in a detached manner at the richness, depth and layers of subtlety involved, we instead have derived a practical response. The aim is not to help managers to craft the perfect strategy. That is impossible. The aim of our book is to help people confronted with strategic responsibilities to find an understandable and workable way to address these challenges.

OVERVIEW OF THE APPROACH

This book makes a clear distinction between strategy at business level, and corporate level strategy. This distinction is made in order to simplify the arguments we shall make. However, although other writers in the field make a similar distinction, most continue to treat the two levels of strategy as involving separate, and unrelated issues. We take a different view. We believe that corporate level strategy needs to be addressed from a competitive strategy perspective, since ultimately it is generally the business units that make the profit and not the corporation. A corporate group can be very successful through the business unit's efforts, without the corporate staff ever seeing any of the firm's products, or meeting a customer, distributor or supplier, let alone a competitor. Nevertheless the corporate officers have important work to do in the areas of selecting, resourcing and controlling business units, as will be described later.

Therefore, in structuring this book we have focused on business level competitive strategy in the first half of the book, and then used many of the ideas and insights gained at business level to inform our exploration of corporate level strategy.

3

COMPETITIVE STRATEGY: SOME BASIC PRINCIPLES

The overriding strategic issue at the level of an individual business unit or firm is how the firm can gain advantage over competing firms. This is not a new argument. However, there is a great deal of confusion in the competitive strategy literature that stems largely from two different economics-based traditions. On the one hand there are theories of competitive strategy that derive from industrial organization (IO) economics (Caves and Porter, 1977; Caves, 1980; Porter, 1980, 1985). In these theories, superior profits stem from the structure of the industry. Where firms face few competitors, and where it is difficult for firms to enter the industry, the incumbent firms should make reasonable profits. An individual firm's profit performance can be further enhanced where it can successfully implement a strategy of either cost leadership or differentiation; these are Michael Porter's **generic strategies**. The lowest-cost producer in an industry must earn above-average profits if he prices at industry-average levels. Above-average profits can also be achieved where the firm can successfully differentiate its products. Here, superior profits are generated because the successful differentiator can charge premium prices.

More recently, a competing school of thought which focuses attention on the firm's unique resources has emerged. This resource-based theory (Wernerfelt, 1984; Barney, 1991) holds that above-average profits stem from resources controlled by the firm that not only combine to deliver valued products, but that are also difficult for other firms to imitate or acquire.

We explore these two approaches in more depth in Chapter 3. There are strengths and weaknesses to both approaches. What we have constructed in this book is an argument which suggests that both the IO approach and resource-based theory are incomplete. In reality it is necessary to understand both the competitive structure of the market and the firm's resource base if viable and sustainable strategies are to be formulated.

In this introductory chapter we set out the basic building blocks of our approach. These foundations are then built upon in subsequent chapters. We begin by explaining our definitions of value. We start here because there is a good deal of confusion in the strategy field stemming from differing and unclear uses of this crucial concept.

SOME BUILDING BLOCKS

Value is Defined by the Customer

Value is used to mean many different things in the strategy literature. The value of a product or a service is defined by the perceptions that a customer has of the usefulness of the product. In judging value, the customer is assessing the extent to which his or her needs can be met by a given product. We call this definition of value **perceived use value**.

Total Value (TV) is a Product of Perceived Use Value and the Customer's Willingness to Pay

Total value is the amount the customer is *prepared* to pay for the product or the service. This will, in most cases, exceed the price the customer pays. Economists call this difference between the amount the customer is prepared to pay and price **consumer surplus**. Thus, our definition of total value is **price + consumer surplus**.

Total Value is Made up of Two Types of Perceived Use Value: Hygiene Value and Motivator Value

This distinction is based on Hertzberg's two-factor theory of job satisfaction. **Hygiene value** refers to those elements of the product or service that all competitors offer. These are the standard **order qualifying** product or service aspects that every firm has to provide just to be a credible player in the game. In order to win some customers, the firm needs to offer **motivator value**. These dimensions of perceived use value are not generally offered, and they would tend to be unique to a particular firm. These motivator values excite customers, and are the sources of differentiation. So, for example, consider a short management course in strategy. Hygiene value would include comfortable accommodation, appropriate refreshments, acceptable course documentation. Motivator value may comprise the presence of a leading industrialist on the programme, or a stunning location for the course, or a brilliant team of lecturers.

Total Value can only be Increased by Increasing Motivator Value

There is no point in increasing the level of qualities that are not order winning, *i.e.*, hygiene factors, as the customer expects those anyway, and only notices if they are absent.

The Power Relationship between the Firm and the Customer Determines who Captures the Lion's Share of Total Value

If customers can choose between many equally-attractive products, they have greater power, and they can extract a lower price. Therefore, the proportion of total value accounted for by consumer surplus would be high. Alternatively, if a firm is able to offer large amounts of motivator value which other firms cannot offer, then they should be able to bid up their price and capture a large portion of total value.

5

Motivator Value Migrates into Hygiene Value through Competitive Imitation

As firms seek to attract customers, they may try to offer motivator value that their competitors are offering. As soon as more than one firm is able to offer these dimensions of value they cease to be motivators, and they migrate to form part of the standard package of hygiene value. This is a continuous process.

The Firm's Activities can be Classified into those that Deliver Motivator Value, and those that Deliver Hygiene Value

Activities that deliver hygiene value dimensions should be managed for lowest costs. Activities associated with the delivery of motivator value dimensions, both now and in the future, should be managed to maximize their effectiveness, but without giving their costs free reign.

Normally, only Motivator Activities can Generate Surpluses.

Hygiene activities can, at best, only pass on their costs to the customer. Therefore, if there is a continuous migration of use value from motivator value into hygiene value, then unless firms are able to create new motivator values they will eventually cease to earn surpluses. Thus, firms need to continually invest in motivator activities. This requires them being able to anticipate future perceived use values, and to manage the relevant activities to achieve excellence in differentiation.

Hygiene activities may well be subcontracted as they become less strategically significant. If hygiene activities are performed at above lowest-feasible cost they actually destroy profits, because their additional costs cannot be passed on to the customer.

Hence, therefore, our argument is a dynamic one. The process of motivator-value migration through competitive imitation is continuous. No firms can have a sustainable competitive advantage in the long-term, unless it is contained in the ability to learn faster than their competitors. They can, however, strive to continually seek new sources of advantage by trying to identify future perceived use values, and by developing the motivator activities to deliver those values.

As motivator activities migrate into hygiene activities, the firm may need to redefine the core of its business. For example, when Boeing developed the 737, the majority of the airframe was developed and built in-house. For the Boeing 777, the company has focused its attention on the front fuselage, the tail plane and fins, and some parts of the wings. The bulk of the rest of the plane has been subcontracted. So, firms have choices about the scope of the value domain. By value domain, we mean the areas which the firm chooses to tackle directly as these are areas in which they believe they can add real value. Similarly, the proportion of BP Oil's upstream activities that they choose to do in-house has been drastically reduced over the last fifteen years. They have focused on the core activities that they believe are critical to developing competitive advantage.

One of the most difficult challenges facing firms stems from the pressure to deliver short-term performance. Short-term profits can be boosted most easily by cost cutting. Whilst this may be appropriate where hygiene activities are concerned, it is a potential disaster where the axe falls on motivator activities. The problem is compounded where the management of the firm is unclear about what the motivator activities are. So, if we return to our business-school example, pressures for short-term performance might lead to cuts in research funding, programme development and in marketing budgets. These may well have serious effects on the school's ability to compete in the future. Part of the reason why these budgets and activities appear more susceptible to cost cutting is that they are perceived to have only a tenuous link to the firm's bottom line. A more sophisticated analytical appreciation of the sources of surpluses would reveal the critical motivator activities, and one hopes, this would lead to them being protected. The future of the firm depends ultimately on them.

However, where motivator activities have been neglected, the firm may end up in a situation which is not recoverable. They then face a messy end-game, where they can only deliver hygiene value, and in order to attract any customers they have to undercut competitors on price.

So, our basic argument concerning competitive strategy recognizes the customer's definition of value. Total value can be estimated by discovering the amount customers would be prepared to pay for a product. In highly-competitive markets, where customers are facing a huge choice of products, customers should be able to capture most of total value, *i.e.*, the proportion of total value made up by consumer surplus will be large. Thus, there is little differentiation, and firms have few advantages to deliver, *i.e.*, the proportion of motivator value in total value is very small.

Alternatively, where customers perceive that there is only one product that really meets their needs, then the power balance shifts to the firm; price will then form a large part of total value, and motivator value forms a large proportion of total value. This is where firms are able to generate surplus revenues over their competitors.

These processes of competitive imitation and innovation determine the relative performance of competing firms. The absolute levels of surplus earned by all competitors is determined by the wider environment. Changes in the wider environment affect the number of customers that demand a given package of perceived use value, and the amounts of money they are prepared to pay for it.

Clearly, managers face considerable problems in coping with the complexities of strategy. The argument developed here assumes a firm producing a single product. This is rarely the case as most firms produce a range of products. However, the basic arguments are the same, although complexity is increased where activities involved contribute to more than one product.

7

CORPORATE STRATEGY

Moving from the single-product case to a multi-product situation involves the same issues as moving from business-level strategy to corporate-level strategy. Although the complexity of the problem is compounded by the scope and volume of differing products, the fundamental issues are the same. If we view corporate-level strategy through our competitive-strategy lens, we would then need to explore the extent to which being part of a corporation helps a business to compete more effectively. This is the basic approach we take in Part II of the book.

The way in which the corporate centre seeks to add value is to carry out effectively the three key tasks of selecting, resourcing and controlling:

■ **Selecting** involves determining in which product/markets it should operate; such decisions to be based on the degree to which corporate-wide and business-unit competences match those required for success in particular markets.

■ **Resourcing** involves ensuring that the existing business units have appropriate means to do their job, and ensuring through strategic alliances, mergers and acquisitions that any perceived deficiencies in this regard are made good.

■ **Controlling** involves setting up and operating a corporate structure and systems to avoid the development of internal inefficiencies in the corporation, and to ensure high levels of motivation and performance. Corporate strategy is dealt with in Part II of the book since we argue that it follows from competitive strategy rather than precedes it, much as Mintzberg (1979) argues that the multi-divisional organization follows from the successful development of the simple organization.

THE STRUCTURE OF THE BOOK

The basic argument set out above provides the underpinning for the structure of the book. We elaborate the customer-driven definition of value through the **customer matrix** (Chapter 2). This device, with its axes of perceived use value and perceived price can be used to locate competing products in a market segment. This positioning requires a sophisticated understanding of the dimensions of perceived use value, how customers weight them, and how they try to evaluate them. We use the customer matrix to explore the consequences of various competitive manoeuvres: cutting price, adding perceived use value, and premium pricing.

We then explore the internal aspects of the firm through a second device: the **producer matrix** (Chapter 3). This matrix has axes of **key competences**, defined as those competences required to be an effective player in the market segment under consideration, and unit costs. This matrix helps us to understand the internal implications of a firm wishing to reposition itself in the customer matrix. Competences are made up of activities, both hygiene and motivator, and these in turn are combinations of resources, systems and know-how. In this chapter we examine the aspects of a firm's activities that deliver motivator values, and that are more difficult for other firms to imitate. Systems and know-how that deliver motivator value, and that are difficult to imitate, give the firm some respite from competition. However, these advantages will inevitably be eroded as other firms acquire or replicate these resources. In Chapter 4 we combine the customer and producer matrices through an exploration of five strategic pathways that a firm could pursue.

We then turn our attention to the competitive structure of the market segment (Chapter 5). This helps us to identify demand and supply conditions, and to explore who captures the lion's share of total value. Total value is shared between the customer, the firm and resource suppliers. Who gets what proportion of total value is affected by the power relationships between these three groupings. We explore shifts of power between these groups.

Staying at the level of the individual firm or business unit, we then consider issues of strategy implementation. Chapter 6 explores the links between strategy and organizational structure. Chapter 7 examines the cultural dimensions of the organization, and in Chapter 8 we draw on Chapters 6 and 7 in an exploration of the processes of strategic change.

In Part II of the book we consider how the corporate centre can add value to the activities of the business units. After an introductory explanation of the approach (Chapter 9) we consider the three, key, corporate-level tasks of selecting (Chapters 10 and 11), resourcing (Chapters 12 and 13), and controlling (Chapter 14). A number of tools are explained, notably the risk and portfolio cubes and the make–buy–ally matrix for the selection process; systems for the resourcing task of carrying out merger–acquisition activity and for setting up strategic alliances and the various management styles for the controlling task. Finally, we discuss two quite distinct corporate strategy concerns, namely, how best to deal with the unpredictable nature of the future (Chapter 15), and how to configure and coordinate the corporation to go global (Chapter 16).

chapter 2

The Customer Matrix

In this chapter we introduce the customer matrix, one of the two basic devices that we use to explore competitive strategy. This matrix is derived from the perceptions that customers have of the products/services offered to them, and the prices that they are being charged. The vertical axis of Figure 2.1 (perceived use value, or PUV) refers to the value perceived by the buyer in purchasing and using the product or the service; the horizontal axis is perceived price (PP). Perceived use value and perceived price represent the two components of **value for money**, and the customer matrix separates these to assist us in analysing competitive strategy. They are distinct in that one is received by the customer (PUV) in exchange for the other (PP). Perceived use value is a similar concept to the economist's **utility**. Perceived price refers to the elements of price with which the customer is concerned. For example, in purchasing a heating system for a house the customer may not be concerned only with the initial cost of the installation (the price of the boiler, radiators, fitting) but may also be interested in the running costs of the system over the years (fuel costs, maintenance *etc.*). Perceived use values are the benefits the customer gains from the transaction, and perceived price is the cost incurred by the customer.

Figure 2.1
The customer matrix.

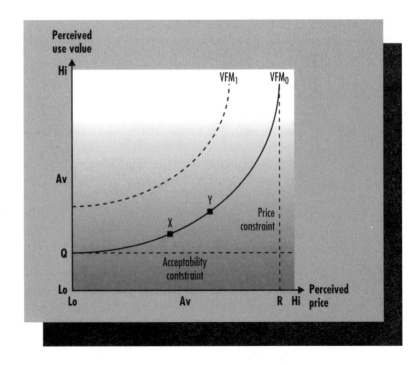

Before we explore the positioning of particular products within the matrix, and the implications of attempts to reposition products in the matrix, we need to elaborate on the customer perspective.

REPRESENTING THE CUSTOMER IN THE MATRIX

In a pure sense, a customer matrix can be derived only from the perceptions of a single individual. We would all have slightly different perceptions of the same collection of, say, family cars. What we would be looking for in terms of perceived use value, or utility, from the purchase of a car would be different from one customer to the next. The elements of price that we pay attention to would also vary. For example, one customer might regard insurance and running costs as a vital cost element, whereas another customer would be more concerned with initial purchase price, and the likely rate of depreciation over two years of ownership. How we individually assess alternative products will also vary. This means that, in trying to understand customer behaviour, we must be prepared to recognize that there may be important differences between potential customers. People don't all see things the same way, and inappropriate assumptions of homogeneity across large groups of buyers will lead to mistakes in competitive strategy.

In Figure 2.1 the solid curve depicts a set of combinations of perceived use value and perceived price that, in the eyes of a particular customer, represent equivalent amounts of value for money (VFM). In other words, the customer is indifferent to where he may lie on this curve. Point X on VFM_0 represents a combination of low levels of perceived use value and low price, whereas point Y combines higher levels of PUV with a higher price. Moving up or down this curve would not increase or decrease the levels of satisfaction experienced by the customer.

This value-for-money curve cuts the PUV axis at point Q. This represents the minimum acceptable level of PUV that the customer would tolerate – the **acceptability constraint**. The curve becomes vertical at a perceived price of R. This means that the customer is not prepared to pay more than R for the product or the service, no matter how high the level of PUV that is on offer. So point R is the customer's maximum-price constraint.

Any curve positioned to the left of this represents higher levels of value for money (VFM). So, the customer is continually seeking to move to higher curves, *e.g.*, curve VFM_1. Moves up or down the same VFM curve represent equivalent levels of value for money, and curves to the right of the existing curve represent lower levels of value for money.

The more price sensitive the customer is, the more steeply the VFM curve slopes. The less price sensitive customer would have a more shallow curve over the same price range (see Figure 2.2).

11

Figure 2.2
Price sensitivity on the value-
for-money curve.

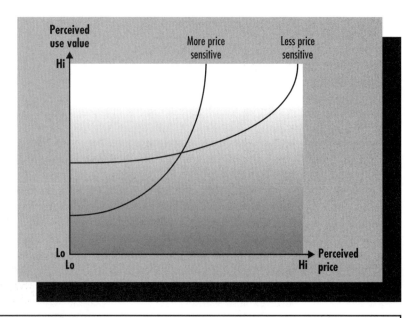

SEGMENTS OF DEMAND

A segment of demand is a group of customers who have similarly-shaped VFM curves. This means that their perceptions of value and their underlying needs are likely to be very similar. Within a segment there will be customers who are more or less price sensitive than the average customer. In order to develop a customer matrix it is necessary to identify a discrete segment of demand; that is, a group of potential customers who share similar needs, and have similar perceptions of use value. A segment, thus defined, might include a quite disparate collection of people. What they share is a set of preferences and similar perceptions as to which use values meet their underlying needs.

When trying to construct a customer matrix it can be helpful to have in mind a particular individual who might fairly-well represent a segment of demand. We have found that approaching the problem in this way reduces the risks of making inappropriate generalizations. At the end of the chapter we explain how a matrix can be constructed.

In Figure 2.3 product positions are represented by points. The points represent the perceptions that an 'average' customer in this segment would have of each of the products perceived to be on offer. The ellipses surrounding each product point represent all customers' perceptions in the segment. We could regard these as **product footprints**. Clearly there is a good deal of variability in customer perceptions of these three products. Perceptions of the perceived use values of products are likely to be more variable than perceptions of price. Variations in perceptions of PUV are caused by:

■ Customers having different underlying needs.
■ Customers having different weightings of the dimensions of perceived use value that could meet those needs, *i.e.*, although

12

Figure 2.3
Product footprints on the
customer matrix.

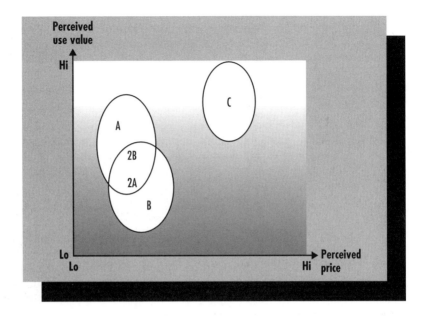

customers might value both styling and performance in a car,
some of them would rate styling as being more important than
performance.

■ Customers having different perceptions of a particular
product's attributes.

If there are wide variations in needs we may conclude that the
market should be further segmented. But, within a segment there
may still be differing perceptions of a product's relative position due
to differences in weightings of dimensions of PUV, and differences
in perceptions of a product's attributes.

In Figure 2.3, customer 2 perceives product B to have higher levels
of PUV than product A, although the average customer would rate
A as offering higher levels of PUV than B. As customer 2 perceives
both products to have the same perceived prices, he would select
product B. This helps us to explain how a product in position A
would not necessarily achieve 100% share of the market. Product
C is seen by all customers as being a high PUV/high price offering.
In some markets, product footprints will be large, with considerable
overlapping. This is likely to occur in emerging markets, and in any
market where the customer is poorly-informed about the products
on offer. In contrast, we would expect commodity markets to display
very small footprints, as customers are likely to be well-informed
about the products available, and the perceived differences between
products will be small.

REPRESENTING PRODUCTS ON THE MATRIX

In order to develop our arguments about competitive strategy, we
shall simplify the customer matrix, so that we show only the positions
of products from the perspective of the 'average' customer. In Figure

13

Figure 2.4
Two basic strategies for
improving a product's position
on the customer matrix.

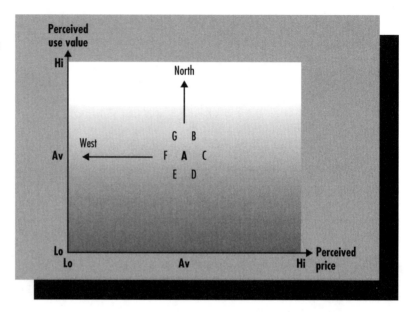

2.4 the letters A–G represent the positions of products in the matrix. In other words, a representative or average customer in this segment would perceive the products on offer to be grouped in this way. As far as this average customer is concerned, all the firms are offering more-or-less equivalent products, and are charging very similar prices. In other words, there is no real difference between the products on offer, as far as this representative customer is concerned. This situation can be found in many industries, not just those that are supplying obvious commodity products like gasoline or potatoes. In any circumstance where consumers perceive the products or services on offer to be more or less the same, the industry approximates to the circumstances depicted in Figure 2.4. This could be the case in, for example, the personal-computer hardware market, or in the choice of real-estate agents.

If firm A is facing the situation depicted in Figure 2.4, what are the options available for improving its competitive position? As things now stand in this industry, it is likely that all the firms will have a similar share of the market, so how can firm A improve its share? There are various moves that could be made in the chart which could improve the firm's competitive position. For example, the firm could cut price, or raise the perceived use value of the products or services it offers, or indeed do both at the same time. These two basic strategy options will now be explored.

CUTTING PRICE

Here the firm moves west in the customer matrix, offering the same perceived use value as the competition, but at a lower price (see Figure 2.4). Such a move should lead to firm A gaining share. However, this may depend on the type of products or services being offered, and on the likely reaction of competitors. In some markets, buyers perceive lower price to mean lower perceived use value. In other words, price is being used as an indirect way of measuring use value, where the customer reasons that 'if it's cheaper, it can't be as good as the others'. If this was the situation facing firm A then a cut in price would move the firm to the south west, to a position offering lower perceived use value at lower prices. The price cut might, then, lead to a disappointing result, where the expected sales increases did not materialize. Managers therefore need to be alert to this possibility. It often occurs where customers are unfamiliar with the purchase situation, and they seek to reduce the riskiness of the purchase by using price as a proxy for value, *e.g.*, when buying wine, dishwashers, cars.

Let us assume that consumers are not using price as a proxy measure of perceived use value, and that the price cut moves firm A due west on the chart. This move should increase sales for firm A and maybe in the industry as a whole, if new consumers are attracted into the market by the lower prices. However, other firms are likely to respond to the move by cutting prices to match firm A so as to preserve their share of the market, or they may even undercut firm A. The net result of the competitors moving west with firm A is to reduce average price and profitability in the industry.

Competitors can, therefore, imitate firm A's price cutting strategy very rapidly, overnight if necessary. How then can firm A hope to gain an enduring advantage from competing on price? In order to achieve a sustainable advantage, firm A must be able to continually drive down prices and be able to sustain lower prices for a longer period than its competitors. This can only be achieved if firm A has either the lowest costs in the industry, or if the firm is able to sustain losses for extended periods, through subsidies from another part of the corporation, or from the government for example. If a firm is not the lowest-cost producer, then the competitor that *is* lowest cost can always cut prices further, or sustain low prices for longer than firm A.

So, if a firm chooses to compete on price it needs to have lower costs than its competitors. This involves exploiting all sources of cost reduction that do not affect perceived use value, *e.g.*, economies of scale, learning from experience, right-first-time quality, just-in-time manufacturing. To be confident of achieving the lowest-cost position, the firm needs to have a clear picture of its own costs, and the costs of competitors. If a firm is able to achieve the lowest-cost position, it could choose to drive out competitors by sustaining very low prices. If, in the course of pursuing this strategy the firm is able to establish barriers to prevent other firms entering the industry it could then opt to raise prices, and hence profits, confident of its ability to see off any potential entrants. If not, however, a subsequent rise in price would lead to re-entry by previously defeated competitors and perhaps by other new entrants.

However, to be sure that the firm is *the* lowest cost producer it is necessary to be aware of the cost levels of competitors. Without cost information on competitors, the management cannot be confident

15

of achieving the lowest-cost position, and unfortunately, this information is usually difficult to obtain.

The risks of competing on price include the following:

- The firm may not be able to achieve the lowest costs in the industry. By definition, only one firm can be in this position.
- The first firm to compete by cutting prices is likely to provoke its competitors into matching its lower-price position as a defensive measure to protect market share. This could lead to a price war with margins for all but the low-cost players being cut to the bone.
- The emphasis on cost cutting encourages management to focus inwards onto the internal operations of the firm. This may mean that little attention is focused on changing trends, tastes and competitive behaviour in the market place.

This last point can lead to a vicious circle for the firm: the inward orientation results in the firm lagging behind changing trends in the market place; the firm's products become less competitive as they have lower perceived use value than the competition; this forces the firm into competing on price; which reinforces the inward, cost-cutting orientation. Ultimately, the firm in this situation may find itself having to offer larger and larger price discounts in order to persuade any consumers to tolerate its inferior products.

When markets are in decline either temporarily due to recession, or permanently due to changing customer needs, firms may find themselves forced to compete on price. But, as we have seen, unless a firm has low costs, preferably the lowest costs, it will inevitably struggle to remain profitable. This would suggest, therefore, that firms should aim to be low-cost whether or not they intend to compete on price, because market conditions outside their control may force them into price competition.

The firm needs to be low-cost compared to those firms the target customer perceives to be alternative providers of perceived use value. This may result in quite different definitions of competition from those typically made by managers and industry analysts, and they are likely to encompass few rather than many competitors. For example, if you are competing in the specialist sports car market you need to be low-cost in relation to other makers of specialist sports cars, not in relation to producers of family cars for the mass market.

If, as is likely, competitors follow the price cutter, this may cause the market as a whole to grow. This is because potential customers, who have similar needs and perceptions of use value, but who were excluded from the market because of high prices can now participate. Previously, their VFM curve turned vertical at a price that was lower than that of all products being offered.

ADDING PERCEIVED USE VALUE

The second basic strategy indicated in the customer matrix is the move north: gaining advantage through adding more perceived use value for the same price as the competitors' offerings. The starting point for this strategy must be the target customer, and the target customer's perceptions of value.

In order to effect this move north rather than it resulting from luck, or trial and error, we must be clear who our target customers are. We must then have a thorough understanding of the target customer's needs, and how that customer evaluates different product offerings (see Figure 2.4).

For example, in choosing a new car, the customer may have a basic need for flexible transportation. He also has other needs which can be expressed through the car he drives. For instance, meeting his status needs and need to belong, may be influential in his selection of a car: 'I wouldn't be accepted as a successful individual if I drove a shabby car'.

These basic needs are translated into a set of dimensions of use value, which are particular to the individual customer. Our status-conscious car buyer requires his car to represent a lifestyle to which he aspires, to deliver good performance, but, at the same time, the car needs to enable him to demonstrate his individuality, albeit within the boundaries of acceptability established by his status and need to belong. So, he is seeking a set of perceived use values that the car must fulfil, and he reasons that if these use values are delivered, his underlying needs will be met. In Figure 2.5 these dimensions of perceived use value are arranged in order of their

Figure 2.5
Perceived use value profile:
executive cars.

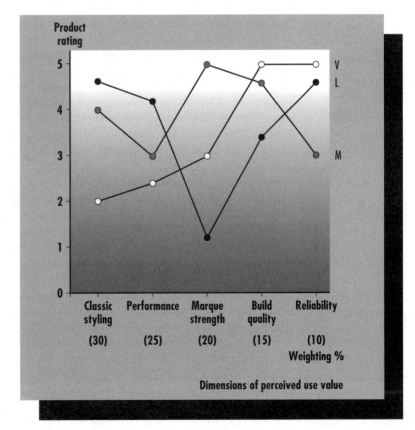

importance, with weightings in brackets, along the horizontal axis. The dimensions of PUV sought are: classic styling; performance; marque strength – which refers to the credibility and acceptability of the brand name; build quality; and reliability – it is important that the car doesn't break down. The strongest competitor in the industry has a benchmark of 5. V, L and M represent different competitive marques of car.

Figure 2.5 indicates that each of these dimensions of PUV is evaluated in some ways. The customer uses various criteria to evaluate the extent to which a particular product can deliver a particular dimension of PUV. For example, how is performance evaluated? For some customers acceleration is critical, and this is assessed by inspecting the 0–60 mph statistics; for others it is top speed that counts. More interestingly, how is build quality assessed? The customer may make inferences about build quality by interpreting the sound the car door makes when it is closed. Build quality might also be assessed by inspecting the alignment of body panels, or the paint finish. These may actually be very poor indicators, or proxy measures of build quality. However, as customer perceptions are paramount, it is essential that the firm understands what criteria the customer does use in making these evaluations, even if he is wrong!

We need to be aware of **substitute** products. Economists would describe a substitute as an alternative way of meeting the customer's needs. So, for instance, the need for up-to-date news on world affairs could be met by watching the news channels on TV, listening to radio, or reading a daily newspaper. There are dangers, however, in adopting narrow, product-driven definitions of competitive products. For example, a chain of pizza restaurants might see themselves as competing with other pizza restaurants: Pizza Hut, Pizza Express, Domino *etc*. But, from the perspective of an individual customer, this may be an inappropriate definition of the competition. Take a family with two hungry sons at midday driving past Burger King, McDonalds, Pizza Hut, and a Kentucky Fried Chicken outlets. These may all be direct competitors, and there is only one pizza restaurant among them!

By exploring customer needs and perceptions systematically through market research and by continually listening to customers, firms can discover what is valued in their products and services and what could be added to them to improve perceived use value. Diagrams like the one shown in Figure 2.5 can be constructed to establish the important dimensions of perceived use value for a particular segment.

It appears that product V is seen to be inferior to the competition on the important dimensions, but it performs well on the less-valued dimensions. If this firm is to move north in the customer matrix, then it either has to significantly shift the consumers' perceptions of its car's performance and styling, through changing the product, or maybe through changing perceptions through better advertising, or a more ambitious strategy might be to try to shift consumers' perceptions of the dimensions of use value. For example, it may be possible to persuade some people that reliability is more important than styling. Either way, unless the firm improves its position relative to the competition on these dimensions of perceived use value it will lag behind its competitors. In a below-average position in the customer matrix, the firm may find itself forced to cut price to try to preserve sales.

WHAT HAPPENS NEXT?

The key issue facing firms pursuing a strategy of adding perceived use value is the ease with which competitors can match their moves. As a firm moves north by increasing perceived use value ahead of its competitors, it should be rewarded with an increased share of the market. The duration of this enhanced position will depend on the ease with which the added perceived use value can be imitated. Over time, it is likely that competitors will be able to imitate the move north, and, as they follow the innovator northwards, the average level of perceived use value in the market is ratcheted upwards.

Thus, in most industries the minimum acceptable standards are being continuously shifted upwards as competitive moves become imitated; order-winning features become order-qualifying features. For instance, anti-lock brakes and air bags, features that were once order-winning, are now required just to be in the game.

In our introductory chapter we suggested that perceived use value is made up of hygiene value and motivator value dimensions as shown in Figure 2.6. Hygiene value refers to levels of perceived use value that all competing products need to offer just to be

19

Figure 2.6
Motivator value and hygiene value.

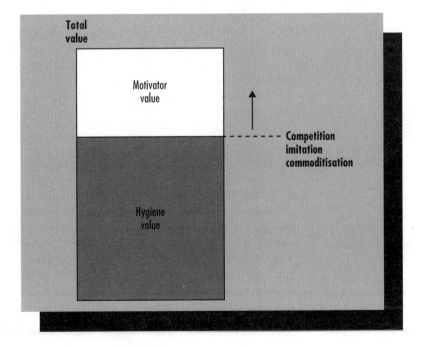

considered as a feasible alternative purchase by the customer. Motivator value refers to those qualities that a particular product offers which differentiates it, in the minds of some customers, from other products. Competing products will offer differing motivator values. Thus, although on average several products may offer equivalent amounts of perceived use value overall, this average perception masks subtle but important differences between groups of customers, and specific products. So, several firms may be able to survive in a particular product market because of small variations in what is valued by customers within the segment, *e.g.*, customer 2 in Figure 2.3.

When motivator value possessed by one product gets embodied into competing product offerings, it ceases to be a unique attribute. Hence, through competitive imitation, motivator value becomes hygiene value.

Thus, the issue of sustainability of competitive advantage needs to be considered against this backdrop of continual northward shifts in the competitive arena. What can the innovator do once the competition has caught up? There are two basic options: keep moving north by staying one jump ahead of the competition through innovation, or move west through a cut in price.

We argued earlier that, in order to compete on price, the firm needs to be the lowest-cost producer in the market. So, can you move north by adding perceived use value, and simultaneously achieve the lowest-cost position? If the move north increases market share, and if these share increases are translated into lower unit costs, through exploiting scale and experience advantages, then there is no reason why the move north could not result in a low relative cost position.

Furthermore, if you really understand what it is that customers perceive as value in your products or services, you can confidently strip out everything that does not feed through to perceived use value. There is no point in offering a range of costly options, if this is not really what customers want. Of course, if you are not confident about what customers' needs are and how they evaluate alternative products then, to play safe, the tendency is to leave everything in the product, because you are not sure which parts of the total package are the valued features.

OTHER MOVES IN THE CUSTOMER MATRIX

If the firm offers higher perceived use value, but demands a price premium for this added value, then this moves the firm's product position to the north-east in the matrix (see Figure 2.7). The success of this strategy depends upon the existence of a group of buyers, who are less price sensitive and so are prepared to pay higher prices for the added perceived value. It also depends upon the ease with which the added perceived use value can be imitated. If it can readily be imitated by competitors, then the price premium may be rapidly competed away.

Figure 2.7
Other competitive moves on
the customer matrix.

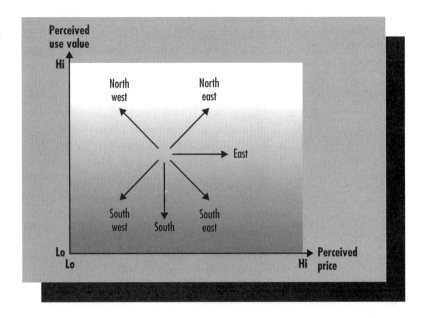

One other point to note with this move to the north-east is that it may well be shifting the firm's product into a new segment. For example, let us assume the new owners of an Italian restaurant wish to move the restaurant up-market. They intended to achieve this by introducing more exotic dishes onto the menu and dropping the more basic pasta main courses, by changing the decor and by increasing the prices by 50%. The price positioning of the restaurant was therefore shifted away from the cheap and cheerful end of the restaurant market. Now, however, the restaurant was being compared to other existing up-market venues. Service levels, location, car parking and ambience were unfortunately perceived to be inferior to these 'new' competitors, and so the restaurant was forced to close. Whereas in its lower price/perceived use value position these aspects of the restaurant experience were not critical, they clearly were important to customers in the higher-price segment.

The move east in Figure 2.7 has the firm increasing price without adding perceived use value. This move can succeed in increasing profitability if competitors follow suit. For example, in the glass container industry in Britain in the early 1980s, all firms were struggling for profitability: input costs, particularly for gas, were rising and firms did not feel able to pass these costs on to customers. Rockware made a unilateral move to increase prices which was followed by competitors, which resulted in the preservation of relative market shares and increasing profits. If the move is not followed by competitors then market share will fall. This move can also succeed if the firm has a monopoly position in the short-term or, less dramatically, can benefit from a temporary supply constraint. Incidentally, if consumers use price as a proxy measure of value then a price increase may shift the firm north-east.

21

Figure 2.8
Raising price on the customer
matrix, and a value for
money curve.

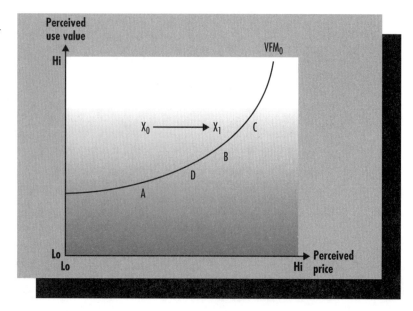

A move east can also be viable if the firm's product is in the position indicated in Figure 2.8. Here, all other competing products are bounded by VFM_0. Firm X's product is priced lower than it needs to be to attract customers. Firm X could increase the price to X_1 without affecting sales, and the difference between price X and price X_1 is additional contribution to overheads and profits. At X_1 it is on a higher VFM curve and should capture most of the market.

The move south-east, increasing price and decreasing value, is only feasible in a monopoly situation, otherwise it is a short route to failure. Reducing value but holding price, moving south, may come about inadvertently:

■ Either through attempts to cut costs which result in customers perceiving reductions in quality; or
■ Through competitors adding value.

These unintended moves can occur when the management is not clear about the dimensions of use value, and how they are weighted by customers. Whatever the reasons for the move south, it is likely to result in a reduction in market share.

Moving south-west, cutting price and perceived use value, is a diagonal move which may well shift the firm into a new market segment. For example, if a car manufacturer located in the middle ground of the car industry, *e.g.*, Ford, took this route it would be moving to a down-market position. Whereas Ford's competitors might have been GM, Nissan and Chrysler, they would now find themselves being compared by potential customers with Hyundai, Daewoo and Proton. This may be a viable shift as long as the relative cost position of Ford enabled it to operate profitably against these low-price competitors.

The only direction on Figure 2.7 that is guaranteed to deliver an increased share is a move north-west, adding value and cutting price. The firm must be the lowest-cost producer, and it must be able to move faster than the competitors to sustain its relative position. Typically, however, a competitive firm may move north initially by adding value; then when competitors imitate the added value the firm shifts west by cutting price. The share advantage gained through moving north may well enable the firm to become the low-cost producer through the achievement of scale and experience economies, making the price cutting strategy feasible. So, the north-west position is reached by moving north, then west. This is a common strategy used by Japanese companies when they move to attack the global market.

As we have argued, moves north-east or south-west may move the firm into new segments of demand. More generally, if a firm wishes to diversify into new markets the customer matrix should be part of the analysis. Before such a move is contemplated, the management should ask the following questions:

- What do we know about customers in this segment? Specifically, what are their needs? What are the critical dimensions of perceived use value? What criteria do they use to evaluate these dimensions of perceived use value?
- What do we know about competitors? Who is here already? How are they positioned in the customer matrix?
- Where would we try to enter the market? Low price with average perceived value, or high perceived value?

The most critical question is:

- What makes us think we can outperform the players who are already in this market?

And, in addressing this question, the management would need to explore the key competences that are required to compete in the industry. This issue is taken up in the next chapter.

Movements in the customer matrix are determined by changes in customer perceptions of price and perceived use value. Shifts of particular products in the matrix can occur even when the producing firm does nothing. If a competitor is able to move its product north by adding PUV, then this has the effect of pushing other competitors' products south in the eyes of the customer. Products can be repositioned through changes in customer tastes and preferences which can alter the dimensions of PUV seen to be important by the customer. This may result in products well-endowed with the preferred dimensions of PUV moving further north.

In addition to these spontaneous shifts in the customer matrix, firms can obviously seek to reposition their products in the matrix through deliberate acts. However, markets are in a continual state of flux, and the outcomes of actions by one producer will be moderated by actions and reactions of competitors. So, the linkages between a firm's deliberate attempts to position its product in the customer matrix and the eventual outcome are complex and dynamic. The linkages are complex because a firm cannot anticipate precisely how a set of internal actions will translate into movements in the customer matrix. The linkages are dynamic because competitors will not stand still; they will be attempting to effect

23

manoeuvres in the customer matrix themselves. Strategists have employed concepts from game theory (Brandenburger and Nalebuff, 1995) to explore competitor actions and reactions. We refer to this literature in Chapter 15.

EXPLORING VALUE-FOR-MONEY CURVES

As we explained at the start of the chapter, within a segment most customers by definition have similarly shaped value for money curves (see Figure 2.9). Indeed, if some customers had radically-different shaped curves they would represent a different segment of demand. The product positioned at point A can improve its competitive position by either a price cut (to A_1) or by offering product improvements delivering higher levels of PUV (a move to A_2). A higher VFM curve is attained in this case by either a small increment in PUV, or a very large cut in prices or some combination of these two. In contrast, the product positioned at point B can attain the customer's higher VFM curve by achieving a substantial increase in PUV (to B_2). However, even a quite modest price cut delivers the same higher level of value for money (a move to B_1).

The **acceptability constraint** (shown in Figure 2.1) moves northwards as the average level of PUV offered to customers increases. This inexorable increase in average PUV comes about as firms strive to outperform their rivals by offering product improvements. As these improvements are imitated by competitors, the minimum acceptable standards in the market are ratcheted northwards. This continual shifting of the acceptability constraint means that firms whose products fail to keep pace with the average level of PUV on offer are forced southwards, relative to the

24

Figure 2.9
Product repositioning and price sensitivity on the customer matrix.

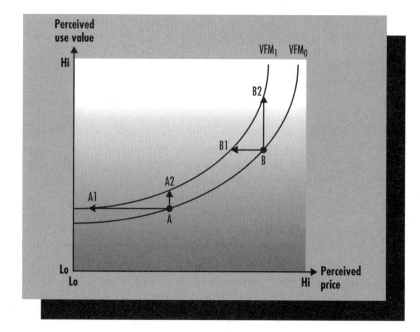

competitors moving north. So, in a developing market, no firm has the option to stand still in the customer matrix. The firm's position is determined by customers and the actions of competitors, and not by the firm itself. Central locking in cars represents such a shift, as no doubt air bags will do too in the near future.

Newly-emerging markets tend to offer products that are high priced and that are low in PUV. Competitive behaviour that develops as the market matures tends to shift the average position of products towards the north-west. As markets mature the average real price tends to fall as the average level of PUV offered rises. What also appears to happen in maturing markets is that products tend to proliferate to fill most feasible combinations of price and PUV.

CONSTRUCTING THE CUSTOMER MATRIX

We have found that the process of constructing a customer matrix is an extremely valuable contribution to strategic thinking. We have worked with many top teams, who, relying initially on their perceptions of customers and their needs, have constructed customer matrices for critical segments of demand. As a first pass at the exercise, it is acceptable to use management's perceptions. The thinking and debating process that is required to reach agreement invariably raises important questions about the firm's products. Consistently, the exercise of constructing the matrix demonstrates forcibly to the management team that they lack reliable and comprehensive information about their target customers and their competitors. This usually stimulates a quest for better market research.

We suggest that a management team should move through the following steps:

1. Clarify the Target Market

We have found it helpful to be very specific in defining the target market. Sometimes it is appropriate to identify a specific customer or type of customer and a specific requirement. This avoids the tendency to generalize, which can lead to rather bland and uninteresting analyses. In selecting a specific customer it is helpful to choose one that might represent a large group of similar people.

2. Identify Dimensions of Perceived Use Value

Top team members must try to put themselves in the customer's shoes. If the team is working together, it must conduct itself initially as individuals. Team members identify what they see to be the important dimensions of perceived use value on their own. They then share their lists. This can often reveal a wide spread of views. This either indicates that there is little real understanding of the customer's needs, or that each manager may be reflecting different sub-segments of demand. Once the dimensions have been pooled, the team should agree on the most critical dimensions: what is most important to this customer?

3. Rank the Dimensions of Perceived Use Value

The selected dimensions, usually about five or six, are sufficient must then be ranked in order of importance to the customer. They should then be weighted by allocating percentages (see Figure 2.5).

4. Rate Competing Products on each Value Dimension

Each product perceived by the customer to be a viable offering can be rated on a 1–5 scale, including the firm's product (as in Figure 2.5).

5. Calculate the Overall Perceived Use Value Score for each Product

This requires some simple arithmetic: for each product, its rating on each dimension of PUV needs to be multiplied by the weighting for that dimension. These are then summed to produce an overall PUV score for each product.

6. Calculate the Perceived Price

Note price factors which the customer would take into account. In the case of a car, for example, the list price, resale value, insurance group, cost of accessories and fuel consumption

7. Plot the Products onto the Matrix

By combining the PUV score with the price of each product, the products can be located onto the matrix (see Figure 2.1). Some adjustments of the axes may be necessary to ensure that there is an 'average' position around which the products will be arrayed.

We have found that the relative simplicity of the matrix means that it is easy for managers to construct and interpret. Managers use it to discuss where they should move, where competitors are likely to move, and what would be required of the firm to shift their products in the matrix. This visual representation of the firm's competitive position in a particular market segment acts as a powerful metaphor and a focus for debate.

In Figure 2.10 we have included some examples of dimensions of perceived use value profile charts. The first illustrates the advantageous competitive position achieved by an oil company (T), against the best of the competition. This success came about through the recognition that, although the lubricants needed by the paper and pulp industry were the same as those used in the truck and bus industry, the needs of the customers were quite different. By

Figure 2.10
Perceived use value profiles.

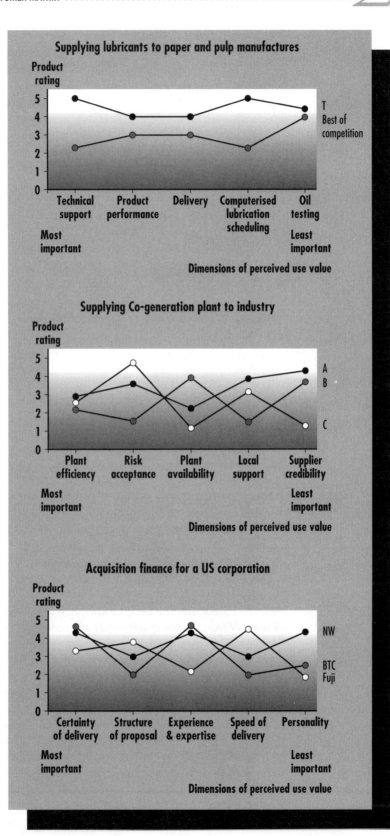

Supplying lubricants to paper and pulp manufactures

Product rating

Technical support · Product performance · Delivery · Computerised lubrication scheduling · Oil testing

T
Best of competition

Most important

Least important

Dimensions of perceived use value

Supplying Co-generation plant to industry

Product rating

Plant efficiency · Risk acceptance · Plant availability · Local support · Supplier credibility

A
B
C

Most important

Least important

Dimensions of perceived use value

Acquisition finance for a US corporation

Product rating

Certainty of delivery · Structure of proposal · Experience & expertise · Speed of delivery · Personality

NW
BTC
Fuji

Most important

Least important

Dimensions of perceived use value

Figure 2.11
Suppliers of consumables to
CD manufacturers.

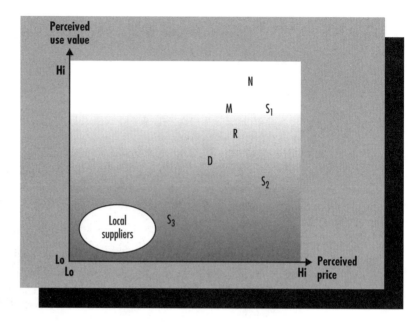

focusing on this narrower segment, firm T have developed specific expertise which is valued by paper and pulp-mill operators.

The second profile refers to customers of co-generation (heat and power) plants. The most important dimension of PUV is plant efficiency, but the profile reveals that all competitors are judged to offer equivalent levels of efficiency. This then becomes a hygiene factor, an order qualifying feature that is required just to be in the game. Therefore, when customers are making a choice, they would focus their attention on other dimensions of PUV such as financial-risk acceptance, plant availability (up time), local support and supplier credibility.

The third profile is from corporate banking. The segment is the lending of acquisition finance to a US corporation, specifically the lead bank in an acquisition. The dimensions of PUV include certainty of delivery and experience. These raise important questions about how the customer evaluates these dimensions. What indirect, proxy measures are used by the customer to assess competing banks on these dimensions? Often, track record is a catch-all measure, which then poses a problem for a firm that has no record at which to point.

In Figure 2.11 we have a complete matrix for the supply of consumables to compact-disc manufacturers. This rapidly growing market illustrates a polarization between the international players (N, M, R and D) and many 'local' suppliers who are very price competitive. The problem for the firm that constructed the matrix was that they had several subsidiary companies, obtained through acquisition, that were located in different parts of the matrix (each marked by an 'S'). Moreover, none of the subsidiaries was in a strong position.

Often, the completed matrix will have competitors located along a diagonal, as in Figure 2.12. In this example we have four consult-

Figure 2.12
Customer matrix for
'Downsizing advice'.

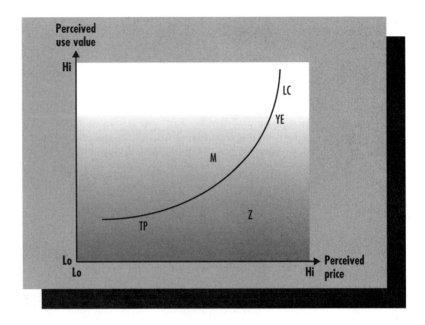

ancy firms each offering advice on downsizing to corporations operating across Europe. Since the market perceives the quality of their advice to vary, but that this is balanced by the levels of their fees, each is considered to give similar levels of value for money. Thus TP, M, YE and LC can all survive in the market as they operate on the same VFM curve. Firm Z, however, could not survive as its price position locates it on a much lower VFM curve. This seems to support the notion of a value-for-money curve, implying that there are feasible positions representing different combinations of price and perceived use value, but where the product of these value-for-money offerings is the same.

To recap, perceived price refers to the aspects of price that the customer pays attention to. This can include the costs of switching from one supplier to another. The effect of switching costs is to increase the perceived prices of competing products. We have had occasions where it was necessary to construct two customer matrices: one representing existing customers, and another representing prospective customers, because their perceptions of price were substantially different.

29

SUMMARY

There are two basic options facing a firm seeking sustainable competitive advantage: either compete on price, or add perceived use value, although both moves can be adopted simultaneously. If the firm opts to compete on price it is vital that the firm has lower costs than its competitors. Otherwise it is likely that, if a price war develops, price levels will reach the point where the firm is forced out of business.

In order to add perceived use value, it is essential to be clear who the target customers are, and what their needs are. From this understanding, the firm can develop approaches to adding perceived use value in ways that are difficult for competitors to imitate.

Whether the firm is seeking to compete on price, or to compete by adding perceived use value, it should strive to be the low-cost producer. The firm needs to be low-cost compared to those firms with which the target customers perceive it to be in competition. Achieving a low-cost position through a strategy of adding perceived use value is attainable if market share advantages enable the firm to realize the cost advantages accruing from sale and experience effects. Moreover, if the firm really understands what the customers value, then all costs that do not feed through to perceived use value can be eliminated.

A move north-east, adding perceived use value, and charging higher prices, may involve a shift from one segment to another. Care needs to be taken to ensure that the firm can achieve a competitive advantage over firms serving this segment.

chapter 3

The Producer Matrix

This chapter introduces the second basic tool used to explore competitive strategy, the **producer matrix**. The customer matrix shows how a firm's products are rated in value-for-money terms in relation to competitors' products. The producer matrix gives a graphical picture of the firm's strengths in terms of the competences required to deliver value to customers, and the level of its unit costs in relation to its competitors. Thus, while the customer matrix illustrates the customers' judgements, the producer matrix illustrates the firm's position within the customer matrix.

Before we explain the matrix, we will address two different theories of firm profitability which have a bearing on our approach. We will then explain the producer matrix and how it can be constructed. Then we will focus on the problems of sustaining advantage, particularly the problem of competitive imitation.

PROFITABILITY: MARKET STRUCTURE OR FIRM RESOURCES?

There are two contrasting explanations of the sources of above-average profitability. The view from the tradition of the industrial-organization economist (Porter, 1980, 1985) holds that firm profitability is largely determined by the structure of the industry in which it competes. So, a firm should earn decent profits in an industry that has few competitors, where the customers have little power, and where it is difficult for new firms to enter the industry.

A different explanation has gained popularity in recent years. It argues that superior profit performance is due to unique assets and resources that a firm has acquired and developed over the years. This is the resource-based theory of the firm (Barney, 1991; Peteraf, 1993). We shall explore these alternative views briefly, as an introduction to the producer matrix.

A third perspective is the game theory (Brandenburger and Nalebuff, 1995) which takes note of the fact that a firm's profitability is as much dependent on competitors' actions as on its own strategic choices. We have allowed for the actions and reactions of competitors already in our customer matrix, and we do so in our producer matrix.

Market Structure

Throughout the 1980s, strategic thinking was strongly influenced by Michael Porter's book *Competitive Strategy* (Porter, 1980), in which market structure is said to play an important part in determining firm profitability. This thinking developed out of industrial organization (IO) theory, in which market structure was seen as largely determining strategic conduct, which in turn was largely instrumental in determining performance. This is the structure–conduct–performance paradigm so influential among industrial economists in the 1950s and 1960s, and associated with the names of Bain, Mason, Scherer and, more recently, Tirole.

Within this approach, the process of formulating a competitive strategy has been most commonly described as follows:

1. Analyse the environment for attractive industry segments.
2. Identify, evaluate and select the appropriate strategies for competing in the chosen industry segments. In Porter's terms these would be low cost, differentiation or focus.
3. Implement the chosen strategy.

The thinking behind this process is that the attractiveness of the industry or market is the main determinant of firm profitability and, therefore, that the prime strategic task for the firm is to identify an attractive market or market segment and then focus on it. Given good management, profits are likely to follow.

However, there is evidence (see Rumelt, 1987 and Buzzell and Gale's PIMs data, 1987) to show that variation of profit levels in firms *within* industries is at least as great as that *between* industries. Furthermore, the undoubted profit record of the Hanson Group and others, the fundamental strategy of which frequently involves investing in apparently unattractive industries and then running companies within these industries more efficiently, casts further doubt on the contention that high profits necessarily have to be made in highly attractive industries.

There is also the danger that a firm that believes it has identified an attractive opportunity, *e.g.*, cable television, will embark on an investment in that opportunity area without paying sufficient attention to whether operating in such an industry actually builds upon something the firm has experience in doing well, and in which it can therefore reasonably expect to have some competitive advantage.

Whilst any modern strategist would probably concede the strategy process can be carried out only by an examination of *both* the external environment and the internal strengths of the firm, the emphasis placed upon the sequence in which this exercise is carried out is, we believe, of some importance.

Firm Resources

The resource-based theory of competitive advantage (Wernerfelt, 1984; Hamel and Prahalad, 1990; Grant, 1991) suggests that competitive advantage is best sought by an examination first of a firm's existing resources and core competences, followed by an assessment of their profit potential in relation to the congruent opportunities presented by the market; strategies based upon the possibilities this reveals are then selected. The task is then to fill whatever resource or competence gap is identified by the inventory-taking of existing resources and competences, in relation to the perceived profit potential of a given opportunity. From this analysis emerges a set of decisions to build competences internally, to form alliances with other firms with complementary competences or to acquire a firm with such competences.

This process would discourage a firm from investing in an enterprise that was not strongly related to its core competences. Only strategies based upon existing competences could, it would hold, lead to the acquisition and maintenance of sustainable competitive advantage. Thus a would-be athlete wondering what event to specialize in, would be more likely to succeed by considering his or her qualities first, before considering the attractiveness of the event. If he is five foot six in height and weighs 200 pounds, neither the high jump nor the marathon seem likely events in which he might expect to excel, however hard he trains. By selecting throwing the hammer or the javelin however, he might well, given training and technique, achieve eminence. Similarly, a company is likely to excel only in areas where it is already highly competent, and for which a strategic opportunity has arisen. If it lacks the core competences, it may become acceptably proficient, but is unlikely to achieve competitive advantage over firms already prospering in the industry.

In contrast to the market-structure view of profit potential, the resource-based theory suggests that above-average profits arise in a firm because it is able to make use of certain resources and core competences better than its competitors, and because these competences mesh better with the current key competences required for success in the industry than do those of its rivals.

The market structure approach assumes the ultimate arrival in markets of 'normal' conditions of equilibrium, i.e., a balance of supply and demand at a price acceptable to both buyers and sellers. Above-average profits will have been competed away, and appropriate rational strategies will have led to the end-game of a commodity product which is produced by a small number of the most efficient firms each with low costs and minimal differentiation. Indeed, some industries do display these characteristics, e.g., the personal-computer hardware industry and many other electronic goods producers, but by no means all do so, and generally not those in which long-run profits are to be made.

The resource-based approach however, has a radically different view of likely outcomes. By contrast, it assumes a state of dis-equilibrium as the norm: that firms differ essentially from each other for reasons of history, of differing asset endowments both inanimate and human, and through the development of distinct capabilities. At given moments, industries will display characteristics that make certain factors key to superior profitability for firms possessing them. The firms able to achieve above-average profits will be those whose competences most closely match the key strategic industry factors. These competences may be called the firms' strategic assets (Amit and Schoemaker, 1993). However, they need to be deployed with an

33

appropriate strategy in order to capitalize on the above-average profits that may potentially be available.

Unfortunately, managers have only bounded rationality (Simon, 1957) and are frequently faced with conditions of high uncertainty and complexity (Williamson, 1975). They also face the problem of resolving potential organizational conflict within the firm arising from the differing personal agendas and ambitions of the firm's executives. The selection and implementation of the most profitable strategy, even by firms possessing the core competences most appropriate in relation to the industry's key requirements, are therefore fraught with risk and there is limited probability of a successful outcome. The supposed predictability in terms of market evolution of the market-based approach, developed from traditional economic theory, is thus replaced by the strategic uncertainty of firms, even with the most appropriate core competences, groping in the fog of unknown futures. Such a description of the 'real' world is not without credibility. However, even with these limitations to the probability of success, if the game is to be played, the search must be for the most valued core competences, and for the key to how to use them most profitably.

THE PRODUCER MATRIX

Using this resource-based perspective, the problem posed for the strategist is how to achieve a superior and sustainable position on the customer matrix described in Chapter 2, through the appropriate use and development of the firm's competences. The matrix below, (Figure 3.1) which we call the producer matrix, illustrates the relationship between relative unit cost (efficiency) and key, value-creating competences (effectiveness), that the strategist must try to manipulate, to improve the firm's position on the customer matrix. The competences on the vertical axis may be called **key competences** as they are most concerned with enhancing value. The horizontal axis refers to the relative unit cost position of the competing firms.

Although in general we subscribe to a resource-based view of the firm, there are some problems with the approach. We believe that although the firm's unique resources help to explain why some firms outperform their rivals, this is only one part of the explanation. A firm may have great skills in producing a product for which there is little demand, so when assessing the value of a firm's resources some account needs to be taken of the context within which the firm is operating. Most contributors to the resource-based view of the firm recognize this problem, but they either tend to *assume* a resource is valuable and they then focus their attention on problems of other firms copying these resources, or they define valuable resources in rather vague and generalized ways.

Resource-based theory can lead to an overly internal perspective that provides little insight into what the firm should try to do to improve its situation. For example, some firms are using consultants

Figure 3.1
The producer matrix.

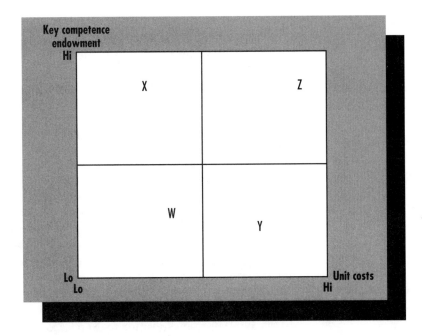

to conduct **competence audits**. One firm of our acquaintance was cheerfully informed by consultants that it had 39 core competences! We believe it is unhelpful to try to identify competences without some reference to a particular product market. **Core competences** are only of interest if they enable a firm to compete more effectively in a given market place.

Therefore, we distinguish between key competences and core competences. Key competences are those required by any firm to be a serious and successful player in a particular market. Core competences are what the firm happens to be good at. Hence, key competences are derived from an understanding of the requirements to compete in a particular market arena, whereas core competences are firm-specific. Clearly, a firm's core competences may coincide with the key competences required to compete in a given market place. Where this happens we would expect the firm to perform well. But also probable is a situation where a firm's core competences have drifted out of line with the key competences required and, unless the firm can develop new competences, or move to another market where its competences may be more effective, it will perform poorly.

So this approach enables us to anchor or benchmark an assessment of the firm's core competences against some external criteria, the key competences required to compete in a given market.

The vertical axis in Figure 3.1 rates the firm's endowment in the key competences required to compete in a given market. The horizontal axis refers to the firm's unit costs. So, a firm which had core competences that were in line with the key competences required would be in a position high up the vertical axis. If this firm also had low unit costs in relation to its competitors, it would be located towards the north-west corner of the producer matrix (position X in Figure 3.1).

If the firm improves its competences, but competitors improve their equivalent competences even more, the firm will go down, not up the vertical axis, and will become less competitive. Of the four competitors shown on the diagram the one in the north-west quadrant is capable of delivering the highest performance in current circumstances, *i.e.*, highest delivery of key competences at lowest unit cost. The south-east quadrant competitor (Y) has the worst potential with high unit costs and low key competence endowment. The north-east (Z) and south-west (W) quadrant competitors may be balanced in relation to each other from a potential performance viewpoint, with Z only able to deliver key competences at high unit cost, and W able to be low cost, but at the expense of its ability to deliver the key competences.

An understanding of both the customer and the producer matrices is vital to achieving competitive advantage, since their linkage is indirect. Competitive advantage can only be achieved as a result of movement on the customer matrix, since that advantage comes at a point of resolution between the buyer's perception of use value and of price. The firm can act directly only on its producer matrix to put itself in a position to exercise flexibility on price. It can do this by either increasing its competences in order to attempt to increase PUV, and/or by lowering its costs through improving efficiency. Competitive advantage is a customer-determined characteristic, and the actions of the producer can at best attempt to achieve it uncertainly through movements in the producer matrix.

We should note that a shift northwards on the customer matrix may come about spontaneously due to a change in consumer tastes, without any core competence improvement at all. Moreover, a firm may move westwards on the producer matrix by reducing its costs, but may judge that market conditions suggest a supply constraint, and may thus opt to increase its margins by *raising* prices; thus causing an eastward move on the customer matrix.

REDUCING COSTS

Reductions in relative costs can be achieved in five ways: exploiting economies of scale, economies of scope, experience advantages, managerial efficiencies, and low factor costs. We shall consider each in turn.

Economies of Scale

Economies of scale are the reductions in unit cost that are achieved by a firm increasing the scale of its activities. These economies accrue where the firm is able to spread fixed or overhead costs over a greater volume of sales, and where the scale of the firm's activities permits it to enjoy other cost advantages, *e.g.*, it is better able to bargain with suppliers to get lower prices for its inputs. There is some empirical evidence to suggest that these scale advantages may not be widespread and, in any event, one would not expect these economies to be universal, *e.g.*, the extent of the advantages accruing to larger scale production will vary according to the technology used in the industry. There is a view that new methods of production such as flexible manufacturing systems and just-in-time systems may be much more important in determining relative costs than the scale of production. Firms that are able to exploit these new methods may achieve lower unit costs at relatively smaller scale than rivals (see Managerial Efficiencies below).

A related concept is **economies of sequence**. Here, cost advantages accrue from linking sequential processes. An obvious example would be locating a hot rolling mill next to the steel blast furnace to avoid the costs of reheating the steel.

Economies of Scope

Economies of scope derive from core competences. If a firm has been able to build up a competence such as brand development skills and if it is able to deploy this competence across several product markets, then it enjoys economies of scope. So scope economies are realized where a firm's core competences match the required key competences in a number of product markets.

Advantages from Experience

Pioneering work by the Boston Consulting Group demonstrated a strong link between experience and unit-cost reduction. Over time, firms accumulate experience in making or supplying products. If the firm learns from this experience, it should be able to deliver products at lower costs by, for example, finding the most efficient ways to assemble components using method study and value engineering. Firms that have a high relative market share accumulate experience at a faster rate than their competitors. If they translate this advantage into lower unit costs, assuming they charge similar prices to their competitors, they should be more profitable.

Managerial Efficiencies

Firms that are not subject to strong competitive pressures may suffer from **X-inefficiency**. This economist's term refers to the increases in costs that can occur if firms are protected from the full rigours of a competitive market. X-inefficiency can result where firms are essentially in a monopoly supply position, where there is a cartel, or where a firm is protected from competition by, for example, import restrictions. Absence of competition leads to a slackness in the way the firm is managed leading to increases in input costs *e.g.*, labour, excess capacity, administrative slack and the persistence of inefficient production processes.

Some economists would argue that X-inefficiencies will exist unless there are pressures from the market place that force the firm's management to take action. This survival of the fittest argument assumes that the firm can only react to external pressures and, in the absence of these pressures, unit costs will inexorably rise.

However, a more managerialist view would suggest that firms are capable of achieving efficiency through the exercise of good management practice. Over the past decade, a wide variety of management prescriptions have been proffered which could help a firm lower its costs, and which are not directly connected to scale or experience effects: *e.g.*, total quality management practices, business process redesign, delayering, downsizing, just-in-time, materials requirements planning, Kanban *etc*. These cost advantages can accrue where the management of a firm actively and continuously seek to drive costs out of the productive process. Even when a firm may face benign market conditions, the exercise of managerial efficiency will yield even higher levels of profit. Note that other sources of cost efficiency from scale, scope and experience effects still require the active intervention of knowledgeable management if they are to be realized. None of these volume- and scope-related advantages accrue automatically. Managerial efficiencies offer cost advantages over and above the volume-related effects.

Factor Costs

Some firms will enjoy cost advantages over their rivals because they have access to cheaper resources. Many of these advantages are locational: lower wage costs; proximity to bulky raw materials; cheap power sources; low social costs, taxes; having a low-valued currency *etc*. Some of these factor–cost advantages can be considered as managerial efficiencies, *e.g.*, where a firm has deliberately located an assembly plant in a low-wage country, but others accrue through no proactive behaviour on behalf of the firm's management. However, factor–cost advantages can outweigh all the hard won benefits exploited from scale, scope and experience effects.

So, in order to assess the profit outcome of a competitive strategy we would need to be able to assess the impact of the strategy on these five cost drivers. It is difficult to identify generalizable relationships between competitive strategy options, the cost drivers and the likely profit outcome. Each situation needs to be assessed on its own merits.

CONSTRUCTING THE PRODUCER MATRIX

The method for constructing the producer matrix is similar to that required to construct a customer matrix. As with the customer matrix, it is necessary to derive an intermediate device, in this case the **competence profile**, which is then used to position firms on the vertical key competence endowment axis. In constructing the producer matrix, the management team will probably discover that the firm lacks adequate information about competitors. It is

Figure 3.2
Activity-chain power-service
manufacturer.

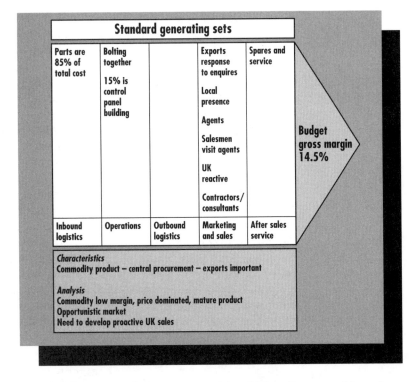

suggested that initially the matrix should be constructed based on the collective experience of the team. The following structured approach should then be taken:

1. Prepare an Activity Cost Chain Analysis

It is generally helpful to prepare some form of activity cost or value chain analysis (Porter, 1985) of the product/market under review. This involves plotting the activities within the company that take the product from its raw material state which could be in the form of bought-in components, through the manufacturing stage, if appropriate, and on to after-sales service. In each of these activities costs can be noted and the key characteristics of the activity carried out. This clarifies what the firm actually does to get the product onto the market, and may then give insights into how the process could be improved. Figure 3.2 illustrates the activity chain of a power services manufacturer in producing standard back-up generator sets.

The analysis reveals that the company adds little value since 85% of total cost is bought-in. It also notes the high level of maturity of the market. It can be perceived therefore that the product is largely a commodity one, and therefore that cost efficiency will be crucial to success.

2. Agree Segment Definition

It is important to be very specific about the market segment being addressed, since different competences with different weightings will be applicable for different segments. It may be possible to develop a more generic matrix of the company's competences at a later stage. This will be useful when judgements are being made on which new segments to enter.

3. Identify Key Competences

The firm's management team needs to answer the question: what does a firm need to be really excellent at to win in this segment? For example, in the corporate banking sector, an individual competitor may need key operational skills in dealing, market making, lending and investment. It may also need a strong reputation, track record and a strong balance sheet.

4. Construct a Competence Profile

A key competence profile should be drawn up (see Figure 3.3) which weights each key competence according to its importance, and rates competitors on a scale of 1–5. The profile in Figure 3.3 refers to a part of the industrial insurance market. The most critical competence is the IT system, followed by experience of working in the client's industry sector. Product innovation is important as is having a motivated sales team. The four competitors plotted in the profile clearly have different key competence endowments. Competitor X is in the strongest position, with competitor Y as the weakest player.

5. Construct a Unit Cost Profile

In order to locate the firm and competitors on the horizontal axis of the producer matrix, some relative cost information is required. In our work with top teams, this tends to be the area of greatest weakness. Managements seem to have little idea about their relative cost position. This is partly because of an overly inward orientation that focuses attention down inside the firm. This leads to a lack of effort and resources being devoted to benchmarking costs against the competition. However, there is progress being made with groups of firms pooling cost data in benchmarking agreements. But even without this level of effort, some approximations of the firm's cost position can be derived by techniques such as reverse engineering, scrutinizing publicly available cost information, assessing input costs, *e.g.*, wages and power, and combining this with employment data and hiring competitors' employees.

If there is some understanding of cost-drivers such as economies of scale, experience effects *etc.*, further insights may be gained into competitors' costs. But it seems the biggest stumbling block to assessing relative costs is the low priority the exercise is given in many firms. Given the critical importance of being low cost, irrespective of whether the strategy is to add value or to compete on price, a failure to form at least some understanding of your relative cost position appears foolhardy. A unit cost profile similar to the key competences profile illustrated in Figure 3.3 needs to be constructed in order to determine the firm's position on the horizontal axis.

6. Plot Firms on the Producer Matrix

The scores and weightings from the competence and unit-cost profiles can then be used to locate competitors on the axes of the producer matrix. Information from the competence profile in Figure 3.3 has been combined with cost information to locate the four firms in the producer matrix as in Figure 3.1. Firm X is in a very strong position. It has been an established player in this market for many years, and has built up a sound reputation. The only weak spot seems to be the sales staff who are viewed as rather complacent.

Competitor W is a new entrant to this market. They have excellent IT skills and have invested heavily in their systems. They are a strong player in life, motor and household insurance markets, and they intend to leverage their systems advantages into the industrial insurance market. They are a low-cost player largely due to the sophistication of their systems, but they lack experience in the market, and they have yet to develop skills in developing innovative products.

Firm Y is the weakest player. It has suffered from under-investment, and the uncompetitive nature of the firm's products and prices has led to a demotivated sales force. Firm Z is mainly held back by its high cost base. This is connected to a lack of investment in IT systems.

41

Figure 3.3
Key competence profile of the industrial insurance market.

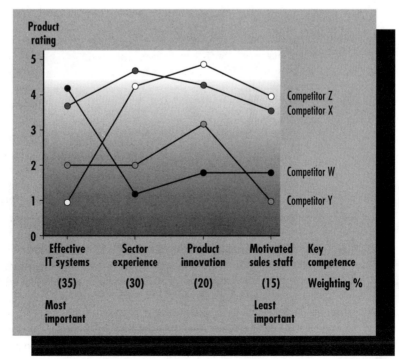

SOME CASE EXAMPLES

In Figure 3.4 we have two key competence profiles from an analysis undertaken by the top management team of an actuarial consultancy company. They saw themselves competing in five different market segments. The competence profiles for two of these segments are presented in Figure 3.4: one segment was concerned with giving advice to relatively wealthy individuals on tax planning and

Figure 3.4
Key competence profiles:
actuarial consultancy.

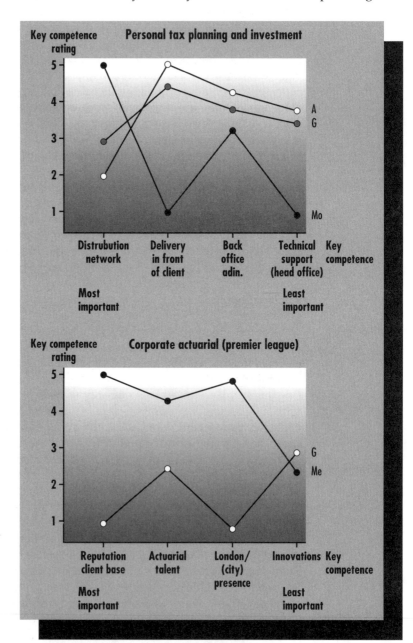

investments; the team referred to the other segment as the premier league of corporate actuarial work, advising large corporations about their pensions policies.

The team identified what they saw as the key competences required to compete effectively in each segment. They then weighted each competence to reflect its relative importance, selected competitors and rated each competitor and themselves on how well they performed each key competence. From the personal-tax planning segment it would appear that our firm (G) is reasonably well endowed with the required competences. The only area of weakness would seem to be distribution network. This prompted a discussion about the ways in which this competence gap could be closed. Three basic options were considered. The first involved an extension of their branch network to regions where they were poorly represented. The second option involved purchasing a rival firm (M_o) which had the strongest representation across the whole country. The third idea was to form an alliance with a firm in a related, but not competing, financial services business.

The first option was dismissed on the grounds that the branch development costs would be prohibitive. There was a view that G was already a relatively high cost firm, and that they would be unable to recoup the expansion costs through higher prices or greater sales volumes. Buying Mo was a possibility as, although the firm had a good distribution network, it had suffered bad publicity due to its aggressive selling style, causing a fall in share price. Option three, the alliance, generated most enthusiasm, as it was seen to be a low-risk way of solving the problem.

The competence profile for the corporate actuarial advice market is substantially different in two respects. The first is that the key competences required to compete in this market are quite different to those required in the personal tax planning segment. Second, G's position is very weak in this segment. This analysis provoked a very uncomfortable debate about whether the firm should try to stay in this market. It revealed that not only were they poorly endowed with the required key competences, but that there were enormous obstacles preventing them from improving their position. G had recently relocated out of London to reduce accommodation and staffing costs, but their provincial location was preventing them from being considered as a serious player in this top end of the market. Moreover, there was little prospect of them attracting the best graduates to train into the best actuaries whilst they remained outside London.

These two analyses raised fundamental questions about the firm's strategy. The contrasting sets of key competences shocked the team. They prompted reactions which questioned the viability of competing in two quite different segments with the same organization. On the positive side, some suggested that they reorientate their efforts towards medium-sized organizations, for which a London presence may actually be seen as a disadvantage.

43

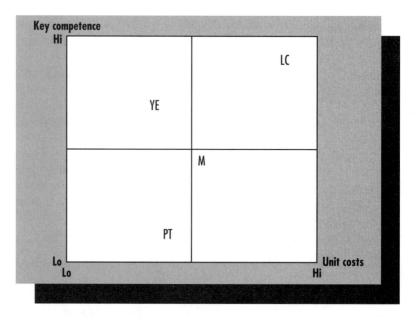

Figure 3.5
Downsizing advice: European
multinationals.

The producer matrix in Figure 3.5 refers to a market served by a group of large human-resource management consultancies. The market segment is 'giving downsizing advice to multinationals in Europe' and the matrix was based upon a key competence profile that ranked the following key competences: a wide European network, a strong client base, business acumen, project management skills, and back-office administration. The four firms in the matrix are the leading players in the European market. LC is clearly a capable but high-cost player. They are able to survive as their brand enables them to charge a premium price. PT are struggling largely because they do not have the coverage across Europe, although they have a strong presence in three countries. The biggest threat to firm M would appear to be YE who have been able to reduce their costs dramatically without it reducing their competences. At present YE price similarly to LC, which suggests that this must be a profitable segment for them, and one they are likely to aggressively protect.

The customer matrix indicates the current situation in a particular product/market. The producer matrix, being a firm-level device, reflects the relative situation with regard to competences that are required to compete in this product market. In practice the same or very similar competences may be required in a number of different but related product markets. For example, in the insurance industry, competences in systems, underwriting, and managing relationships with brokers and with reinsurers may be required in most insurance product markets. However, different analyses will need to be made for each segment as competitor positions, and the importance of key competences, are likely to vary.

Because the producer matrix reflects the relative positions of the firm's competences in relation to its rivals, it can provide some indication of how competitors may be able to manoeuvre on the customer matrix in the future. For example, a firm may have been building its core competences to achieve a strong relative position on the producer matrix, which may enable it to move aggressively on the customer matrix. In this sense, the customer matrix reflects the situation today, whereas the producer matrix provides indications of how the customer matrix may evolve in the future.

However, a firm may be able to improve its position in the producer matrix, but the resultant advantages may be short lived if other firms are able to imitate these improvements. We now focus our attention on the problems of maintaining an advantage.

COMPETITIVE IMITATION

In Chapter 1 we distinguished between motivator value and hygiene value. To recap, hygiene value dimensions were aspects of the product or service that customers would assume to be present. These order qualifying value dimensions enable the firm to play the game. They do not, however, motivate customers to buy their particular offering. Motivator dimensions of value, on the other hand, are those that are not only valued by customers but are also specific to the firm. These dimensions help to explain why several firms are able to coexist in a particular market.

As firms strive to increase or hold their sales in a given market, a process of competitive imitation ensues. As one firm offers new perceived use values or higher levels of existing value dimensions, they attract more customers. This forces competing firms to match these higher levels of perceived use value. This process of competitive imitation has the effect of converting motivator value dimensions into hygiene value. Features that were once unique to one competitor become order qualifying dimensions offered by all firms.

The key competences required to compete in a given market are delivered through a complex set of activities undertaken by the firm. Some of these activities are crucial to the firm's ability to deliver exceptional performance of key competences. Other activities are nevertheless essential, but they do not feed through to exceptional competence performance.

The aim for a firm must be to create a bundle of activities capable of producing a unique product which is difficult to imitate. Grant (1991) suggests that to sustain competitive advantage, strategic resources and competences need to score well when screened for four characteristics, namely:

Appropriability.
Durability.
Transferability.
Replicability.

Grant (1991) argues that the key task of the strategist in internal analysis is to identify the firm's core competences and strategic resources and to screen them against the four defining dimensions of sustainability.

Appropriability

This is concerned with the degree to which the profits earned by a particular strategic asset can be appropriated by someone other than the firm in which the profits were earned. The lower the appropriability of the asset, the more it may be able to sustain profits for the firm. An asset is difficult to appropriate if it is embedded deeply within the firm. The problem arises because of the fact that firms own fixed assets, but not the skills of individuals. For example, if in a soccer team a star with high goal-scoring ability develops, he owns that skill and is empowered either to take it to a competitor, or to use it to gain, in salary or other benefits, a high percentage of the profits from the owners of the team he represents.

Similarly, certain film stars are able to appropriate to themselves a substantial percentage of the profits of films in which they appear, as they are able to convince the films' producers that without their star name the profits would not be achieved. In the business world, certain well-known chief executives of major corporations are similarly successful in appropriating high compensation to themselves with these arguments.

If, however, the profits can be ascribed confidently to the routines and team excellence developed by a wide range of managers and staff within the company, then the profits cannot be so appropriated, as the loss of any individual will not be perceived as affecting profits to any large extent. When a firm has been performing excellently over a period of time, the competence may even transcend individuals or teams, and become a competence of the firm itself in an **organizational learning** way. Low appropriability of the strategic asset therefore means high profit sustainability.

Durability

This characteristic of a strategic asset applies not so much to its physical durability, but rather to its durability as a source of profit. The more intangible aspects of durability are therefore more important. Shortening product and technology life cycles make most assets less durable than they were, even a decade earlier.

However, if tangible assets are proving of declining durability as sources of sustainable profits, the more intangible distinguishing characteristics of firms are not suffering in this regard. Firms' routines and team methods can, and do, survive passing generations of products. Firms' reputations do not decay with the years, so long as they do not decline visibly in their essential, perceived, innovative, productive and high quality characteristics. Similarly, leading brand names prove remarkably durable. As products come and go, such household names as Kellogg, Nestlé, Du Pont, and Xerox continue with undimmed reputations in the public's eyes.

Any one of these can, however, all too easily prove to have a reputation of perishable durability, after no more than a year of poor performance. The recent diminishing reputation of IBM is a salutary illustration of this. However, the more durable the core competence, the higher the profit durability.

Transferability

The easier it is to transfer the core competences and resources, the lower the sustainability of their competitive advantage. Some resources are obviously easy to transfer, *e.g.*, raw materials, employees with standard skills, machines and to some extent factories, where the transferability may be through change of ownership rather than physical transportation. In this sense, such assets are of less strategic significance, due to the ease with which they can be bought and sold. Again, the essential characteristic of a strategic asset is the degree to which it is firm-specific: embedded within the fabric of the firm, within its culture and its mode of operation. Such capabilities represent the profit sustaining assets of the firm. The less transferable these assets, the greater their strategic profit-sustaining quality.

Replicability

If the competence or resource cannot be transferred easily, it may be possible by appropriate investment or simply by purchasing similar assets, for a competitor to construct a nearly identical set of competences. If so, the original firm possessed no real durable competitive advantage. Equilibrium theory operates here, and a profitable company will find its profits competed away, as new entrants replicate its resources and competences, and produce similar products, thereby reducing price through competition, moving the product inexorably towards commodity low profit status. The easier the replicability, the lower the strategic importance of the resources and competences in question.

Competences that qualify as strategic assets with profit-sustaining capacity need to have high durability, but low appropriability, transferability and replicability. It should be noted that this taxonomy could be collapsed from four into two, *i.e.*, durability and the various forms of imitability.

Hence, Grant and others in the resource-based field would argue that advantage can be sustained if the firm has competences that not only deliver valued products, but that the resources involved in developing these competences must be difficult for other firms to imitate. We agree with this view up to a point. We would argue, however, that no firm has sustainable competitive advantage for ever. All advantages are transitory and ultimately all resources can either be imitated or by-passed, *i.e.*, they cease to be uniquely required to deliver value. The issue then shifts away from the prevention of imitation towards the continual development of new sources of advantage, a continuous process that firms neglect at their peril. Perhaps the only truly sustainable advantage, as has been suggested by some commentators, is the ability to learn faster than one's rivals.

We now turn our attention to the problem of continual regeneration of sources of advantage.

RENEWING SOURCES OF ADVANTAGE

Using the arguments developed in Chapters 1 and 2, we can classify the firm's **activities** into those that deliver motivator value and those that deliver hygiene value.

If there is a continuous process of use value migration from motivator value into hygiene value, then unless firms are able to create new motivator values they will eventually cease to earn surpluses. Thus, firms need to invest continually in motivator activities. This requires that they are able to anticipate future perceived use values, and to manage the relevant activities to achieve excellence in differentiation.

Hygiene activities should be managed for lowest cost. Hygiene activities can, at best, pass on only their costs. If they are conducted at above lowest feasible cost, they actually destroy value, because their additional costs cannot be passed on to the customer.

Therefore, our argument is a dynamic one. The process of motivator value migration through competitive imitation is usually continuous. Few firms can have a sustainable competitive advantage that lasts forever. At best they can try continually to seek new sources of advantage by identifying future perceived use values, and developing the motivator activities to deliver those values.

As motivator activities also migrate into hygiene activities, the firm needs to redefine continually the core of its business. We used the example of Boeing in Chapter 1 to illustrate this. So, firms have choices about the scope of the value domain.

Where motivator activities have been neglected, the firm may end up in a situation which is not recoverable. It then faces a situation where it can deliver only hygiene value, and in order to attract any customers it has to undercut competitors on price.

Some activities undertaken by the firm may actually destroy value (see Figure 3.6). These are activities that do not deliver products that are of interest to the customer, and so customers are not prepared to pay for them. Firms that engage in these activities are unable to pass on their costs to customers. So, costs are incurred which cannot be recovered in the price charged to the customer. There may be a surprisingly long list of these activities. Consider the case of a manufacturing organization making airframe components. Activities which produce hygiene and motivator value may include cutting and machining, heat treatment, packing and dispatching. Activities that add no value might include internal movement of component parts, storing material, chasing an order, reworking, batching for internal convenience or inspection. We could argue this further by including activities to do with controlling imperfections in the firm's

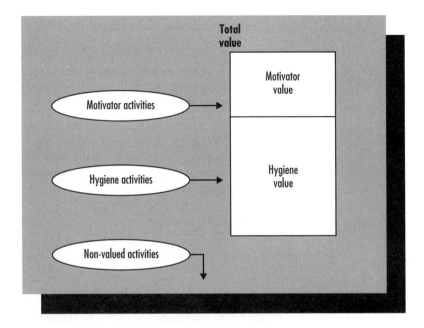

Figure 3.6
Classifying activities.

systems: costs of supervision, management time spent in dispute resolution, budget setting, the costs of managing performance-related pay systems *etc.*

Delayering, just-in-time systems and even employee empowerment can be regarded as attempts to eliminate activities that destroy value. In simple terms, activities either add to total value, or they destroy value in that they have costs but few, if any, benefits. The challenge is to know how to categorize activities and to manage them accordingly.

RESOURCES, SYSTEMS AND KNOW-HOW

Activities combine to deliver key competences. Activities themselves are combinations of three factors: resources, systems and know-how, each of which typically has different characteristics.

■ **Resources** are the basic factors of production involved in the creation of a product or service. Thus, materials, machinery, technology, location, premises, labour, brands and reputation may all be regarded as factors of production that are necessary before a product or service can be manufactured or performed.

■ **Systems** are the methods by which the resources are brought to life, *i.e.*, coordinated and deployed in the value activity. Systems are usually explicit and well understood, and they can often be codified into written procedures.

■ **know-how** is the term used to represent the individual or group capability to work the systems. It is present in individuals and can be embedded throughout the organization, but is not codified. As soon as it becomes so it has to be reclassified as a system.

49

Figure 3.7
Competences and imitability.

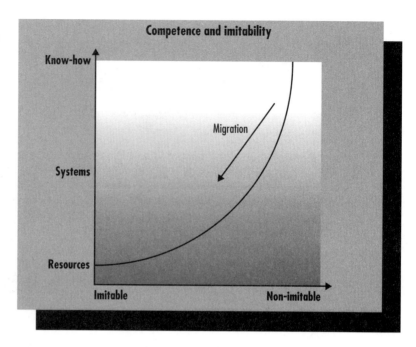

In general, as time passes there is a tendency for know-how to migrate into systems and then often to basic resources (see Figure 3.7).

Thus, resources are generally tangible and visible, with a few exceptions such as reputation. At their simplest, they are land, labour and capital – the traditional factors of production of classical economics. They are, however, generally inert and to be activated need the systems to put them to work. To be called a system, a process needs to be able to be codified and subject to reduction to a set of rules, manuals, standards and modes of inspection and audit for efficient operation. Systems cannot be activated unless operated by an individual or team of individuals with know-how. This is immediately obvious if you sit a computer-illiterate person, *i.e.*, without relevant know-how, in front of a personal computer and set them a task to be completed. Without the help of someone with know-how, they are unlikely to make much progress.

Resources are generally imitable, but in rare cases may not be, *e.g.*, a diamond mine or a very strong brand name. Systems, by definition, tend to be imitable since they are rule dominated, and can be explained and described in manuals. However, if the system is understood but not made explicit in the form of procedures or manuals, for a time at least it is protected against imitation.

Nevertheless, the lowest level of imitability is generally found in the know-how category. At an extreme, only Stradivarius proved capable of making violins to such a standard that they would still be sought after by concert virtuosi hundreds of years after their manufacture. Try as he might to pass on his know-how to his apprentices, so much of the knowledge was tacit that he succeeded in teaching them to make only excellent violins, not superb ones.

In general, as time passes there is a tendency for know-how to migrate into systems and then often to basic resources (see Figure 3.7).

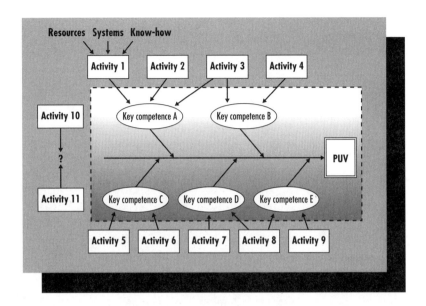

Figure 3.8
A means—end chain.

Thus, the know-how of the expert is observed and turned into a system by an acute analyst and system designer, and with the passage of time this system may become a basic resource encapsulated in machinery or software, now no longer unique and inimitable.

Therefore, firms need to invest continually in activities that deliver motivator value. Firms first need to understand what customers perceive as value. They must then recognize those activities that deliver motivator value dimensions, the qualities in the product or the service that excite customers. But, in order to sustain a more enduring advantage the investments should enhance know-how, as this is the most difficult component for other firms to imitate.

In Figure 3.8 we bring together the concepts discussed so far in this chapter. To recap, **key competences** are a market driven set of capabilities required by any firm to deliver perceived use value to a market segment. Competences are delivered through ongoing **activities**. These activities are combinations of **resources, systems** and **know-how**. Note that some activities undertaken in the firm may not contribute to perceived use value (activities 10 and 11 in Figure 3.8). These activities incur costs that cannot be passed on to customers, and they therefore destroy value. Also note that some activities contribute to the delivery of more than one key competence (activities 3 and 8). So, Figure 3.8 is a **means—end chain**, and by constructing such a chain the management team should be able to identify value-delivering activities, and they should be able to understand more clearly which activities are difficult for other firms to imitate. These will be activities that not only deliver key competences, but also embody special know-how or resources unique to the firm.

These activities should be managed in ways that enhance their performance, as they are likely to be delivering motivator value.

51

Attention must be focused on protecting and developing these unique assets. Other activities, those that are imitable and hence deliver hygiene value, must be managed for lowest cost.

ANALYSABLE AND CRYPTIC SPACE

In Figure 3.9, the producer matrix has been divided into two areas, labelled **analysable** and **cryptic**. The analysable space refers to areas of the matrix that can be understood by a management team engaging in normal analysis. By working back from a sophisticated understanding of the dimensions of PUV valued by customers, the management team can derive the key competences required to deliver this bundle of PUV at low cost. As we have explained, these key competences are combinations of activities, which in turn are made up of resources, systems and know-how. The analysable space represents levels of performance that can be attained if the firm is able to understand and to match the resources and systems required to deliver the key competences.

The cryptic space refers to know-how, the ability some firms will have which enables them to perform the key competences exceptionally well and/or at low cost. The reason that these areas of the producer matrix are labelled cryptic is that they cannot necessarily be understood through established techniques of analysis. know-how has qualities which render it difficult to understand, explain and develop. Often this knowledge is tacit (Polanyi, 1958, 1966), *i.e.*, it is difficult for even the possessor of know-how to explain quite how they do what they do. Where know-how is spread across the organization in the form of embedded routines (Nelson and Winter, 1982) it makes it even more difficult for outsiders to understand what is going on.

This does not mean that it is either impossible to identify and explain this area of the matrix, nor does it mean that a firm cannot

Figure 3.9
Cryptic and analysable space.

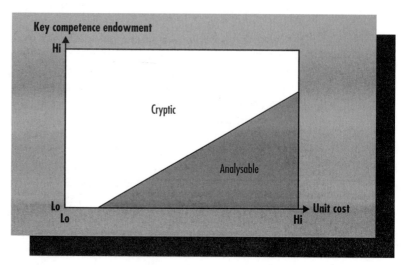

manage a way into this area. However, it is highly likely that a firm may actually be in this zone without any one person in the firm being able to explain the special know-how the firm possesses. This may explain why some attempts to redesign the organization come unstuck, as crude redesign, *e.g.*, delayering, downsizing, may inadvertently destroy know-how.

The way we have drawn Figure 3.9 suggests that positions in the cryptic space are advantageous, and that the sources of advantage can derive from low costs and/or higher levels of key competences.

Given this distinction between different areas of the producer matrix, we can now incorporate this extension into our exploration of competitive strategy. The goal of competitive strategy is to steer the firm into the cryptic space of the producer matrix, and to keep it there. By so doing the firm is able to create competitive advantage over other firms in a particular market segment. This is not to say that firms cannot operate successfully in the analysable regions of the matrix. There are acceptable above-average positions in the analysable space that enable firms to earn reasonable returns relative to competitors. But these positions of advantage are potentially accessible to competitors as competing firms are able to analyse the resources and systems required to be in these positions, which may mean that they can replicate them.

A firm can steer its way into the cryptic space by developing special know-how that delivers motivator value to customers. The extent to which these sources of advantage can be sustained depends upon the ease with which competitors can imitate this know-how. As know-how becomes more knowable, and hence imitable, it migrates into systems. This moves the firm back into the analysable space. If this movement continues, the firm will lose advantage and the best it can hope for is that it will be an efficient 'me too' player.

The size of the cryptic space of the producer matrix will vary over the life cycle of an industry. As a new market emerges, one or two firms begin to exploit the new opportunities available. The cryptic space is likely to be large, as it represents know-how developed by the emergent firms, which is not understood by other potential entrants. The form this know-how takes may be technical, pertaining to the technicalities of a new product area, or it may be marketing expertise which has enabled the early movers in the emerging market to exploit these opportunities. Perhaps these firms are more able to detect weak signals of a change in tastes or needs, and to rapidly respond to them, than follower firms.

As the market grows, and the 'rules of the game' emerge, the taken-for-granted, shared assumptions about how to compete in the market, the cryptic space, typically shrinks. What was once special know-how protected by the few, becomes systematized knowledge, codified and proceduralized and available to many. Unless a firm achieves a product or a process breakthrough, the end-game of the industry is typified by a minuscule cryptic space, with competing firms understanding and possessing all the resources and systems required to deliver the key competences.

At this stage, quite small differences in resource and system endowments can be leveraged into major share and performance advantages. For example, as the market matures all players understand the technologies required to function in the market, so access to this expertise cannot be a source of advantage. But some firms may be able to source cheaper labour, or cheap power, or to have lower transport costs by virtue of their location, and although the systems and technologies deployed by all competitors may be identical, the firm with the cheaper inputs can gain a big advantage. This is nothing to do with know-how. Every player knows how this firm has been able to undercut them on price; they just cannot match that firm's cost levels.

As the market matures and know-how degrades into systems, the cryptic space shrinks. Firms can still, however, build a defensible position in the analysable space, if they have resources and systems that are difficult to imitate. But these advantages are not know-how advantages: they can be due to a firm's advantageous access to resource inputs, like labour or materials, or they could be due to the firm possessing resources that, whilst being knowable, are nevertheless difficult to imitate. Here we would include a strong brand or reputation. It is no secret why the firm outperforms its competitors, so it is nothing to do with know-how, they just happen to have the strongest brand.

Firms may be in the cryptic space without realizing it. This would typically be the case in an emergent industry, where all is know-how, and there are few well-understood ways of delivering value to customers. The more successful emerging players will have gathered and developed know-how without them necessarily being consciously aware of it. Often the know-how is embodied in one individual, the entrepreneur. Unless this expertise is passed on to others, *i.e.,* unless it is made explicit and codified, the firm is vulnerable when the entrepreneur departs the scene. If this transfer of expertise is not effected, the firm may find itself drifting inexorably from the cryptic space to the analysable space. However, paradoxically, the codification of the entrepreneur's intuitive expertise renders this special knowledge more accessible to others outside the firm. This may well result in the firm being pushed out of the cryptic space anyway as other firms are able to access and replicate what was once the entrepreneur's know-how.

Either way, firms need to manage the transition from entrepreneurial to professional management extremely carefully. The firm needs to develop other ways of sustaining advantage once it can no longer rely on entrepreneurial expertise. Either the firm has to protect this now codified expertise closely to slow down its acquisition by rival firms; or it has to develop a sustainable position in the analysable space of the producer matrix by developing resources and systems which cannot easily be replicated, even if they are analysable and knowable.

Figure 3.10 contains a key-competence profile from work we did with teams from a large brewing corporation. We were dealing with

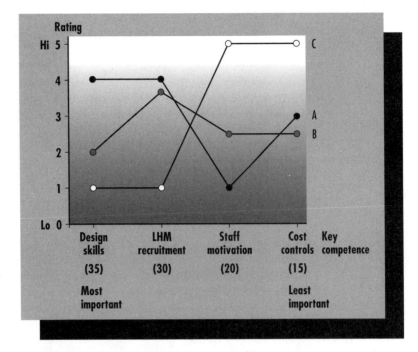

Figure 3.10
Competence profile: pub
management.

the division that owns and manages a large number of pubs. The key-competence profile illustrates that design skills, licence-house manager (LHM) recruitment, staff motivation and cost control are critical to success. Our client (B) rated low on design skills, but it scored well on LHM recruitment. This rating prompted a vigorous discussion into why B was so good at recruitment.

This revealed that, to a large degree, identifying good potential pub managers was something of a mysterious black art. Managers relied on intuition, instinct, and gut feel: we were told that 'you can always spot a winner'. In an attempt to demystify this selection process we asked a large group of regional and divisional managers to select their three most successful pub managers, and to sketch out a profile of them, background, age, education *etc.*

This produced surprising results. Although some of the successful managers conformed to a stereotypical, male, pub-manager profile, a significant number of very successful managers were female, divorced with children, and had previous experience with major retailers such as Marks and Spencer or Boots. These had often ended up running the pubs through family upheavals, so they were in these positions through chance events. Most of the traditional and accepted ways of recruiting managers would have bypassed these women.

The intuitive approach to recruiting managers would be classified as know-how, and it would be firmly lodged in the cryptic space of the producer matrix. By prompting some systematic reflection and analysis, some of this know-how can be captured, passed on to others, and maybe incorporated into recruitment procedures. The questioning of these experienced managers also raised the possibility that new knowledge could be developed about recruiting different types of manager, which could be a source of advantage.

FILLING COMPETENCE GAPS

In Figure 3.11 we have set out a logical sequence of analysis that links the arguments we have developed so far. Once a target market segment has been clarified, we need to understand what the dimensions of perceived use value are to these customers. Then, the key competences required to deliver this package of value at low cost need to be identified. Finally, the firm's relative endowment in these competences needs to be assessed. This will reveal the nature and extent of any competence gaps that are preventing the firm from competing more effectively.

In the event of a firm's core competences not matching the key competences required, the firm must seek to acquire or develop the additional resources, systems or know-how, either by internal development, by strategic alliance or by acquisition. The caveat here, however, is that the resources or skills sought must be only a small proportion of the existing resources, or the risk exists that the newly-acquired competences will so outbalance the existing ones as to

Figure 3.11
Deriving a competitive
strategy.

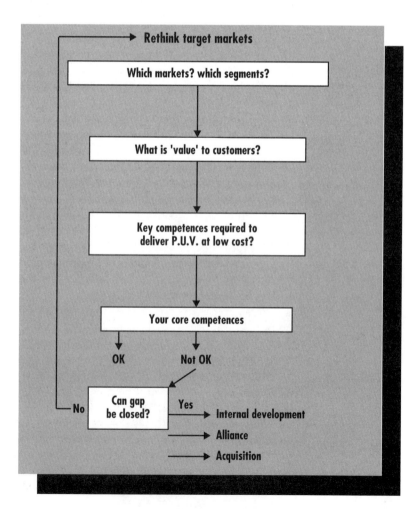

change the nature of the firm, and thereby reduce the effectiveness of the existing competences. So long as the acquired competences are restricted to this small proportion of the whole, the firm can continue to develop its competences effectively and incrementally. Thus a firm, or in an alliance more than one firm, seeks to develop a range of core competences that potentially enable it to match the key competences necessary to succeed in its chosen markets.

To return to our example of a producer matrix on downsizing advice consultancies in Figure 3.5, firm M needs to close a competence gap it has, particularly in relation to YE. Firm M is quite a small consultancy, and it is unable to improve its branch network through internal development. If it set up branches across Europe its unit costs would rise in relation to the other competitors. This is because, compared to YE, PT and LC, firm M is narrowly focused, and is therefore unable to spread the overhead costs of its branches over a wide range of consultancy assignments. At the moment, firm M is able to pick up business by pricing significantly below LC. This source of advantage would be eroded by branch expansion.

So the management team faces a dilemma. To compete with YE and LC for this attractive business they lack the key competence of a wide network and a presence in all the countries that the client corporations operate in. Internal development of the network was ruled out on cost grounds. One idea that emerged in discussion was to target multinationals whose European network mirrored Firm M's, redefining their target market. Another was to use their competences in project management, which is where the firm started out, in more creative ways to overcome the network problem.

The preferred solution was to accept that their coverage would never be as extensive as LC's or YE's, but to achieve excellence in 'business acumen'. This key competence was vital in delivering reassurance to customers that the consultants understood the clients' problems, a critical dimension of perceived use value. By focusing on just three client industries, pharmaceuticals, construction, and distribution, firm M's management felt they could build up this competence to the point where they would convince clients that the lack of coverage was not critical. Thus, they decided to redefine their target market in ways which enabled them to be a more effective competitor.

SUMMARY

The market attractiveness theory suggests that all major possibilities for profit emerge from the market. The key to success is therefore to identify an attractive area in which to compete. The resource-based theory, in contrast, hands the power to win above-average profits to the firm and its ability to develop unique inimitable competences that it can profitably direct to an appropriate market.

This chapter argues that both the market and the resource sides of the equation are relevant to the achievement of sustainable competitive advantage. However, it suggests that the development of a unique, firm-specific and deeply embedded set of core competences matched to a market opportunity is more likely to lead to competitive advantage and above average profits than a strategic approach that concentrates primarily on identifying a market need and then sets out to meet it, without concern for the need to develop capabilities in the firm over time.

The construction of a producer matrix with axes of key competence endowment and unit cost provides a producer's mirror on the internal company side to reflect, in successful cases, the market determined customer matrix on which, ultimately, sustainable competitive advantage is measured.

To add the quality of sustainability to that of competitive advantage, the firm's excellent key competences need to be as close to inimitable as possible. A breakdown of these competences into resources, systems and know-how is likely to reveal where the quality of inimitability is most likely to reside. Generally, this is more likely to be in the tacit know-how of individuals and teams, than in the readily codifiable systems, or inert resources.

Strategic Pathways

In the previous chapters we have explained the two devices which are central to our arguments about competitive strategy. To recap briefly, the customer matrix (Chapter 2) with its axes of perceived use value and perceived price represents the customer's view. It is possible to locate the range of products, perceived by a typical customer as viable alternatives in this matrix, and we explored the implications of a firm attempting to position or reposition its product in this matrix.

In contrast, the axes of the producer matrix refer to aspects of the firm's activities which are not directly visible to the customer, unit cost and key-competence endowment (Chapter 3). The producer matrix can be regarded as representing the means required to deliver the ends valued by the customer. For instance, in order to offer a superior product at low price, the firm would need to be well endowed with the relevant key competences and to have low unit costs in relation to competitor firms.

Key competences provide the link between the two matrices. These competences are, therefore, a market-driven concept. In order to assess a firm's competitive position in any given market we would need to understand these key competences, and then be able to rate the firm's ability to deliver them; the firm that is well endowed with the required key competences would be the most effective competitor.

In this chapter, we first explore various combinations of positions in the customer and producer matrices in which a firm might find itself. Secondly, we consider five **strategic pathways** that a firm might follow in the producer matrix. We then explore the implications of firms competing across a number of market segments. This leads onto an examination of competitor responses. At the end of the chapter we have included a theoretical appendix which develops the value-for-money curves introduced in Chapter 2.

COMBINING THE CUSTOMER AND PRODUCER MATRICES

The customer matrix at a general level can be used to represent the overall company strategic stance, *e.g.*, Rolls Royce – very up-market and expensive; Skoda – rather down-market and budget-priced. However, to be usable for specific strategy formulation, the matrix needs to be constructed for a particular product/market situation. It represents the firm's position relative to its competitors in relation to PUV and perceived price. Any movement on it refers to the same product in the same market.

The producer matrix, however, is concerned with key competences and cost efficiency competences as they apply to a particular product group and market, but may well reflect the firm's overall competences in a variety of areas to a greater degree than the customer matrix can. There are potentially a large number of combinations of positions on the customer and producer matrices. In Figure 4.1 we have set out six possible combinations.

We shall examine each of these briefly to explore what strategic response might be appropriate to them. Note, however, that we are not advocating a crude and simplistic set of prescriptions; we are merely pointing out some potentially viable options that might be explored.

The Up-Market Operator

Here, the firm is currently premium pricing on the basis of offering higher-than-average PUV. On the producer matrix we can see that the firm, perhaps not surprisingly, compares favourably with its competitors with regard to its level of key competences. However, the firm's unit costs are high, presumably because it incurs high costs to produce the up-market offering which commands premium prices.

Figure 4.1
Combinations of customers
and producer matrices.

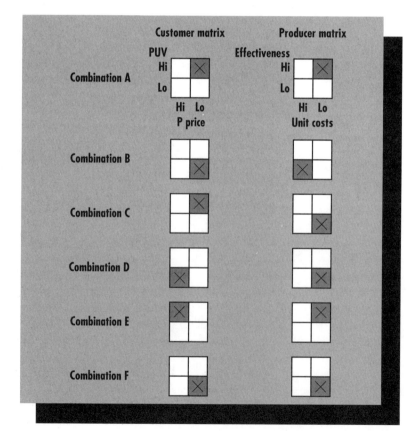

This can have three effects:

1. Price premiums tend to allow the firm to operate at less-than-optimal levels of cost efficiency.
2. Beliefs in a strong brand image and/or quality reputation can encourage the management to think that cost reduction is not a pressing priority.
3. An effect of premium prices might be that relative market shares are smaller, reducing the firm's ability to benefit from any cost advantages that might accrue from scale or experience effects.

An important issue here is the sustainability of the price premium. If this is based on market-specific competences *e.g.*, leading edge technology development, then the issue is how reproducible this competence is. If a competitor could acquire this competence, then the firm might find itself under threat. If the competence is, say, a strong brand image, then the premium-price positioning may be more defensible, as long as the brand's image can be sustained.

If the advantage is derived from more generic competences, *e.g.*, value-assurance processes, then the likelihood of a competitor matching or surpassing the firm may be lower, as these competences are built into the fabric of the firm and inherently difficult to imitate.

Of course, once a competitor offers equivalent PUV, the price premium is likely to be competed away. The resulting positioning for the firm would be average price, above-average or average PUV depending on how many competitors could imitate the higher levels of PUV, combined with an above-average cost position. Relative profitability would then be poor. However, it might be possible for the firm to shift perceptions of price, so that it achieves a move west without actually cutting list prices, *e.g.*, Mercedes attempts to shift price perceptions away from initial purchase price to overall costs of ownership, which includes the resale value of the car.

So, prescriptions for a firm in this position might be:

- Defend the bases of differentiation, *e.g.*, the brand or the ability to innovate.
- Pay greater attention to cost reduction, factor costs, or improved coordination and control in order to improve relative position on the horizontal axis of the producer matrix.

The Uncompetitive Down-Market Performer

Low relative PUV and above-average pricing in this example will lead to decreasing market share in all circumstances other than a severe supply constraint, *e.g.*, a monopoly supplier. Such a position can be avoided by cutting price, as the firm has the low-cost position to permit this. However, if the level of key competences on the producer matrix cannot be improved, the firm will be restricted to a down-market positioning.

Unfortunately, if the competitors leverage their relatively stronger key competences into the offering of higher and higher levels of

PUV, this firm may find itself having to discount prices heavily in order to persuade customers to accept the inferior package of PUV being offered to them.

One option may be to explore other markets, where the firm's products would not be seen to have relatively low levels of PUV, *e.g.*, sell the Rover Montego in Russia. But then the firm would be facing another producer and customer matrix, and the relative cost position on the producer matrix might present a problem, *e.g.*, the factor costs of indigenous Russian car producers might be much lower. Alternatively, the firm may be able to improve its effectiveness competences through alliances.

The Inefficient Up-Market Producer

In this example, the firm has achieved the position of a premium-priced differentiator. However, it has below-average key competences and above-average unit costs. This situation can arise when past levels of investment in, say, product development, R&D or brand-image building have been strong, but have not been sustained into the present. The firm has, in effect, been resting on its laurels. The higher relative cost levels cannot be explained away by higher current expenditures on developing the firm's effectiveness. Higher relative costs resulting from poor cost disciplines would mean that profit margins would be no better than average. This situation can also arise where a firm is good at innovation but it is unable to transfer these developments into saleable products. As with the EMI Scanner, the inventing company, EMI, scored highly on innovation, but was unable to capitalize on this in profit terms, due to its deficiencies in marketing.

The fact that competitor firms have higher competences would suggest that it is only a matter of time before they will move north on the customer matrix. The prognosis for this firm is not good. The urgent need to improve both effectiveness and efficiency with only average levels of profitability presents a major problem.

Interestingly, the managers' perception of the firm's situation may be quite different to that revealed by this analysis. If, as is often the case, managers are not sufficiently well informed about their position on the producer matrix because the required information on competitors is not routinely collected, they might see their firm as being in a very strong position. They would make this judgement from their current ability to sell at premium prices. Therefore, in the absence of a sense of crisis, the tendency would be to maintain the status quo in an atmosphere of complacency.

If, however, the management are aware of the firm's predicament, then it is probably necessary in the short-term for them to prioritize either improving key competences or reducing unit costs, *i.e.*, trying to move either north or west on the producer matrix, rather than attempting to do both things simultaneously. Unless there is focus on either effectiveness or cost efficiency, the danger is that efforts will be dissipated over too broad a set of actions. Typically, cutting costs is easier to achieve as a short-term strategy than building competences. A major focus on cost reduction will signal that radical change is necessary, and this may help to build a momentum for the introduction of further changes designed to improve effectiveness.

An alternative approach may be to subcontract some activities to more efficient suppliers, thus reducing the amount of work done in-house, and enabling the firm to concentrate on improving its key competences in areas it decides to continue to handle directly.

The High-Cost Down-Market Firm

The firm in this example is offering low PUV at a low price, but it has high costs coupled with a low level of key competences. If it is to survive in this market position, it needs to get its costs down to a level to give it acceptable margins, otherwise it will run into unsustainable levels of debt, or its other profitable operations will be heavily subsidizing this product area.

Even if it succeeds in doing this it may need to question whether the route to success does not lie in improving its key competences and thereby enabling it to position itself in a more profitable part of the market. Only firms with naturally low costs and skills in maintaining them can prosper in the southwest quadrant of the customer matrix and this does not seem to be one of those firms.

Japanese companies have shown that this entry strategy need not prevent the subsequent development of the required competences to design and build high quality products, *e.g.*, cars, hi-fi equipment, cameras, and photocopiers. Strategic alliances may be one route to gaining the required competences that the firm currently lacks.

The High Value-for-Money Firm

This position on the customer matrix is the one to aim at to beat the competition. However, it can be sustained only by firms in the northwest quadrant of the producer matrix. Firm 5 will have inadequate profit margins as its highly-competitive pricing is not matched by a low enough cost base to generate the necessary margins for sustained success. It needs either to work on its cost base or to hope that it will gain such market share that scale economies and the experience curve will cure the unit-cost problem. Alternatively, it might raise prices and hope it does not lose too many customers as a result.

The firm might also explore other product markets where its core competences might confer similar advantages, since a strong producer matrix position may well be transferable into an equally strong one in other segments without the need for major changes of emphasis.

The Loser

This combination reflects high prices and low PUV, linked with low competences in both cost efficiency and effectiveness. A firm in such

63

a position faces a fight for survival. The key question must be: how difficult is it for the firm to move northwest on the producer matrix, i.e., to increase both its relative effectiveness and cost efficiency? It may be possible to institute a programme of cost cutting, coupled with the recruitment of some additional expertise to close the gap with competitors.

If the task is too large to achieve by internal development, the solution may be approached through alliances or even merger, acquisition or being taken over. The position reflected by this combination requires drastic measures if it is to be converted into one from which profitable survival may be confidently predicted.

STRATEGIC PATHWAYS

It is not necessarily the case that the dilemma in which firms find themselves in, such as in some of the combinations described above, needs to be solved in one move. In this section we explore five **strategic pathways** that might be travelled by a firm in a particular product market. We also examine the likely profit outcomes associated with each pathway.

Towards the end of the last chapter we devoted some attention to operationalizing the producer matrix – one of the areas of difficulty being the problem of identifying the key competences. The reader may recall that although it was relatively straightforward to identify the more obvious resources and systems required to compete in a given product market, the more subtle areas of know-how proved more difficult to deal with. We made a distinction between analysable and cryptic areas of the producer matrix.

When a firm is not well endowed with even the more obvious resources and systems required to be effective, then management attention should be focused on improving this position. As we explained in the previous chapter however, there is a strong argument in the strategy literature that suggests that know-how and its continual regeneration through learning is likely to be the only source of sustainable advantage over time. Our approach therefore needs to accommodate this crucial aspect of competitive strategy. We return to this issue in Chapters 6 and 7 where we explore some of the structural and cultural issues involved in know-how generation.

Effecting Movements in the Customer Matrix

Movements in the customer matrix are determined by changes in customer perceptions of price and perceived use value. Shifts of particular products in the matrix can occur even when the producing firm does nothing. If a competitor is able to move its product north by adding PUV, then this has the effect of pushing other competitors' products south in the eyes of the customer. Products can be repositioned through changes in customer tastes and preferences

Figure 4.2
Strategic pathways.

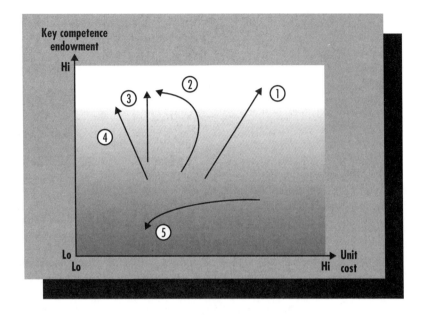

which can alter the dimensions of PUV seen to be important by the customer. This may result in products well endowed with the preferred dimensions of PUV moving further north.

In addition to these spontaneous shifts in the customer matrix, firms can obviously seek to reposition their products in the matrix through deliberate acts. However, markets are in a continual state of flux, and the outcomes of actions by one producer will be moderated by actions and reactions of competitors. So, the linkages between a firm's deliberate attempts to position its product in the customer matrix, and the eventual outcome are complex and dynamic. The linkages are complex because a firm cannot anticipate precisely how a set of internal actions will translate into movements in the customer matrix. The linkages are dynamic because competitors will not stand still; they will be attempting to effect manoeuvres in the customer matrix themselves.

Deliberate attempts to add PUV to products in the customer matrix can be achieved only through the firm improving its ability to deliver the key competences. And, although shifts in perceived price can be effected overnight by simply communicating the lower prices to customers, the ability to sustain lower prices rests on the relative cost position of the firm. So, deliberate repositioning of products in the customer matrix is achieved by changes in the firm's key competence endowment and its relative cost position, *i.e.,* movements in the customer matrix result from the firm moving in the producer matrix.

Strategic pathways are consistent and logical evolutionary outcomes of attempts to improve the competitive position of a firm. In their simplest form, they evolve largely from actions taken by the firm. We will consider these pathways first (see Figure 4.2). Later, we consider more complex pathways which take more account of the likely reactions of competitors.

Pathway 1: Natural Improvements in Key Competences

A natural pathway for improving a firm's ability to deliver key competences would involve the firm investing in the acquisition of resources, systems and know-how. These investments are likely to lead to increases in unit costs. So, the natural pathway moves the firm north-east in the producer matrix, *i.e.*, increasing effectiveness is naturally associated with increases in unit costs.

Pathway 2: Improving Key Competences with Volume Effects

If the move north-east links through to a northward shift in the customer matrix, *i.e.*, the outcome of increased effectiveness is that customers now perceive the firm to be offering higher levels of PUV, the firm should sell more, assuming the move is not immediately imitated by competitors, and that the market is not in decline. The increased volumes may be translated into lower relative costs if there are significant scale and experience economies that can be exploited. So, a second pathway may see the firm moving north-east initially, but then tending north-west or west as the volume-related economies begin to take effect.

Pathway 3: Improving Key Competences without Increasing Costs

The most obvious way in which a firm can increase effectiveness is through a thorough understanding of what exactly are the key competences required to compete in a particular market. A rigorous analysis of PUV, leading through to a clearer insight into the competences required to compete in this particular market can help management focus on those activities that really matter. The resulting increase in effectiveness need not result in any cost increases.

A good example of such a move is provided by the brewing corporation we mentioned in the last chapter. One of the divisions owned and controlled a large number of pubs. One of the challenges facing the industry is the problem of segmenting the market and targeting the pub offer to defined market segments. Where this issue has not been confronted, the pub offering is likely to be a compromise which serves no segment particularly well. We discovered a pub success story based on one astute manager's appreciation of his target market.

The pub, located in Bristol in the west of England, was performing adequately, serving the local community in the evenings, with a few business people using it at lunchtimes. Despite the local area housing a large number of students, few used this pub. The young manager set out to attract students by tailoring the offer to meet their needs. He achieved this by buying a few board games, arranging quiz competitions, and by buying some music CDs that he believed students would like. These investments cost about £120, and over period of months he was able to more than double the turnover of the pub.

This illustrates the importance of targeting a particular segment, and trying to understand what it is that these customers perceive as value. As a result of this attempt to target a specific market, the pub now has no business customers at lunchtimes. This is viewed as a success, because if they were in the pub then the students might feel less at ease. Another interesting outcome has been the way other, more experienced, managers have reacted. Some regard this as a fluke, this manager was just lucky. For others this case represents a severe challenge to the accepted wisdom in their trade. The usual formula for reviving the fortunes of a pub is an extensive refurbishment costing between £50,000 and £100,000. This case challenges the recipe; indeed, if such a refurbishment were undertaken on this pub it might well damage it severely.

Another way of achieving a costless improvement in effectiveness results from corresponding improvements being effected in managerial efficiencies. These efficiencies result from the exercise of good management practice such as using total quality management, re-engineering processes, and just-in-time systems. Key competences can be enhanced through the application of superior technologies which, again, may not involve increases in unit costs.

Pathway 4: Improving Key Competences with Scope Economies

Where the firm is able to exploit a core competence over a number of product markets, the unit cost of performing the competence declines. Achieving these advantages requires excellent coordination across business units that serve different, but related, product markets. This source of advantage can be reduced if, in leveraging the competence across several product markets, it results in compromises being made through a loss of focus. This could lead to lower costs being combined with reducing abilities to deliver the key competences in a particular product market.

Pathway 5: Natural Reductions in Unit Costs

If a firm embarks on a cost-cutting strategy, the natural pathway in the producer matrix may be an initial shift to the west followed by a gradual move southwards. This may occur for two reasons:
- The firm may damage its effectiveness through crude cost-cutting efforts, although the effects of this may not appear immediately.
- The firm may end up being pushed south as competitors pursue strategies concerned with enhancing effectiveness.

Crude cost cutting may have the effect of an immediate boost to the bottom line, but the longer-term effects can be catastrophic: blanket cuts in budgets, *e.g.*, 'all departments have to shed 20% of staff', the slashing of softer budgets, *i.e.*, those that do not have an immediate impact on current operations, like training, research and development, and simplistic delayering where vital experience may be pushed out the door. As relative effectiveness declines this feeds through to the customer matrix as lower PUV. Low relative PUV forces the firm to compete on price, which adds further pressure for cost cutting. The longer-term prognosis for a firm in this position is not good.

Hence, the risk of a strategy which just focuses on cost cutting is that it may result in a reduced ability to deliver key competences, a position that may well turn out to be irretrievable.

Strategic Pathways and Profit Outcomes

Each strategic pathway is associated with a particular pattern of profitability, as it unfolds over time.

Pathway 1, natural improvements in key competences, is likely to lead to an uncertain profit outcome. The increases in effectiveness result in relative cost increases. This shifts the firm to the north-east in the producer matrix. If the firm is unable to pass on the cost increases to customers through premium pricing, then the likelihood is that profits will decrease. If the firm can increase prices, profits may stabilize or improve depending on the price sensitivity of customers and on how many of them are willing to pay more for higher levels of PUV.

In pathway 2, as the firm increases its key competences, it incurs a cost increase in so doing, but over time it is able to exploit scale and experience benefits to reduce costs. We might expect this to lead to an initial drop in profits as costs increase, followed by a gradual improvement as the scale and experience benefits take effect. As with pathway 1, the firm may attempt to introduce a premium price. If they are successful, this should reduce the impact of the initial cost increases incurred with the enhancement of competences. If the firm can maintain higher prices, profits should improve substantially when volume advantages from scale and experience take effect.

However, there is a trade-off here. Higher prices will deter some customers. So, premium pricing will have an impact on sales volumes, which in turn will reduce the scale and experience advantages that are potentially available. In judging how to price, therefore, some understanding of the price sensitivities of customers is desirable.

Pathways 3 and 4 permit the improvements in key competences to be accompanied by reductions in costs either through managerial efficiencies, or economies of scope. The profit outcome is likely to be attractive: the improvements in key competences should feed through to increases in PUV. These PUV improvements should lead to increases in relative market share and, as relative sales rise and unit costs fall, the profit volumes generated will increase. The rate of profit growth will vary according to the extent of the PUV gap

Figure 4.3
Rumelt's capability matrix.

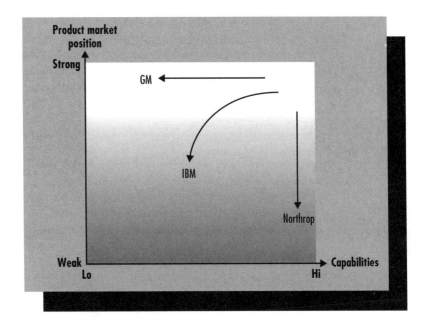

that is created by the improvements in key competences, and by the pricing strategy of the firm. It may choose to price aggressively to capture the market, and in so doing it may be willing to sacrifice short-term profits for longer-term strategic advantage.

Pathway 5 is the natural cost-cutting strategy. As the cost cuts take effect, a short-term boost to profits is likely to result. But, over time the concomitant reductions in key competence endowment that result are likely to lead to falling sales, falling prices and falling profits.

A similar and complementary approach to the notion of strategic pathways has been suggested recently by Rumelt (1996). He constructs a matrix which has product/market position as the vertical axis, and firm capability as the horizontal axis (see Figure 4.3). He presents three illustrative examples that have followed different paths in the matrix. General Motors have pursued a focused-product market position in the car industry, but have not been able to develop the required capabilities to be the strongest player. Hence, they have lost share to other firms, notably Japanese corporations. Northrop have excellent capabilities in producing Stealth aircraft. Unfortunately for them, this capability no longer matches customer requirements, so although their capabilities in stealth-bomber production are unparalleled, their product/market position is weak. Finally, Rumelt suggests that IBM have lost product market position, and have deteriorating capabilities, so they have moved from a dominant position to an increasingly weaker position in the matrix.

There are clear links between Rumelt's model and our two matrices. We would measure product/market position with the customer matrix, and use the producer matrix to assess capabilities. Rumelt's view of capabilities would align with our definition of core

69

competences, not key competences, as he is referring to a specific firm capability which is not related to a particular product market.

So far we have restricted our analysis to firms competing within one market segment. We made this assumption to simplify the argument. We now consider the more typical case of firms competing in several market segments.

COMPETING ACROSS SEGMENTS

In Figure 4.4 below, we have represented the situation of a firm competing in four different market segments. The key competences required to compete successfully in each segment are represented by the letters A–M. So, the key competences required in segments 3 and 4 are similar in that competences A, B and C appear in both competence profiles. The firm is well endowed with competences A, B and C relative to competitors. We can justifiably refer to these then as its **core competences.**

We would expect the firm to perform well in market segments 3 and 4, as its core competences match three of the key competences required. It may be less well positioned in segments 1 and 2, although it may be that none of its competitors is particularly strong in the delivery of these key competences.

By leveraging its core competences across four market segments the firm may be achieving economies of scope. And, as indicated at the foot of Figure 4.4, there may be possibilities to explore other markets which require key competences A, B and C. Hence, here it would be an approach to diversification which is driven by an understanding of the firm's core competences.

However, there may be some dangers in over-extending the scope of the firm in this way. For example, let us assume that a major grocery retailer has a core competence in negotiating with suppliers. This competence may have been developed over time through the corporation's dealings with large food manufacturers and household product suppliers.

They then diversify by stocking clothes in their larger stores. To succeed with this diversification the firm needs to possess the appropriate key competences, which includes competence in negotiating with suppliers. However, these negotiations with clothing manufacturers have peculiarities outside of their experiences in dealing with grocery suppliers: for instance, most of the clothing manufacturers are located in the Far East, and the style of negotiation is subtly different. So, although the retailer has competence in negotiation, this is not a generic competence; it is actually specific to certain market segments. Moreover, attempts to develop a generic competence may reduce the firm's ability to perform in one specific segment.

We consider the issues and challenges of diversification further in Part II.

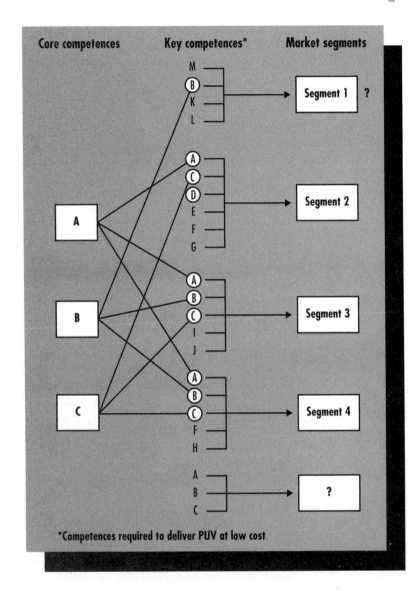

Figure 4.4
Core and key competences.

*Competences required to deliver PUV at low cost

As well as assuming that firms compete in a single product market, we have also tended to simplify competitor actions and reactions to the firm's strategic manoeuvres. We now extend our exploration of the five strategic pathways by considering likely competitor responses to the firm's actions.

COMPETITOR ACTIONS AND REACTIONS

Both the customer and producer matrices recognize the dynamic nature of all product markets. In this section we consider pathways where the firm's situation with respect to competitor behaviour is critical. These pathways can find the firm in one of two basic postures: proactive or reactive.

In the first four of the five pathways considered above, the firm is assumed to be proactive: the firm acts to achieve above-average positions in key-competence endowment. In the fifth pathway, the outcome is less attractive. The cost-cutting drive is often a reactive strategy, almost a knee-jerk response to an ailing competitive position. In the four proactive pathways, we adopted the convenient assumption that competitors would allow the firm to achieve these advantageous positions without retaliation. This is of course unlikely to happen in the real world, so we now need to move closer to reality by including likely competitor behaviours into the pathways.

The first mover in an industry is usually able to achieve a strong and lasting competitive advantage over laggard firms. We can see from our consideration of cost advantages where some of the first-mover benefits derive from. The first mover is able to build a large market share early on. This allows the firm to exploit volume-related economies of scale and experience earlier than followers, permitting a more aggressive pricing strategy, which builds more share *etc*.

But, if a competitor is also playing an aggressive game, although the absolute advantages from volume effects may accrue, there may be little or no *relative* cost advantage. In other words, as the strategic pathway moves the firm west, the average cost level in the industry is moving west at the same or maybe even at a faster rate. So, the outcome may be lower unit costs for the firm, but no relative cost advantage.

Similarly, strategic pathways concerned with improvements in key competences may result in no relative advantages accruing. The key issue here is the ease with which competitors can improve their competence endowments. Moves north in the producer matrix that can be easily matched by competitors lead to no *relative* improvements. So, imitability is a central feature of these pathways.

Here again, first-mover advantages can lead to moves north which cannot be readily imitated. It may be the case that a particular firm has been able to improve its competences in a way that is very difficult for other firms to emulate. This could be due to the particular path pursued by the firm over time, which has enabled it to accumulate valuable know-how. This can mean that rival firms need to follow similar patterns of development over time, and that there is little scope for followers to compress the time it takes to acquire this learning.

Changes in technology, resulting in a shift in the mix of key competences required to compete in a market can wrong-foot a firm, pushing it rapidly southwards in the producer matrix. New entrants can have a similar effect, especially if they are able to acquire the most efficient and effective resources to compete. This will raise the average level of competence endowment, and lower average unit costs, which will push some firms south-east in the producer matrix.

Scope advantages can also permit some firms performing in a product market to achieve effectiveness and cost positions that cannot be matched by more narrowly focused competitors.

PLAYING TO WIN

Our analysis would suggest that as long as a firm can achieve above-average performance of key competences at below-average unit costs, it will be profitable. Therefore, the firm does not need to 'win' or be the most effective, or indeed provide the lowest cost in order to make a reasonable level of profits. This view contrasts with other writers on competitive strategy who argue the need to win the competitive race, and that coming second or third is not acceptable.

Porter argues the need to be *the* lowest cost producer, and Hamel and Prahalad (1994) stress the need to lead the field, otherwise the firm is forced to play 'catchup'. Some practitioners have pursued similar approaches, *e.g.*, Jack Welch's policy of selling off all business where GE was not in first or second place. This tough message implies that, unless you win the race, there is no point in taking part.

We take a different view for three reasons:

■ There is no finishing line in this race: firms that may be leaders at one point in time may be followers later on.

■ No-one knows enough about how the world works to be able to deliberately manage their business to sustain a leadership position. Firms that have managed to remain in the forefront of their industries may be well managed or just lucky, and often case-studies of winning businesses owe a lot to rationalizations after the event, *e.g.*, Honda's entry into the US motorcycle market.

■ Firms seem to able to make an honest and acceptable living for their stakeholders without being the leaders in their markets, and there may be some merit in being a less conspicuous follower.

The playing-to-win may be product of US culture, which seems to value only winners, or it could stem from sporting and military metaphors that seem to be overused in the strategy literature. Whatever the source of these sentiments, the results are a rather simplistic and unhelpful conception of the commercial world. Since the race never ends and therefore cannot be won , the best that we can say is that a particular firm seems to be leading its rivals today; whether this situation persists is a point of debate. Certainly many of the 'excellent' firms singled out by Peters and Waterman (1982) in the early 1980s do not look so excellent today. If we want to use the sporting analogy, the losers live to run another race another day, and as the circumstances of the race will be constantly changing, they well may find that they have the capabilities to win in these changed circumstances. So, survival is all, as firms that achieve temporary leadership can come only from the population of survivors.

Proponents of resource-based theory have a tendency to attribute almost mystical properties to successful firms. By emphasizing the importance of tacit knowledge, embedded know-how and unknowable entrepreneurial capabilities, the routes to competitive success become arcane and intangible. These ephemeral attributes

73

have paradoxical properties. For instance, if you are able to articulate and explain what gives your firm advantage, you have probably destroyed the essence of your uniqueness, because if you can explain it, others may be able to copy it. If these arguments are taken to their logical conclusion, sources of competitive advantage become unmanageable, because in order to manage these resources they have to be explicitly recognized, and deliberately enhanced. These processes inevitably make the sources of advantage more replicable.

We would like to argue the case for the mundane follower in an industry. By dint of diligent management, by giving the customer a fair deal, and by trying to keep abreast of the times a firm can carve out a good living for its staff and shareholders without being the leader in the industry, especially in industries not dominated by brand names.

SUMMARY

In this chapter we have linked the customer and producer matrices to help us explore combinations of positions in each matrix that a firm may find itself in. We then suggested five generic strategic pathways: routes through the producer matrix that firms might follow. Four of the five can be considered to be proactive, where the firm's management deliberately embark on the pathway. A pathway was traced which began with reactive cost cutting, leading eventually to a loss of key-competence endowment. The profit outcomes of each pathway were considered, and towards the end of the chapter we explicitly addressed the actions and reactions of competitors. Finally, we extended the analysis to consider situations where the firm competes in a variety of product markets. This anticipates the exploration of diversification in Part II of the book.

APPENDIX

In this appendix we explain some theoretical extensions of the customer and producer matrices. We have placed these in an appendix as they may not be of interest to practioners, but they help to underpin some of the arguments set out in Chapters 2, 3 and 4.

In Chapter 2 we introduced the value-for-money curve, explaining that it represented combinations of perceived use value and price that were equivalent in the eyes of the customer. So, each value-for-money curve represented a level of satisfaction: higher curves, *i.e.*, those nested to the north-west of the matrix, delivered more satisfaction.

We argued that a firm needs to position its product on a higher VFM curve to attract more customers. This could be achieved by either cutting price, or by adding perceived use value, or by combining the two in a move north-west in the customer matrix.

Figure A.1
Value-for-money curves.

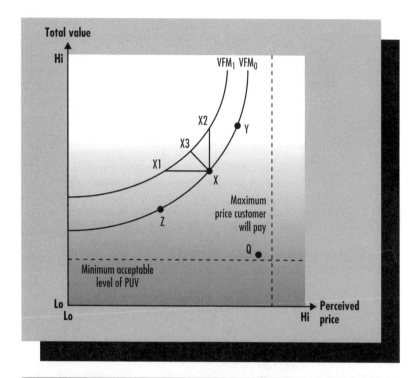

Figure A.2
Equal levels of consumer surplus.

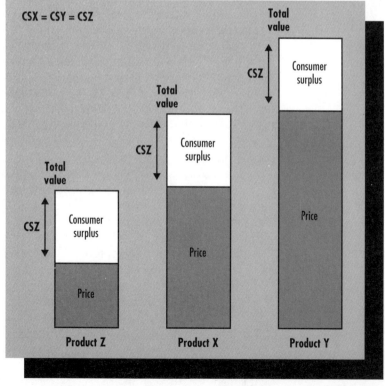

In Figure A.1 we have located three competing products (X, Y and Z) along the same value-for-money curve (VFM$_0$). In Figure A.2 we have represented these products as columns of value. Total value (TV) is the amount of money the customer is prepared to pay for a product. Product Y delivers higher total value than products X or Z. Total value is made up of price plus consumer surplus. So, to put this another way, consumer surplus is the difference between the amount the customer is prepared to pay for the product, and the price he is charged. Figure A.2 refers to a single customer. Operationally, in the customer matrix, customers with similar required levels of PUV are grouped together. In this case, the economists' demand curve, sloping downwards from left to right, will apply to the consumer surplus part of Figure A.2, as it will include consumers with decreasing, but still acceptable, levels of PUV.

As can be seen from Figure A.2, although product Y delivers more total value, because the customer is charged a higher price for the additional use value gained, the customer reaps the same amount of consumer surplus as he does from buying products X or Z. So, the value-for-money curve can also be viewed as a consumer surplus isoquant: each point on the VFM curve represents the same amount of consumer surplus.

Let us assume that product X could be repositioned onto a higher VFM curve at points X1, X2 or X3. In Figure A.3 we can see that the outcome in each case is an enhanced and equal level of consumer surplus. So VFM curves nested to the north-west of VFM_0 represent increasing levels of consumer surplus.

If we take as a starting point a new, emerging market, there will initially be a single monopoly supplier. If this supplier is aware of the average customer's price constraint, it could choose to price up to this point (Q in Figure A.1). The price constraint is the maximum price the customer is prepared to pay for this new bundle of use values. In this sense, the price constraint is a measure of total value potential in this new segment, as we defined total value as the price the customer is prepared to pay.

As the customer has no choice of products, and as the monopolist is aware of this price limit and can price accordingly, point Q in Figure A.1 confers no consumer surplus on the customer. The bargaining position of the monopolist has ensured that the supplier captures all the value in the form of price.

As competitors enter, either through pricing below the monopolist or by adding perceived use value, consumer surplus increases. Fierce competition will move the market to the north-west, where customers will enjoy increasing amounts of consumer surplus.

So the presence or absence of rival products determines:

■ The level of total value delivered to the customer, so at point Q the customer receives a low level of perceived use value.
■ The amount of total value captured by the customer in the form of consumer surplus, and the proportion of total value captured by the producer in the form of price.

Although our monopolist would be able to price at point Q, whether the firm makes profits at this point cannot be determined from the

Figure A.3
Repositioning a product on a
higher value-for-money curve.

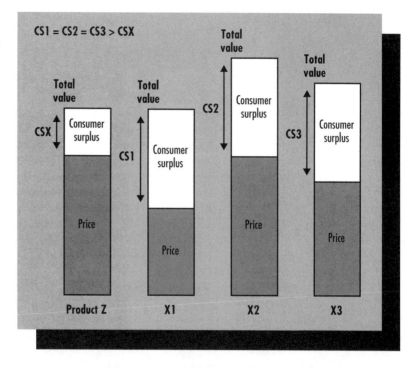

Figure A.4
Components of total value.

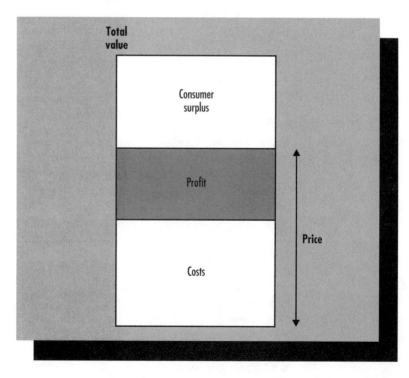

customer matrix. To answer this question we need to know the
firm's costs. So the total value columns of Figure A.2 can be further
subdivided to represent costs and profit margins (see Figure A.4).

The Competitive Environment

In this chapter we explore techniques that can be used to develop insights into the competitive situation in a particular strategic market segment. A strategic segment is defined as a group of customers who have similar needs. Thus a segment of demand could span across geographic boundaries, *i.e.*, there might be people with very similar needs ranged across the globe. What unites them are perceptions that they have the same or similar needs and that there are no barriers to prevent them being offered the same range of products.

There are two critical issues at segment level:

1. What is the nature of the effective demand in the segment? What are the needs of customers? What is the volume of demand? Is demand growing or shrinking?
2. Competence imitability. How easy is it for firms to replicate the key competences required to meet the demand?

These two issues are the most important in determining the overall attractiveness of a particular market segment. The level of demand in the segment influences the prices charged by firms serving the segment, relative to other segments; it also affects the relative cost levels in the segment, via economies of scale and experience effects.

Prices and cost levels combine to indicate the overall mass of profit that might be generated by the aggregate of firms operating in the segment. Firm-level profitability will be critically affected by the ease with which the key competences required to compete in the segment can be imitated. The easier it is for the competences to be imitated, the more firms are likely to be attracted into serving the segment. If demand is increasing in the segment, prices and profits may be rising as well. If it is relatively easy for a new firm to enter the market segment, the number of firms will increase, the likely outcome being a reduction in profitability for each individual firm.

The ease with which other firms can enter a market affects the balance of power between an individual firm and customers. More choice of suppliers gives the customer bargaining power over the firm. Using our argument set out in Chapter 1, we can see how the power relationships between firms and customers affect who gets the greater part of total value.

If the firm is in a strong position, perceived by customers as offering a unique and valued product, the firm is able to capture a large proportion of the total value available. To recap, we defined total value as the amount customers were *prepared* to pay for a

Figure 5.1
Who captures the value?

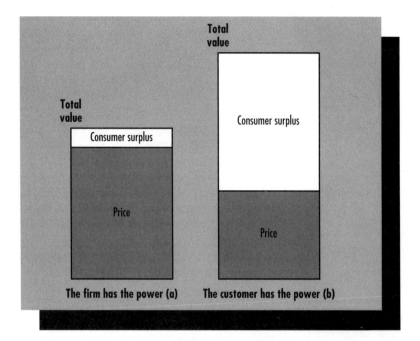

product or service, which is made up of price plus consumer surplus.

In Figure 5.1 we depict two extreme situations. In (a), we have a monopoly supplier. The amount of total value on offer is not high; the monopolist does not have to try too hard to please the customer. The monopoly firm has captured the greater part of total value in the form of price. In (b), the customer can choose between many alternative suppliers. In an effort to win business, firms have tried to offer higher and higher levels of perceived use value, which has increased the total value available. But competition has also had the effect of driving prices down. The net result is a happy customer receiving the larger proportion of total value in the form of consumer surplus.

In order to understand the situation within a particular market segment, it is necessary to be able to identify the **drivers of demand**, *i.e.*, what factors affect the level of effective demand in the segment, and we also need to understand the factors that affect competence imitability. We shall refer to these as the **drivers of imitability**.

DRIVERS OF DEMAND

We need to know what determines the level of demand within a particular segment. This question can be broken down into two further questions:
1. What influences customer needs in the segment?
2. What influences the number of customers in the segment?
In trying to assess the influences on customer needs, we require to know a good deal about the customer. A straightforward distinction

can be made between customers purchasing on behalf of businesses, *i.e.*, business customers, and customers purchasing for their own or their family's consumption, *i.e.*, personal customers. Typically, business customers are purchasing goods and services as inputs to a business process, *e.g.*, components, power, computer software, short-term finance. In order to better understand the drivers of demand for business customers we need to gain insights into their businesses, their needs, and how our products and services can meet their needs. We need to be able to anticipate how these needs may change in the future, and also whether the number of potential business customers will increase or decrease in the future. This requires a sophisticated knowledge of the customer's industry, their competitors, and their customers. In fact, you need to know nearly as much about your business customer's business as you need to know about your own.

Some firms have been particularly diligent in this regard. Major suppliers of computer hardware have been attempting to redefine their businesses from being suppliers of hardware, to becoming providers of systems and solutions to their clients. In effecting this transformation one corporation, AT&T, has realized that it needs to be involved in the very early phases of strategic decision making in client organizations, which has led, in turn, to major training and development initiatives designed to transform their salesforce into credible strategic level consultants. To achieve this, their consultants have to be able to analyse the strategic positioning of their target clients, and to be able to contribute to strategy debates within client organizations.

In personal customer segments we need to be able to understand their needs, and how these might change in the future. We have found that these questions are extremely difficult to answer. To get somewhere with this analysis we need to comprehend the different layers of needs, not just the more straightforward, obvious motiv-ations that drive customers. We then require to identify what trends, social, demographic and economic, affect these needs. This might then suggest how the needs may change in the future, and whether the demand within the particular segment is likely to be increasing or decreasing.

DRIVERS OF IMITABILITY

We have labelled the factors that influence the ease with which firms can imitate the key competences required to compete in a segment the **drivers of imitability**. These will clearly differ from one segment to another, but based on our discussion in Chapter 3 they will stem from:

- The transparency of the process, *i.e.*, how easy it is for an outsider to understand the business processes required to operate in the segment.
- Access to critical resources and systems including resource inputs, brands, reputation, installed base, and access to channels of distribution.

■ Economies of scale, scope and experience.

■ Technical know-how.

These factors have been variously referred to as barriers to imitation, mobility barriers, or barriers to entry (Bain, 1956; Mason, 1957; Scherer, 1980; Rumelt, 1984, 1987). As we argued earlier, the ease with which new firms are able to enter a market is a critical determinant of the overall attractiveness of segment. We therefore need to understand, for a particular segment, what affects these barriers to imitability.

There are some existing frameworks and techniques that can help us to shed some light on the two issues of demand and competence imitability:

■ The structural analysis of industries which analyses the five forces of competition within an industry.

■ Competitor analysis, *i.e.*, a detailed assessment of individual competitors.

■ Strategic group analysis – this helps us to understand the way competitors are grouped, and the mobility barriers that restrict movement between these groups.

■ PEST analysis, for analysing the macro-environment.

■ Scenario building – this helps us formulate consistent pictures of the future environment, and the effect different futures may have on our firm.

The first three of these techniques should help us address primarily the issue of competence imitability. PEST analysis and scenario building can help us explore how segment demand may change in the future. We explain the first three of these briefly in this chapter, treating them as stand-alone pieces of analysis, and then at the end of the chapter we try to integrate these approaches and examine the extent to which the techniques have been able to illuminate the two critical issues of demand– size and nature – and imitability.

STRUCTURAL ANALYSIS OF INDUSTRIES

In his book, *Competitive Strategy* (1980), Michael Porter develops what is now a very popular framework for analysing the structure of an industry or market segment, from the viewpoint of its attractiveness to a player already in the industry. For the purposes of this analysis, an industry is defined as a group of firms producing similar goods or services for the same market. Porter's approach concentrates on the competitive forces operating in the industry, with the outcome of the analysis being an assessment of the attractiveness of the industry, defined by how profitable the industry is likely to be for the firms already in it. The real benefit of the approach is that it forces the management team to view the industry from a broader perspective than would typically be the case. The discipline of assessing the relative strengths of the forces operating in the industry can develop new and important insights into the competitive environment, which can help in the construction of better competitive strategies.

Figure 5.2
The five competitive forces.

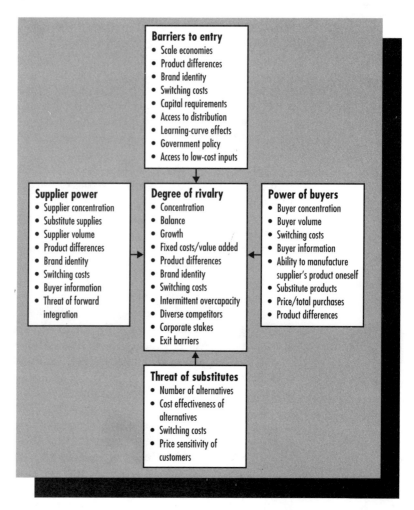

Porter argues that there are five competitive forces which operate in an industry and together determine the potential profitability of that industry. The five forces are:

1. Rivalry among existing firms.
2. The barriers to new entrants.
3. The bargaining power of buyers.
4. The bargaining power of suppliers.
5. The threat from substitute products or services.

Each will be considered in turn. Figure 5.2 sets out a schematic check list of the forces.

RIVALRY

Rivalry refers to the intensity of competitive behaviour within the industry. It addresses such issues as whether firms are continually seeking to outmanoeuvre their rivals through price cuts, new product innovations, advertising, credit deals, or promotional campaigns. Perhaps there is little competitive activity, with firms content to stick with their shares of the market, and unwilling to upset the balance of the industry by, say, instigating a price war. There are a number of factors which, Porter suggests, determine the probable intensity of rivalry in an industry:

- Slowing growth of demand, or declining demand: if demand slows, firms can maintain historic growth rates only by gaining market share from competitors. This tends to intensify rivalry as firms battle for share by price cuts or other attempts to boost sales. Declining demand will lead to further intensification of competitive activity, particularly if there are exit barriers to the industry. These barriers can take the form of large investments of capital that has no alternative use, few transferable skills, and high costs of plant closure, including redundancy costs. It is important to note that this factor refers not to slow growth itself, but to the slowing of growth in the absence of the exit of any competitors.

- High fixed costs: if the cost structure of the industry is such that there is a high fixed cost, and a low marginal cost component, then firms will be under intense pressure to produce at near full capacity. So, if demand fall off, firms will use price cuts and other weapons to maintain sales. Similar behaviour can occur in industries with highly perishable products.

- Unpredictable and diverse competitors: if the industry is made up of a diverse group of firms, their behaviour is likely to be unpredictable. If there are new entrants from other countries or industries that do not play by the rules their maverick behaviour is likely to lead to an extremely volatile competitive arena.

- Low switching costs: switching costs are costs incurred by the buyer in moving from one supplier to another. For example switching costs are incurred if an airline moves from an all Boeing fleet to a mixed Airbus/Boeing fleet, *e.g.*, the need for crew training, spares inventories and so forth. If switching costs are low in an industry, buyers are able to switch between suppliers without any penalty. Switching costs may be tangible as in the airline example, or may be composed of the intangible costs of being accustomed to working smoothly with a particular supplier.

- A commodity product: the more a firm is able to differentiate its product either by establishing a strong brand name, or offering clearly distinct PUV, the less it needs to fear its rivals, as it is laying claim to the argument that it alone supplies a given market need. Correspondingly, the nearer its product is to being a commodity, the greater is likely to be the rivalry it faces. Brand names therefore tend to reduce rivalry since they emphasize differentiation, and establish, at least, psychological switching costs for the consumer if he/she is to move to a different brand. IBM has 100% of the market for IBM computers after all, and always will have!

- Cycles leading to periodic over capacity: during these periods of spare capacity, rivalry will be intense as firms fight to fill their factories.
- High corporate stakes: in difficult times, the options are 'fight or flight'. If the market is an important one to the main players in it they will be inclined to fight. This will also be the case if exit costs are high.

BARRIERS TO ENTRY

If new firms enter an industry they bring additional capacity. If demand is not increasing to absorb this additional capacity, then the new entrants will have to compete for a share of the existing demand. To gain entry they may either compete with lower prices, with enhanced product features, or both. The net effect of these new entrants will probably be to lower the overall level of profitability in the industry. Entry is deterred by the presence of barriers to entry, which can stem from a number of sources. We have already considered some of these barriers in our discussion of imitability, but for completeness we set out the barriers identified by Porter:

- Economies of scale: if there are major cost advantages to be gained from operating on a large scale, then new entrants will either have to match that scale or have higher unit costs, and suffer lower margins. Scale economies are usually thought of as a production phenomenon, but may also exist in advertising, purchasing, R&D and after-sales services and elsewhere.
- Experience benefits: low unit costs can be achieved by accumulated learning, *i.e.*, finding progressively more efficient ways of doing things, which if they are significant would place by definition inexperienced new entrants at a unit cost disadvantage.
- Access to know-how: patents can protect firms from new entrants, and access to process knowledge and particular skills can make entry difficult.
- Customer brand loyalty: customers may have preferred brands, or they may have strong relationships with their existing suppliers, which they are reluctant to break. New entrants would have to persuade customers that it was worth their while incurring the switching costs involved in moving to the product of a new entrant. This may provide a strong barrier to entry.
- Capital costs of entry: if capital costs are high, this will limit the number of potential entrants. Such costs include setting up production facilities and research and development costs, establishing dealer networks and initial promotion expenses.
- High switching costs: if customers will incur high switching costs if they move to a new entrant's product, this constitutes a barrier to entry. Thus if IBM have a high installed base in the mainframe computer market this constitutes a very effective barrier to the entry of other potential rivals, as winning orders against the supplier of the installed base would require a really

special advantage to overcome the switching costs of changing computer systems.

■ Government policy may also provide a barrier to entry as the government seeks to regulate the industry by restricting licences, issuing exclusive franchises, or establishing regulations that are onerous and costly to implement.

■ Access to low cost inputs may also provide a barrier to entry by potential competitors without such access. Low labour costs in the Far East thus have provided barriers to the development of, for example, textile industries in the developed world.

BARGAINING POWER OF BUYERS

Buyers or customers can have considerable bargaining power for a variety of reasons:

■ When there are few buyers, and they purchase in large quantities.

■ When the buyers have low switching costs, and therefore probably low loyalty. Thus, highly differentiated products offer less opportunity for the exercise of buyer power than do relatively undifferentiated products.

■ When buyers face many relatively small sellers.

■ When the item being purchased is not an important one for the buyer, and therefore he can take it or leave it.

■ When they have a lot of information concerning competitive offers, which they can use for bargaining.

■ When there is a real risk that the buyer may decide to integrate backwards, i.e., to make the product itself rather than buy it in.

Thus, where buyers are faced with many alternatives, and the cost of switching is low or non-existent, buyers have power. The more concentrated the buyers the greater the power. Buyer power is normally evidenced by the ability of the buyer to bargain the price downwards.

BARGAINING POWER OF SUPPLIERS

Correspondingly the ability of suppliers to increase prices without losing sales illustrates their power. Such power may come about when:

■ The purchase is important to the buyer.

■ Buyers have high switching costs.

■ There are few alternative sources of supply.

■ Any particular buyer is not an important customer of the supplier.

■ There is the real risk that the supplier may integrate forward, e.g., instead of the car maker supplying his independent dealers, it may decide to set up its own dealer subsidiary.

Examples of powerful supplier relationships would be gas supply to the glass container industry, and microchip suppliers to the computer industry. The term 'suppliers' includes the providers of capital and of specialist skills. Hence, if an industry is dependent on particularly skilled people, these individuals can bargain up their pay levels, *e.g.*, advertising agencies are highly dependent on a few creative individuals and their pay is accordingly high.

If suppliers are powerful they can increase the prices of their inputs, thus extracting potential profits from the industry. If firms are facing powerful suppliers and buyers, profits will be severely squeezed, as input cost increases cannot be passed on in higher prices to buyers. Such a situation is likely to make the industry unattractive to potential entrants.

THREAT OF SUBSTITUTES

Industries are usually defined in terms of the products or services they provide. Hence, we have the aluminium can industry, the sugar industry, or the pizza restaurant industry. This enables us to identify a group of firms doing similar things who are in competition with each other. However, if we define industries from the buyer's perspective, we might come up with a quite different set of firms, who do not provide similar products, but who do nevertheless meet the same types of buyer needs. The buyer who likes sweet coffee might consider manufacturers of sugar and of artificial sweeteners to be in direct competition. A lunchtime shopper may see a pizza restaurant, a hamburger outlet, a pub and a delicatessen selling sandwiches as being in direct competition for her custom.

Substitute products are alternative ways of meeting buyer needs. In this respect the fax machine provides a substitute for the letter but not for parcel post. The effect of substitute products on the previously product-defined industry is to place a ceiling on prices, since a price rise may cause a previously loyal customer to shift to the substitute product. In this regard no purchase at all may have the same effect as that of a substitute product, as both represent a reduction of effective demand from the industry.

The threat of substitutes is high when:
- There are a number of equally cost-effective ways of meeting the same customer need.
- The customer faces few switching costs in moving to the substitute product.
- The customer exhibits high price sensitivity, and the substitute is low priced.

Defining the boundaries of an industry is more an art than a science, and is crucial to an accurate assessment of industry attractiveness. If an overly narrow product-based definition is adopted there are risks that the analysis will miss critical aspects of the competitive environment. Some industries are geographically fragmented with each locality having just one or two producers, *e.g.*, quarries, cinemas, zoos and regional newspapers. In most respects such firms in different regions are not direct competitors. Therefore one of the key decisions to make in a five-force analysis is the choice of industry boundary. The market is not an arbitrary one, it is a **strategic market**, *i.e.*, one supplying a distinct customer-determined need to a geographically-defined customer group. Whether it be local, regional, national, or pan-national, the characteristics of the market will determine which of these types of market is appropriate for a particular analysis. Thus, although the corrugated cardboard market is said to be limited to a fifty mile radius of the producer for reasons of transport costs in relation to an undifferentiated product, the market for video-recorders can be legitimately regarded as global. The five-force analysis boundaries adopted must reflect these different facets if the analysis is to be useful for generating insights into possible competitive strategies. Firms can of course redefine their industry by operating on the five forces themselves, *e.g.*, developing brand names, creating switching costs and so forth.

ADVANTAGES OF THE FIVE-FORCES FRAMEWORK

The main benefit of using this technique is that it provides a structure for management thinking about the competitive environment. Each force can be examined using the check-list set out above. Some aspects will be highly relevant to the industry and some less relevant. Some useful insights into the nature of the industry will usually emerge from such analysis.

It can also be useful if two or more groups of managers carry out an appraisal independently. Differences of perceptions can then be identified and discussed, and where agreement is reached some confidence can be placed on the judgements.

It is often useful to carry out several industry/market analyses. The first would be for the industry as a whole, subsequent analyses would focus on particular segments, and a third round might consider the industry at some defined point in the future in order to introduce a dynamic element into what so far had been an exercise in analysing the current situation. The framework can be valuable then in helping to define strategic segment boundaries, in revealing insights about the key forces in the competitive environment, and in revealing which force can be transformed into advantageous ones by operating proactively upon them, *e.g.*, by creating switching costs, or establishing stronger barriers to entry by building strong brand names.

It can sometimes be helpful to rate the strength of each of the five forces to help focus attention on the main competitive factors in each segment, and in order to compare the attractiveness of each segment. A simple points system would be 1 = a weak force, 5 = a strong force. Under such a schema an attractive industry would be one scoring 12 points or less. The disadvantage of such a simplistic system is that it ignores the weighting of certain forces that may be necessary. Note that if such a points system is used, 'barriers to entry' should be redefined as 'threat of entry' so that the points scores all face the same direction. Thus in a patent dominated industry, or a defence industry, barriers to

87

entry, or supplier power respectively would merit about average weighting. However, this could be allowed for in such a system.

COMPETITOR ANALYSIS

The market environment is obviously key to the identification of opportunities and constraints facing the firm. However, for accurate competitive positioning, a more detailed and specific analysis of the rivalry category of the five-forces analysis needs to be carried out by means of an accurate profile of each of the firm's major competitors.

It is important to understand your competitors in order:

■ To try to predict their future strategies.
■ To assess accurately their probable reactions to your strategic moves.
■ To estimate their ability to match you in the quest for competitive advantage.

Competitor analysis is more important in some industry structures than in others. In terms of five-force analysis, the stronger the rivalry force the more important it is to understand your rivals, since only then can you combat them successfully. In very fragmented industries like hairdressing, for example, competitor analysis may not be crucial to success. Firms are typically small, the product or service may well be undifferentiated, and the key to success is not a distinctive competitive strategy, but the provision of a valued service at an acceptable price to a number of locally semi-captive clients. Or the product may be a commodity, *e.g.*, concrete, and price at the required quality the only thing that matters in the buying transaction.

In a concentrated industry, however, competitive analysis is important, since the competitive battle is essentially between a small number of relatively large companies, normally with differentiated products, and often with strong brand names. In such cases, relative market share becomes crucially important, in order to be able to keep down costs by taking advantage of the experience curve, of scale economies and of scope economies as described in Chapters 2 and 3.

Competitor analysis is concerned with five basic attributes of the competitor:

1. Its comparative market strength in relation to the key competences required in the industry.
2. Its resources and core competences.
3. Its current and possible future strategy.
4. Its culture, and hence the assumptions it makes about itself and the industry.
5. Its objectives and goals both at corporate and at business unit level.

Comparative Market Strength

This can be assessed by using the producer matrix described in Chapter 3. In order to complete this matrix it is necessary to identify the essential elements of perceived use value (PUV) on the customer matrix (see Chapter 2), and from this derive the key competences needed to be able to provide these elements of PUV in the product offering.

The next step is to identify the company's main competitors, and collect sufficient data and opinions in relation to them to make a comparative assessment of each of them and of the company itself. The competences are then assessed for relative importance and given a weighting accordingly. If low cost is judged to be twice as important as the other competences, which are judged about equal with each other, low cost is weighted at two and the other competences as one.

It is common to include market share as an internal criterion along with the more direct factors. This is because a strong market share, although more a result than a cause of strength, may help the company achieve low costs through the experience curve and scale economies in particular and, as the PIMS analysis has shown, will lead to higher profit than average for the market leader (Buzzell and Gale, 1987).

Competitor analysis needs to be carried out on a segment-by-segment basis. In this way the specific key competences necessary to achieve competitive advantage in each segment are compared firm by firm. Where the key competence profiles for related segments are similar, this allows firms to enter adjoining segments without substantially needing to build new competences, *i.e.*, it reflects a broadly based set of core competences.

This form of comparative competitor analysis is inevitably imprecise, as it is generally based on judgements rather than on precise data. However, the producer matrix and its back-up profile charts provide a valuable, graphic way of comparing all the members of a strategic group in terms of the key competences relevant to producing what the market requires. Its precision can be improved in direct proportion to the firm's efforts and abilities to collect accurate data on their competitors.

Resources and Core Competences

The resources and core competences of the competitor need to be determined by the same method as that used for the analyst company, as set out in the previous chapters. The only major difference is that gathering the necessary data from a competitor is inevitably far more difficult than for one's own firm.

Current Strategy and Possible Future Strategy

The current strategy of competitors is discernible partly from what the company has to say, but more importantly from what it does. To assess either factor, a positive effort will need to be made at competitor data collection, in excess of the information that will easily come the company's way through a conscientious reading of the press. Effective competitor analysis requires the creation of a file on each competitor, and its active maintenance in an up-to-date condition by an enthusiastic executive who can act as 'champion' for the specific task. In the absence of such conditions, the file is likely to become outdated after a few months.

The company's *intended*, or at least declared, strategy can usually be discovered from the chairman's message to shareholders in annual reports, and by interviews in the press given by competitors' senior personnel. The competitor's *realized* strategy is, however, the more important, and this can be discovered only by tracking the competitor's actions over a period of time, and scanning them for consistency of purpose. Such direct observation can be supplemented by deliberately seeking out comment from suppliers who deal with both the analyst company and the competition, by interviewing buyers, by recruiting and debriefing executives from competitor companies, and by talking to journalists and other industry analysts. It is particularly important to gain early information of a competitor's possible change of strategy, and this may be signalled in a number of ways: by comment, by an unusual acquisition, by announced personnel changes at the top and so forth.

Competitor's Culture

The competitor's culture is normally an important factor in setting limits to the actions the competitor is likely to take in a market. An understanding of that culture will reveal the way the company operates, and the constraints within which it operates, often subconsciously. A company's culture embodies the core values that executives in the company take for granted. An understanding of this can be very valuable to a competitor. In Chapter 8 we explore organizational culture in more depth.

Competitor's Objectives

The objectives of the competitors are a fifth factor to be assessed in a competitor analysis exercise. A company concerned to achieve short-term financial objectives, for example, is likely to react quite differently from one with longer-term, market-share objectives willing to take perhaps a ten-year view to establish its position in the market.

If the competitor is a subsidiary of a major corporation, it is also necessary to understand the basic objectives of the parent. A company owned by the Hanson Group, for example, is likely to be far more constrained in terms of research and development expenditure, or in adopting a new initiative with a long gestation time, than would a company that is part of the Shell Group, accustomed as it is to the high risks associated with oil exploration. The level of autonomy that the competitor possesses, in seeking to achieve its objectives, is also relevant to the competitor assessment exercise.

Equipped with competitor information, the analyst will be in a strong position to address such key questions as:

- Is the competitor satisfied with its current market position, or is it likely to become aggressive in the near future?
- Where is the competitor most vulnerable?
- Is the competitor likely to change strategy soon? If so, how?
- What action by us is likely to provoke the greatest/least retaliation by the competitors?
- In what areas might it be possible to cooperate with the competitors?
- How might we shift the basis of competition in the market towards qualities in which we have excellence?

It is based on answers to questions such as these that new ideas for achieving competitive advantage may be developed.

STRATEGIC GROUP ANALYSIS

There may be what are often described as clear strategic groups of companies in competition. This situation will lead members of such a group to need to understand the essential strengths and weaknesses of the other members of their group, if they are to succeed competitively.

Strategic groups have been defined in a number of different ways. However, perhaps the most useful definition is that of groups of companies who are aware of each other as competitors in a particular market, and who are collectively separated from other such groups by mobility or imitability barriers. Such barriers vary widely in nature from group to group, and different companies within a group may relate to them to varying degrees. These barriers are the structural characteristics of a market that prevent, or at least inhibit, one strategic group from merging into another. Mobility barriers may include scale economies, proprietary technology, possession of government licences, control over distribution, marketing power and so forth. Different mobility barriers will be dominant for different strategic groups. The essential importance of the strategic group concept, is that it is towards the other members or perhaps potential members of the group that competitor analysis need to be directed. Rolls Royce, for example, will not spend its time most valuably by carrying out competitor analysis of Hyundai which is in a quite different group, but it would do well to understand Mercedes Benz's capabilities in some detail.

ASSESSING THE VALUE OF THE TECHNIQUES

At the start of this chapter we suggested that there are two basic issues that segment level analysis needs to address. These are:

1. What is the nature of the effective demand in the segment, i.e., what are the needs of customers? What is the volume of demand? Is demand growing or shrinking?
2. Competence imitability. How easy is it for firms to replicate the key competences required to meet the demand?

Having explained a number of techniques, we are now in a position to assess how useful they might be in addressing these two issues. The first point to note is that all the techniques are essentially driven from a producer perspective. The focus is firmly on the firm, competitor analysis, small groupings of firms, strategic groups, or industries in five-forces analysis. The main problem with this perspective is it might not be an appropriate way to analyse a segment of demand, which is clearly a customer-driven perspective. As we explained earlier, mistakes can be made in the identification of who the real competitors might be if an overly producer-driven approach is adopted. Do Pizza Hut compete with other pizza restaurants, or do they compete with McDonalds, Burger King, *etc.* Our view is that the most appropriate definition of a firm's competitors is the customer's definition, which may be quite different from that assumed by the management of the firm.

Some recent research (Daniels *et al.*, 1994) has indicated that managers within a firm may hold significantly different views about who their firm competes with, and these views can again be quite different from those of other firms seemingly in the same industry. Clearly, as far as competitive strategy is concerned, forging some real understanding of who we actually compete with is crucial, and we would argue that the safest approach to defining competitors is to work back from customers, and their views of who offer them alternative ways of meeting their needs.

None of the techniques described above sheds much light on the nature and strength of demand. The five forces analysis perhaps comes closest in that it includes buyers and buyer power in its framework. Market research needs to be undertaken in order to get some deeper insights into segment demand. Commissioning market research can be expensive, particularly if the management have not clearly thought through the questions they want answered. Often, the quantitative data that is routinely collected is not particularly helpful as it tends to be too aggregated to provide much of an insight into the nature of demand at segment level. The size of the segment can be fairly readily estimated if product sales information can be accessed, but again this can be frustrated where defining a segment in terms of products is not really appropriate.

To gain some deeper understanding of customers' needs, purchase motivations, and their perceptions of products on offer the most appropriate technique is the focus group. Focus groups involve a small group of existing or potential customers coming together with a skilled researcher to talk about products, and their needs. This technique is superior to questionnaire-based research in probing for more subtle motivations and perceptions.

The industry oriented techniques considered in this chapter do, however, offer more assistance in addressing the second issue: imitability of key competences. The five-forces framework addresses this issue explicitly when it considers barriers to entry, as does strategic group analysis where the term is **mobility barriers**. Competitor analysis should also help in the identification of firms that may have core competences which would enable them to develop the key competences required to compete in a particular segment.

Overall, these techniques can play a useful role in forcing a management team to address issues and questions that are not routinely discussed. The techniques can be adapted to suit differing environments. For example, we have used the five-forces framework with management teams from public sector organizations, *e.g.,* government departments. Here 'buyers' may not be the recipients of the service, *i.e.,* the clientele of a public hospital; it can be more useful to think of the buyers as the politicians and influential civil servants who determine budget allocations to the organization.

SUMMARY

We believe that there are two critical issues at segment level: what is the nature of the effective demand in the segment, and how great is the competence imitability? We explored some commonly used analytical approaches – the structural analysis of industries, competitor analysis and, more briefly, strategic group analysis – to assess the extent to which these techniques can help us answer questions of demand and imitability.

We concluded that these techniques were helpful, although they did not address our two concerns of demand and imitability in particularly direct ways. Their main benefit would appear to be in structuring and broadening strategic discussions and in prompting managers to try to gather better quality information about their competitors.

chapter

The Future

A lthough a thorough analysis of the current environmental situation is helpful in determining both corporate and competitive strategy, having a view of how the future environment might unfold can provide even more valuable insights, which can help the firm achieve an additional competitive edge. However, as Michael Naylor of General Motors once said:

> *Strategic planning faces one big problem. There are no facts about the future, only opinions.*

If the world were logical and predictable, forecasting the future could rely on statistical techniques, extrapolating trends discernible from the past. However, research has shown that econometric models are typically unreliable for more than two quarters into the future, and judgmental forecasts are as good or even better. Economic forecasting in fact has much in common with long-range weather forecasting. The number and variability of the strength of the forces impacting on the economy are so great that the probability of accurate prediction must generally be very low. But, of course, a general understanding of the ambient climate is possible.

This view is borne out by a consideration of some of the major, largely unforecast, world events of recent years, notably the dissolution of the Soviet Union, the reunification of Germany, the movement of the developed nations from largely social welfare economies to market-led ideologies, the democratization of Latin America and the crushing of the democracy movement in China and, until recently, the rapid acceleration of EU economic integration.

This record is counterbalanced, of course, to some extent by the list of correctly forecasted major world trends, notably the continuing rise of Far East economic power, the dramatic improvements in communications, due largely to microchip technology, the ever-increasing level of automation in a growing number of industries, and the continued globalization of consumer tastes and markets. Some useful forecasting may therefore be worthwhile so long as it is not single point forecasting, and does not attempt to be too precise. Trends, it would seem, are easier to forecast than events. Changes in the customer and producer matrices are likely to be more predictable over the short term, *e.g.*, 1–2 years, based on the current knowledge of customers and producers. However, in order to assess changes in the medium- to longer-term future, say 2–10 years ahead, other approaches may well be required.

A TURBULENT WORLD

A major problem of strategic management tools is that most of them have difficulty in adapting to the dynamic nature of a changing world. Scenario planning makes an attempt to overcome this problem to some extent by encouraging the strategist to explore alternative scenarios, and thereby avoid at least the single point forecast weakness of traditional planning methods. What, however, if the environment is not just dynamic (i.e., changing) but turbulent (i.e., changing in an irregular, unpredictable way)? How do we cope then?

In trying to account for such environments Emery and Trist (1965) put forward three possible influencing factors:

1. The growth of organizations so large and powerful that they are able, by their actions, to bring about fundamental changes in the economic environment itself.
2. The growing interdependence between the economic, political and other major institutions of society, leading to situations where any action by economic or other actors may have major consequences on those institutions with which it is interdependent.
3. The increasing growth of technological change which shortens product life-cycles and heightens economic uncertainty and unpredictability. Today's market leader may have tomorrow's obsolescent products.

Summarizing the problems of turbulent environments, they state:

> Turbulent environments exist when organizations are quite unable to select a viable course of action because environments are richly interconnected and interdependent. Interdependence per se is not a problem. However turbulence results from environmental interdependencies that are obscure to a focal organization. Environmental sectors lying beyond the purview of a focal organization become related to each other. Because a focal organization is unaware of their existence, it cannot plan to cope with their ramifications. Moreover, independent action only worsens the situation. When organizations act independently, in many diverse directions, they produce unanticipated and dissonant consequences in the overall shared environment – dissonances that mount as the common environment becomes more densely occupied.

Emery and Trist were of the view that the onset of the turbulent economy was visible as early as the mid-Sixties. Terreberry writing a few years later (1968) builds on Emery and Trist's taxonomy, suggesting an alternative definition of a turbulent field, namely one in which:

> ...the accelerating rate and complexity of interactive effects exceeds the component systems' capacities for prediction and, hence,

control of the compounding consequences of their actions;
turbulence is characterized by complexity as well as rapidity of
change in causal interconnections in the environment.

Terreberry notes further that the frequent failures of long-range
planning may be due to forecasting the future by extrapolation of
a non-comparable past. Thus, she wonders whether the rapidity and
complexity of contemporary change preclude effective long-range
planning. Such change, she concludes, clearly suggests the emergence of a change in the environment that is suggestive of
turbulence. Modestly claiming no great new insight however,
Terreberry cites Cyert and March (1959)

> *... so long as the environment of the firm is unstable – and*
> *predictably unstable – the heart of the theory of the firm must be*
> *the process of short-run adaptive reactions.*

Metcalfe (1974), seeking solutions to coping with turbulent systems
moves in a macro-interventionist direction towards the creation of
damping macro-organization systems. He sees a role for second-
order and network organizations in formulating and implementing
macro-policies to limit and control the turbulence through collaboration. He concludes:

> *At a practical level, the problem of environmental turbulence*
> *appears to be at the root of the crises which organizations in a*
> *variety of institutional spheres are experiencing.*

Drucker, in *Managing in Turbulent Times* (1980), took up the banner
of turbulence and announced the arrival of the pluralist society. He
provides much anecdotal evidence to support the contention that
global market forces, whilst increasing international trade and in the
economist's sense increasing 'welfare', also led to an increase in
economic turbulence. He cites, in support of this thesis:

- ■ The Eurodollar, which was, he claims, effectively invented by
  the Soviet Union in the 1950s. Because of the escalation of the
  Cold War, the USSR became afraid that their US$ balances
  might be frozen in the US, so they moved them to London.
  Thirty years later, the so-called Eurodollars amounted to
  US$1000 billion, and substantially financed world trade, and
  exceeded the total liquid resources in all the developed
  currencies combined. They therefore provide a source of high
  potential volatility. They are held by the main manufacturing
  exporters, *e.g.*, Japan and Germany, and by the OPEC countries.
- ■ That the OPEC countries increased world economic turbulence
  with their price hikes in 1973 and 1978, leading to a substantial
  change in the terms of trade between the developed nations
  and the petro-nations and creating more instability and
  inflation.

■ The end of sovereignty as an absolute entity for a nation in charge both of its political and its economic territory. The growth of supra-national entities such as the European Common Market as it was then called, and the concomitant growth of supra-national bureaucracies like that of the European Commission in Brussels, made national governments less master of their own domains, however much they might protest to the contrary to their electorates. For the nineteenth-century nation state, sovereignty meant control over both economic and political matters. Now, economic matters are becoming increasingly global, hence sovereignty cannot anymore be more than partial.

The emergence of transnational money may signify a major turning point in political history and political theory. It may signal the end of 'sovereignty'.

■ That, whilst economies are coming together and thereby causing turbulence, political entities in some parts of the world are fragmenting, *e.g.*, recently Chechnia, Bosnia and elsewhere, thereby causing political turbulence.
■ The growth of 'almost developed' countries as a stimulus to increased turbulence. He believes they represent a very risky phenomenon. He believes that the growth of the East is likely to be the touchstone of economic development in the next few decades, but notes that:

Adolescence and rapid growth are always turbulent.

■ Within companies there is also an increase in turbulence brought about by: the dramatic development of information technology, and, in the factory, of automation; the re-engineering of business systems; downsizing or rightsizing; de-layering; and the redundancy of much of middle management. In 1987, Auster, writing in the *Columbia Journal of World Business*, supported Drucker's thesis that management must now regard a turbulent environment as the norm, rather than as a period of instability before the economist's stable equilibrium returns. He writes:

Over the last fifteen years, and in particular over the last five years, there has been significant and ongoing changes in business environmental conditions. Improved information and communication systems allow rapid global transactions. Improved transportation systems give companies easier access to faraway markets. Both of these factors accelerate the rate of technological diffusion and create increasing socio-economic, technological and cultural exposure.

97

Rapid technological change has created complex products with shorter product life cycles making competitive positioning difficult to achieve or sustain. In addition these technologies seem to be converging, and consumers often demand fully integrated and compatible lines of product such as office systems, and stereo-TV-VCR systems which are extremely difficult for individual companies to cover.

Simultaneously, complicated international political relationships emerging from domestic competitive threats have created ever-changing trade regulations and barriers.

These pronouncements led to the application of the newly-fashion-able scientific theory of chaos to the realms of economic affairs. Stacey, writing in *Long Range Planning* in 1993, adds weight to the school that would write off strategic planning as an impossibly ambitious process doomed to failure, since the future in chaotic and turbulent conditions is too unknowable to be planned. Chaos, of course, is not turbulence. As applied to the economic sphere, Stacey (1993) explains chaos theory in the following way:

Chaos is unpredictable variety within recognizable categories defined by regular features; that is an inseparable intertwining of order and disorder. It is this property of being bounded by recognizable qualitative patterns that makes it possible for humans to cope with chaos.

Chaos is different from turbulence, where the patterns, if they exist, may be very difficult to discern. However, chaos theory has similar qualities in that it describes a world far from the determinist one of the traditional neo-classical economist. The world of the strategist then, seems to be moving towards the world of the physicist with quantum theory, the mathematician with Gödel's theorem, and the philosopher with Heisenberg's Uncertainty Principle. The existence of chance and chaos (Ruelle, 1991), whether described as turbulence or uncertainty, emphasizes the impossible task of the long-range planner.

Max Boisot (1995) summarizes the dilemma brought about by what he sees as the growth of the turbulent global economy thus:

As if competition in global markets were not enough, the experience of the past three years has confronted strategists with a radically new kind of turbulence – the geopolitical kind.... Of what strategic value is forecasting or competitor analysis in the face of geopolitical discontinuities of such seismic proportions as the disintegration of the Soviet Empire? How helpful are these analytical tools in coping with turbulence?

TURBULENCE: AN ASSESSMENT

On balance, then, do we live in a clearly turbulent world or is the supposed turbulence largely in the eyes of the beholder? There is, unfortunately, no generally accepted turbulence index or coefficient, as there is for inflation. It is not possible to say that turbulence has increased, because an operationalized set of turbulence economic indicators have shown wider-than-normal variations over a determined period of time. In theory, such an index might be constructed. It might cover fluctuations in the level of demand in major industries, interest rates, investment rates, foreign exchange rates; ever shortening product life cycles, and technology cycles; growth in the levels of innovation, and a noticeable increase in the boom and bust nature of stock markets.

Unfortunately, no such agreed list exists among economists, as it does in relation to retail prices and hence inflation. A view on turbulence must therefore for the moment remain analytic, and anecdotal, leaving Mintzberg (1989) the right to say 'I see no turbulence' without his being able to be refuted in an unqualified way.

What can we say then even within these qualitative limits? First, it would seem that the simpler and more confined the economic system, *e.g.*, the self-sufficient, small-holder family, the lower the probable level of turbulence. The risk of turbulence seems to increase as systems become more complex, more interdependent and more subject to apparently chance destabilizing events.

If this thesis is accepted, the contention that the level of turbulence in the world economy has increased dramatically over recent years becomes a convincing one for the following major reasons:

- An increasing number of industries have become global in levels of demand and in tastes.
- Technological change has become more rapid and it too has become global in nature.
- The globalization of markets has been further encouraged by the decline in national tariffs, through GATT, the EU and other free-trade institutions.
- The era of the vertically integrated company is in decline, to be replaced by the outsourced system, or even the virtual corporation. This dramatically increases the level of inter-company complexity.
- There are no political institutions able to control more than partially the economies that fall within their borders, since the globalization of markets has not been matched by a corresponding globalization of polities. National governments therefore habitually claim a degree of control over economic affairs that they do not in fact possess.

For all these reasons, even in the absence of an agreed turbulence index, it seems reasonable to declare the current times turbulent, and to state with confidence that we live and do business in an age of particularly strong uncertainty.

If this is the case, then strategic management tools that encourage the taking of a long view based on narrow-range predictions of the current and future state of the environment are unrealistic. The tools suggested in this book should be applied to a world known to be uncertain and at times turbulent. Small steps are therefore encouraged rather than large one, and reversible rather than irreversible ones. Flexibility of strategies is to be preferred to narrow commitment, and visionary corporate strategies are to be probably of more use as a guide than detailed business or functional strategies based on a assumptions that may prove false. For these reasons, the tools should be used more often with varying assumptions and the data constantly updated as new information arrives. Scenarios should be reviewed regularly and new ones developed as necessary rather than to a timetable, for truly the most accurate forecaster is he who forecasts frequently and late!

As markets become more competitive, and as the pace and scale of technological, social and political changes increases, firms are facing increasingly turbulent environments. This would suggest that the complexity of managing strategy must increase; fewer variables are predictable, and the future is increasingly uncertain and unpredictable. How can firms manage in turbulent environments? Possible coping mechanisms might be to engineer flexibility and stability in the firm's operations, and to engineer stability in the firm's environment.

■ Engineering stability in operations: here, the firm settles on strategy, in the full knowledge that it cannot be the perfect strategy for its situation, but the management reasons that by setting and sticking to a coherent view of where the firm should be heading, and by articulating a vision of what the firm should look like in the future, the firm is able to engineer some stability in its internal operations. This approach assumes at the outset that the firm will perform sub-optimally; but this is accepted as a realistic strategic posture given the uncertainty in the environment.

■ Engineering flexibility in operations: in contrast to the first posture, here the firm plans to cope with turbulence by building flexibility into the firm. This can be achieved by investing in skills, and by systems that can adapt and cope to changing circumstances. But, as with the engineering of stability, the outcome is likely to be a sub-optimal strategy. The capability that the firm has developed which enables it to adapt means that it inevitably has resources and skills that are underused at any particular point in time, thus raising its unit costs. This would suggest that, in turbulent times, most firms will be performing sub-optimally, but we can see that rather than this being a symptom of poor strategic management of the firm it could actually signify a recognition of the realities of the firm's environment. But a successfully implemented competitive strategy may sometimes be able to *impose* stability on the environment.

■ Engineering stability in the environment: here, the firm acts strategically to create some environmental stability. This can be attained by targeting particular market segments, delivering outstanding value in ways that cannot be easily imitated. This locks customers in and sets up entry barriers. If the firm can then begin to manipulate customers and control entry it has achieved some degree of stability.

In this chapter, we put forward an integrated set of techniques, which can be used to probe the future industry environment. We begin by examining how the two basic matrices introduced in previous chapters, the customer matrix and the producer matrix, may change. Then the broader environmental context is explored using two well-established techniques: PEST analysis, and scenario building.

CHANGES IN THE CUSTOMER MATRIX

To recap, the two axes of the customer matrix are perceived price and perceived use value. Once the relative positions of competitors' product offerings have been established (see Figure 6.1), a number of questions should be addressed:

■ Is demand in this segment expanding or contracting?
■ In which direction are the existing individual products likely to move?
■ Will the dimensions of PUV change, either through a change in the relative importance of the PUV dimensions, or through the introduction of new ones? Remember that a shift in the

101

Figure 6.1
The customer matrix: looking ahead.

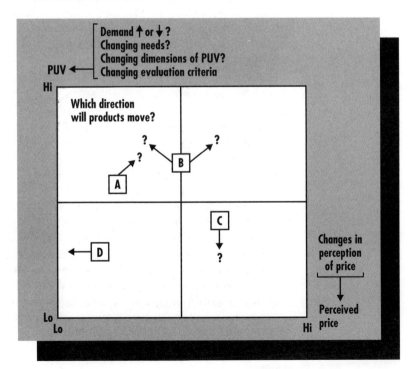

dimensions of PUV will most probably alter the relative positions of competitors on the customer matrix.

■ Will the elements of perceived price alter, e.g., away from concern with purchase price towards the long-term cost of ownership? Again, shifts in the elements of perceived price are likely to affect the relative positions of competitors on the matrix.

CHANGES IN THE PRODUCER MATRIX

A similar set of questions can be addressed in relation to the producer matrix (see Figure 6.2).

The axes of this matrix are key competence endowment and unit costs, and they reflect the strength of the core competences of the firm in relation to those of its competitors. An important issue concerning the producer matrix, and hence the customer matrix also, is the likelihood of new competitors entering the market. A new competitor can enter and gain advantage either through being able to undercut the existing players on unit costs, or through the possession of superior key competences, or both at the same time. In order to assess the likelihood of entry, the two axes of the producer matrix need to be analysed into their constituent parts.

The ability of firms to move on the producer matrix and the ease with which new firms can enter the industry are determined by a firm's ability to control the activity cost drivers, and to develop the relevant key competences. New competitors are more likely to enter from existing industries that have similar competences. For example, the Taiwanese high-tech sports-goods company Kunnan has recently entered the personal computer market under the Arche brand name, basing its competitive claims on its competence in procurement, its marketing skills, and its lean, high-tech manufacturing processes, including excellent quality assurance.

The relative cost positions of firms in the industry are determined by the factors underlying costs, many of which may stem from the state of the macro-economic environment, and from the existing state of the dominant technology in the industry. In order to develop a fuller picture of the evolution of the customer and producer matrices therefore, the wider environmental context must be considered.

Using existing information on competitors, and current understanding about customers and their needs, it should be possible to develop a view about how firms will move on the customer and producer matrices in the near future, as indicated by arrows in Figures 6.1 and 6.2. These probable shifts will affect the competitive balance in the market, leading to changes in relative market shares.

However, in order to gain insights into the medium- to longer-term development of the industry, say 2–10 years ahead, it is necessary to explore the broader environmental context of the industry. This can be done firstly by carrying out a PEST analysis, and then by developing a number of alternative scenarios of possible futures for the industry.

Figure 6.2
The producer matrix: looking
ahead.

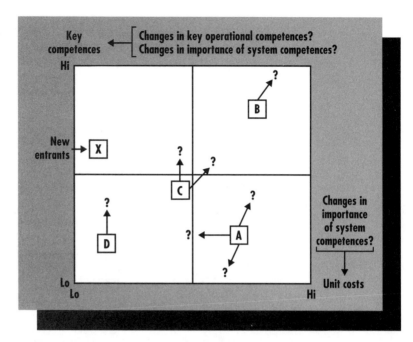

PEST ANALYSIS

A PEST check-list helps the analyst to carry out this process. Perhaps trends can more easily be predicted than events, and the PEST check list (a list of Political, Economic, Social and Technological factors) , provides a useful list of factors to consider in trying to forecast the changing nature of the forces likely to have an impact on the industry over the next few years. PEST analysis can be combined with five-forces analysis described above to develop a view of the future structure of an industry. It is also a useful start for planning the development of a number of possible scenarios (cf Figure 6.3).

103

SCENARIO PLANNING

In many forecasting situations, scenario planning is a useful technique to adopt. Scenario planning is most appropriate for industries that have a high level of capital intensity, and a relatively long lead time for product development. Industries that involve a high level of risk also benefit from the scenario approach. Only in such industries is it necessary to take a fairly long-term look into the future. If the lead time for product development is short, it is possible to react to events as they appear, and a 'trading' type of mentality may be more appropriate than a crystal gazing one. If the industry is not capital intensive, an incremental approach can be taken to development, the essence of which is to maintain flexibility. In these circumstances, therefore, time spent on scenario planning may not be well used. Both characteristics should be present in an industry to

Figure 6.3
Current and future
environmental factors of
importance.

**WHICH ENVIRONMENTAL FACTORS ARE
THE MOST IMPORTANT AT THE PRESENT TIME?
IN THE NEXT FEW YEARS?**

Economic Factors
• Business cycles
• GNP trends
• Interest rates
• Money supply
• Inflation
• Unemployment
• Disposable Income
• Energy
• Availability and cost
• Trade cycles

The Markets
• Market size and trends
• Market shares (by market segment)
• Changes in customer expectations/usage
• Price/volume relationships

Technological
• Government spending on research
• Government and industry focus of
  technological effort
• New discoveries/developments
• Speed of technology transfer
• Rates of obsolescence

Socio-Cultural Factors
• Population demographics
• Income distribution
• Social Mobility
• Life-style changes
• Attitudes to work and leisure
• Consumerism
• Levels of Education

Political/Legal
• Monopolies legislation
• Environmental protection laws
• Taxation policy
• (Foreign) trade regulations
• Employment law
• Government stability

at least a moderate degree before scenario planning becomes a necessary strategic tool. Thus, service sectors like management consultancy, public relations, advertising or market trading may have little need for scenario planning. For the oil, steel, or engineering industries however, the technique is becoming increasingly vital, if the chances of major investment mistakes are to be minimized.

Generally, where the risks are high, the development of more than one scenario provides some hedge against error, although inevitably such a hedge can be only a limited one. You can still get it badly wrong even with scenario planning.

A scenario is a self-contained envelope of consistent possibilities which describe the future. A scenario contains events that the strategist cannot control. If they can be controlled they represent strategic choices. There are two main types of scenario, the quantitative and the qualitative. The quantitative method of scenario building is based on mathematical econometric forecasting, using computer models and a number of simulations using different values of the parameters. Probability estimates are attached to each scenario. The relationships between the variables are assessed, as is the likely impact on one variable of a change in the value of another. Attempts are made to structure and formalize what must initially be judgemental forecasting of the key parameters. Using such quantitative methods, a large number of alternative scenarios can easily be generated on a computer. The quantitative method, however, suffers from the weakness that the seeming precision of the models tends to make the scenario planner forget that all models are built on past relationships, which may well not be future relationships. Furthermore, the model is only as good as the initial parameters allow, and these are necessarily judgemental, and thus subject to an indeterminate band of error.

The qualitative approach is most commonly traced back to the 1950s and the work of Herman Kahn. Believers in qualitative methods tend to distrust the value of quantification, considering that well-judged underlying assumptions are much more important than sophisticated methodologies. They contend that the future carries an infinite number of variables and values, and therefore any attempt to select a few and compute their implications is quite pointless. They put their faith instead in intuition, and the value of an integrative and holistic approach. They are conscious that the possibility of predicting the future in even a rough and ready way is very remote, and therefore believe that the best way forward is to make intuitive guesses structured around known trends, plus selected possible themes for consistent views of the future.

Scenario planning serves three major purposes:

1. It looks into the future and thus attempts to anticipate events, and to understand risk.
2. It provides the ideas for entrepreneurial activity, by identifying new, possibly unthought-of, strategic options.
3. It helps managers to break out of their established mental constraints and become aware of possible futures other than those which merely represent a measured extrapolation of the present.

It enables managers to gain a better understanding of the forces driving business systems, to develop a feel for the direction of those forces, to understand the logical implications of events already in the pipeline, to appreciate the interdependencies in the system, and to become able to rule out the impossible, whilst accepting the inevitable. It is, for example, probably impossible for the UK economy to grow at 10% a year like the Chinese economy seems to be doing, and it is probably inevitable that the UK will face the need to support an ageing population over the next quarter century.

A PROPOSED SCENARIO PLANNING METHOD

The following seven-step methodology for scenario planning is based on the qualitative approach. It is built around the requirement to generate three possible scenarios for the future, each of which represents an internally consistent view of the world often usefully expressed in the form of a theme, *e.g.*, the 'Green' revolution. It uses two central concepts for identifying scenarios, and for relating them to the company concerned, namely **macro-economic factors** and **company-impact factors**.

Macro-economic factors are the major events or trends predicted to happen in the future in relation to the economic world. The events following from the GATT negotiations will be key determinants, for example, as would be a recession in continental Europe. More specifically, a downward or upward trend in interest rates would be a macro-economic factor.

Company-impact factors, however, reflect the likely impact of the macro-economic factors on the enterprise. A macro-economic factor of an interest rate rise would have a company-impact factor effect of an increase in the cost of capital, probably coupled with fall in demand, and a decline in investment.

Macro-economic factors and company-impact factors do not necessarily, or even usually, have a one-to-one relationship. One macro-economic factor may impact a company in several ways and, contrastingly, one company-impact factor may change as a result of a number of macro-economic factors.

Thus, a rise in interest rates will have an impact on a company by raising the cost of borrowing, by reducing investment, and lowering demand, *i.e.*, three impact factors from one macro-economic factor key determinant. The reverse may also apply, and three or more macro-economic factors may affect one company-impact factor. Thus, sharp economic growth, lowered taxes, and a change of tastes in the market may, as key macro-economic factors, affect the company-impact factor level of demand.

Step 1. Scan the Environment

The first step in scenario planning is to develop a profile of the current environment. This would include the following components:
- A five-forces environmental analysis.
- A short-list of relevant economic inevitable and impossible factors, to provide boundaries to the crystal-gazing.
- The identification of key trends currently discernible from world events, derived from a PEST analysis.
- The identification of key macro-economic factors.

It is often useful to employ a panel of experts to help in the completion of this step, since it sets the scene for the scenario development, and is therefore important to get right. Delphi techniques may be useful here. Thus, the experts give their uninfluenced opinions. They are then informed of the opinions of the other experts, and asked to revise their opinions in the light of this new information. By such a method, some of the problems of 'group think' often encountered in expert panels are avoided, *i.e.*, all the participants thinking in accord with the dominant personality or leader figure.

Step 2. Conduct an Internal Analysis

Although scenario planning is concerned with the external world and not specifically with the company, it is nevertheless important, before developing the scenarios, to prepare a summary profile of the company. The reason for this is to enable the scenario planner to choose the most relevant and appropriate key determinants and principal impact factors, as they should be factors with a potentially large effect on the company. For example, if the company has no borrowings, an interest rate rise and consequent increase in the cost of borrowing might not be chosen, respectively, as key macro-economic factors and company-impact factors. If the interest rate rise is steep however, even for such a company, the company-impact factor might be a decline in the level of demand resulting from it. The company profile should include:

- An activity cost analysis of the firm and its linkages both upstream and downstream to suppliers and retailers respectively.
- Identification of the company's core and key competences and its specific corporate competences.
- Data on the company's financial, marketing, production, technology and personnel resources.
- Mission statement and objectives.
- Key strategies.
- Culture and leadership style.
- Competitive position within its major markets, and a list and assessment of its key competitors. These could be in the form of customer and producer matrices for its major markets.

Step 3. Develop Three Scenarios

Although there may be good reasons for developing a considerable number of possible scenarios, it is recommended that only three scenarios be developed, of which one should be a no surprises scenario, developing the implications of current economic trends, adjusted to take note of known current and future inevitable events. The other two scenarios should depict possible alternative views of the future. The key macro-economic variables of the scenarios should be identified at this stage. For example, a possible scenario-planning exercise for the private health-care market in the UK in the medium-term future might go as follows:

- **Scenario 1: No surprises.** The government would continue to fund the health area as at present. The growth of demand in the private sector would be slow, due to static economic conditions, and hence limited real income growth. The ageing population, however, would lead to increasing pressure on resources, although this would be mitigated to some extent by increased fitness lifestyles incrementally reducing some key killer diseases like heart disease. Technology advances would continue to make surgical invasion less traumatic, but at considerable cost in new capital equipment. Finally, the consumer would continue to become more sophisticated in the choice of health-care provision.
- **Scenario 2: The government underfunds health.** This would probably lead to fast growth in the private sector to

compensate for the government's under-provision. The healthy life-style movement shows a reversal, and increasingly stressful living leads to an increase in stress-related diseases. The ageing population continues to increase demand for health provision. Technology development in the sector slows down. Consumer demand becomes less sophisticated as there is a scramble for health-care services.

■ **Scenario 3: The private health-care market becomes very expensive.** The economy declines and incomes to buy health insurance become insufficient for the average target family. The government, through increased resource provision, generous payments to budget-holding GPs and active development of NHS trust hospitals, causes a steep decline in the private medical insurance market. Fitness life-styles improve the health of the nation despite the ageing population. Fast advances in technology continue. Finally, the decline in demand makes the consumer extremely selective in his private health-care investment.

For each scenario, the company-impact factors and the macro-economic factors identified above should be listed. In order to arrive at the most appropriate scenario themes, it may be necessary to identify the macro-economic factors first, before deciding upon a theme. An iterative process may be necessary, between theme selection and macro-economic factor identification, before internally consistent scenarios can be agreed upon.

It is important *not* to select three scenarios characterized as optimistic, medium and pessimistic, for the following reasons: such titles do little more than place a band of error around the medium scenario, which is not the aim of the exercise. Second, a scenario depicts a set of world events. It cannot be classified as optimistic, or otherwise, until the firm's strategy has been determined. It cannot be said for example whether a Europeanization scenario, or a Green life-styles one is optimistic or pessimistic. This depends upon how effectively the firm responds to the unfolding events.

Whilst it is important not to select simplistic optimistic, medium and pessimistic scenarios, it is probably useful to select scenarios that do represent opposite ends of the spectrum in relation to such company impact factors as demand levels. If only strongly growing demand is considered, there will be no contingency plans for potentially more difficult conditions.

Step 4. Apply Company Impact Factors

The next stage in the process is to apply the impact factors to each of the scenarios, as shown in Figure 6.4.

The principal areas of concern in the private health-care sector are judged to be:

■ The level of costs.
■ The level of prices.
■ The level and nature of competition.

Figure 6.4
Scenario theme: the UK
private health-care market.

Scenario theme – The UK private health market			
Company impact factors	**1**	**2**	**3**
A - Costs	Slow Rise	Slow rise	Fast rise
B - Level & nature of competition	Slowly increasing	Decreases short term	Tougher competition
C - Market prices	Downward pressure	Rise	Downward pressure of demand
D - Level of day care	Increasing	Up	Up
E - Opportunities for expansion	Limited	Good	Poor
F - Demand	Static	Rise	Fall

■ The extent of the growth of day-care.
■ The opportunities for expansion.
■ The strength of demand.

The movement of these impact factors is then judged in relation to each scenario, given the forecast nature of the macro-economic factors. For example, scenario 3 predicts a situation in which private health-care prices itself out of the market; this impacts on competitors by making competition tougher as the same number of companies fight for a share of a smaller market.

Step 5. The Scenario Matrix

The next step is to place all the evaluated impact factors on a scenario matrix as shown in Figure 6.5.

The two axes of the matrix are probability of occurrence on the vertical axis, and strategic importance of factor on the horizontal

Figure 6.5
The scenario matrix: the
private health-care market.

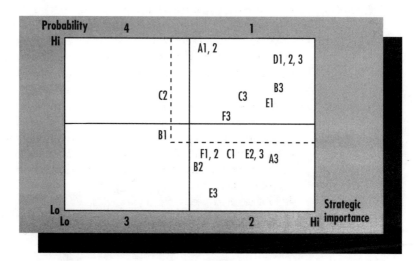

axis. Thus, impact factor A applied to scenario 1 would be coded as A1, a slow rise in costs, and must be assessed for its strategic importance and its probability of occurrence. If both are rated as high, the factor is placed in the top right-hand quadrant of the matrix. Quadrant 1 is that from which the ultimate, chosen, most-likely scenario will be selected. The dotted lines show the quadrant to be larger than a quarter of the whole matrix, since even a 40% level of probability and strategic impact justifies inclusion in the chosen scenario.

When all factors have been assessed for impact and probability for all three scenarios, they may well spread across all four quadrants.

Step 6. Select the Most Likely Scenario

In quadrant 1 and immediately adjacent to it are the factors rated as applying to the most probable scenario, and with the greatest assessed level of strategic importance. The factors in this quadrant will almost certainly be a combination of the factors from two or more initial scenarios. These factors have been rated as both most probable and most strategically important. In the example of the private health-care market, the chosen scenario is characterized at impact factor level as one in which:

■ Costs rise inexorably (A1, A2).
■ Competition becomes tougher (B3).
■ Prices face downward pressure, largely because of weakening demand, and increasing competitor provision (C3).
■ Day-care increases, exacerbating the downward pressure on prices (D1, 2, 3).
■ Opportunities for expansion are limited (E1).
■ Demand falls (F3).

The above impact factors from the chosen scenario after some screening and adjustment for consistency, form the basis of the scenario on which strategy is to be based.

Step 7. Prepare Contingency Plans

Any factors in quadrant 4 would be likely to happen but are judged to be strategically unimportant. They should therefore be accepted as congruent with the chosen scenario, but not highlighted as important factors in the strategic process. Factors in quadrant 3 would also be unimportant strategically, but they are also unlikely to occur. They should therefore be discounted.

The factors in quadrant 2, however, should not be discounted. They are not regarded as likely to come about, but if by chance they do – and scenarios can by their very nature be no more than best guesses – then their strategic importance is great. Contingency plans that are able to cope with these factors should therefore be prepared. In the illustration, contingency plans should be prepared for factors A3, B2, C1, E2, E3, F1 and F2. This means plans should be prepared for the contingencies that costs rise faster than expected, and that competition becomes far tougher. Downward pressure on prices has already been allowed for in C3. Opportunities for expansion should be responded to sensitively even if they are unexpected, and the firm should not be caught napping if demand expands dramatically contrary to expectations.

This is the great strength of the scenario planning process. It enables strategy to be changed to activate ready prepared contingency plans, in the event that a scenario different from the chosen one starts to develop. It cannot be guaranteed that the deviation from the selected scenario will necessarily be in the direction of the contingency plans, but at least the preparation of such plans establishes the mind-set that accepts strategic change in response to unexpected outcomes as a normal event.

THE BENEFITS OF SCENARIO PLANNING

The major benefits of scenario planning are then:
- It challenges the conventional wisdom.
- It demonstrates the possible impact of a lot of 'What if?' questions.
- It enables contingency plans to be developed for strategically important, but low probability, events.
- It helps to clarify the inter-relationships between key impact factors that affect the company.
- Finally, it establishes the mind-set that accepts uncertainty, and finds it less of a threat, and more of an opportunity to profit at the expense of a less far-sighted competitor.

Understanding the forces likely to create the future is crucially important to a strategist. Consideration of the customer and producer matrices, and how they will change, enables the strategist to look towards the future in a structured way. The PEST check list is also useful in this process and can help with scenario development. Scenario planning goes some limited way to cope with the problem that exists because the future cannot be known, and strategies have to be selected in conditions of uncertainty. By developing three different scenarios around consistent themes, and analysing them by macro-economic factors and company-impact factors, strategists are able to construct a more robust strategy than by the use of single-point forecasting. They are also, through consideration of alternative scenarios, able to develop contingency plans to deal with some unexpected eventualities.

GAME THEORY

PEST analysis looks at macro-economic variables in a systematic way, and scenario planning similarly attempts to make some sensible predictions about an inevitably uncertain future. However, it is not only the uncertainty of the wider environment that concerns the strategist, but the uncertainty of the prospective behaviour of those with whom he most closely interacts: his customers, suppliers, competitors and purveyors of complementary products. This also can not be known with any certainty, but the application of game theory may give some helpful insights.

Game theory is a systematic way of attempting to understand the most personally advantageous behaviour of non-altruistic players in situations where their fortunes are interdependent, information is incomplete, and fellow players' actions are uncertain.

An illustration of such a situation may be described as follows: a group of players are asked to choose a number between 1 and 10 and to write it on a piece of paper. A substantial prize will be given to the player whose number chosen is closest to half of the average of all the numbers written down. The issue is what number to write down. Clearly there is no definitive information on what numbers the other players will write down, so a player not employing a game-theory cast of mind may be excused from assuming that the problem is similar to that of the lottery, and may choose a number at random.

A game-theory thinker, however, might approach the problem in the following way: if everyone chose the maximum number then the average of all, apart from my choice, would be 10, and half this is 5, so there is no point in writing any number over 5. However, the other players can think this far too, so if they write 5 then half the average will be 2.5. But if they write 2.5 the average will be 1 (rounding to the nearest whole number), and so the thought process continues to the point of an infinite regress limited only by the rule not to go below 1. So the thinker will choose 1, but it is not certain that this will be the winning number, as it is a very heroic assumption to assume that all the players will have carried out the same thought process. It only needs one to have chosen a high number on the random principle for the game theorist to be deprived of his well-earned prize. Ironically, if all do think game-theoretically, of course they will all choose 1 and the prize will still not be theirs. It will be shared equally by the whole group! The illustration shows how game theory can help constructive thinking in an unpredictable world, but will not necessarily lead to a winning strategy.

The most frequently quoted game theory problem is that of the Prisoners' Dilemma, as illustrated in Figure 6.6.

The story here is that two prisoners are held, unable to communicate with each other, in separate cells, whilst they are interrogated concerning a crime they have committed. The police evidence, however, is very thin, so they are told that if one of them confesses then he will be allowed to walk free and his accomplice will serve ten years in jail, but that if both confess then the term will be seven years each. In the absence of a confession from either, they will get one year each on a lesser charge because of the weak evidence. Clearly if both trust each other and can communicate, they will both keep their mouths shut and accept one year in jail. However, given the impossibility of communication and probable doubt about each

Figure 6.6
The Prisoner's Dilemma.

		Column player	
		Cooperate	Defect
Row player	Cooperate	R = 3, R = 3 Reward for mutual cooperation	S = 0, T = 5 Sucker's payoff and temptation to defect
	Defect	T = 5, S = 0 Temptation to defect and sucker's payoff	P = 1, P = 1 Punishment for mutual defection

other's trustworthiness, the temptation to confess rapidly and hope to walk free is strong. Indeed it can even be regarded as the rational strategy for the unilateral confessor, as the fear that if one keeps quiet he may be betrayed by the other attracted by the offer of his freedom, is a nagging one. The conclusion must be that they are both likely to confess. Yet this will get them seven years, which is a very much sub-optimal solution, better only than the 'sucker's payoff', but far worse than the solution of keeping quiet.

Such a situation can be changed only by either inserting 'commitment' into the equation, or changing the payoff. Commitment may come about by allowing the prisoners to communicate with each other, or providing a strong reason why confessions would be impossible – honour among thieves, perhaps. A changed payoff would apply if the confessor were to know that family of the 'ten-year-sucker' prisoner would kill him shortly after he was allowed to walk free.

This parable is a metaphor for many business situations, particularly situations like joint ventures where trust and commitment get the best mutual results, but there are temptations to cheat. However, game theory thinking is also applicable to all situations that arise between interdependent players in an uncertain world. Game-theoretic approaches are therefore valuable whenever the future is being contemplated, and the uncertain behaviour of other players becomes an important factor in strategic choice.

Most strategic thinking of a traditional nature is concerned with beating your competitor, i.e., establishing a win–lose situation to your own advantage. Game theory shows that there are other possibilities as shown in the matrix in Figure 6.7.

Quadrants 1 and 4 reflect traditional egocentric strategy in which the strategist attempts to find a strategy that will enable him to beat the competition, e.g., producing a cheaper and better product that will take market share from the competitor. Quadrant 4, the strategy in which both rivals lose out, is frequently not considered. Yet it is a very real possibility. For example, in Oxford in 1995–6, a price war was waged between two competitive bus companies. It reached the stage where a day return to London, 60 miles away, was £3 (the rail

113

Figure 6.7
Possible outcomes according
to game theory.

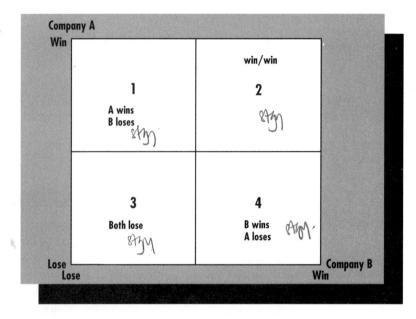

fare was £20). Clearly the bus companies were engaged in a lose–lose strategy, at least until one company left the market, and the other was in a position to dramatically increase its prices. This has now ended and been replaced by tacit collusions on fares which have now doubled in both companies.

Quadrant 2, however, is even less commonly considered, yet attractive strategies are available in this quadrant. Strategies that expand the overall size of a market for example will benefit both the player concerned and his competitors. So will strategies that benefit the sales of complementary products. An increase in the sales of new houses at the same time increases the sales of furniture, paint, carpets and estate agents' commissions without damaging the house-seller's profits. There is clearly an incentive for possible cooperation here.

Game theory expands the identified options that the strategist has available.

Game theory is a key element of trying to deal with an inherently unknowable future since it provides the strategist with a structure within which to carry out what is inevitably probabilistic thinking. It helps the strategist to avoid the most common mental traps in thinking about the future. These are:

■ Believing that you have to accept the current rules of the game you are in. If this were true Direct Line Insurance company would never have become the most profitable insurance company in the UK through direct selling. The rules of the game prescribed the use of commission agents and brokers in the insurance industry as the prerequisite of being a player.

■ Thinking that changing the game must come through beating someone. Many strategies that lead to success require cooperation not competition, e.g., the creation of international strategic alliances as a short-cut to globalization.

- Believing that to win you have to do something that others can't. Imitators have frequently been more successful than pioneers. RC Cola was the innovator of diet cola, but the winners were Coca-Cola and Pepsi-Cola.
- Failing to see the whole picture. In their concern to predict the future for their products, strategists think totally egocentrically. They ignore in particular the possible future and therefore opportunities of producers of complementary products. As Brandenburger and Nalebuff (1995) put it:

Any strategy with customers has a counterpart with suppliers; so any strategy with competitors has a mirror image with complementors.

- Failing to think methodically. This is the great merit of game theory thinking when tackling the unknowable nature of the future. It puts structure on the unstructured and makes some calculable sense of infinite future possibilities. It does this by narrowing the possibilities through adopting reasoned positions for yourself in the face of the reasoned positions of fellow players, all of whom are bent on at least survival.

SUMMARY

In an increasingly turbulent world, predictions of the future carry less and less certainty. The question of the use of the largely static analysis strategic tools has therefore to be questioned. Economists faced with this question tend to opine that it is necessary to assume that the world will remain sufficiently stable for a period of time, with the result that sequential static snapshots reflecting trends can be valuable. The strategic theorist would support this view, but add that by use of PEST analysis, scenario planning and game theory reasoning, some of the uncertainties that have to be faced in making strategic choices may become somewhat less daunting, and thus be less likely to inspire fear, and perhaps even represent a passport to success.

115

chapter 7

Strategy and Structure

Most prescriptive approaches to strategy advocate that the structure of the organization should be in line with the chosen strategy (Galbraith and Kazanjian, 1986; Miles and Snow, 1986; Chandler 1962). Most of the literature concerning the relationship between strategy and organizational structure focuses on large-scale changes in either strategy or structure; for example, a shift from a single-product strategy to a multi-product strategy, or moving from one business towards a diversified portfolio of businesses.

This chapter addresses the complex relationships between strategy, structure and organizational processes. We approach this difficult area by starting with some very basic concepts: specialization and coordination. We then consider the most typical organizational structure, the functional structure. Then the rest of the chapter develops a contingency approach to the strategy–structure relationship, building on the work of Mintzberg (1979). This approach argues that there is no one best way to structure an organizationin all circumstances; it all depends on the situation facing the firm. Is the firm large or small? Is it facing a rapidly changing environment or a stable one? Does it have a huge range of products selling into many different markets, or is it basically a one-product firm? In order to determine the appropriate organizational structure to suit a particular strategy we need to identify the key variables that influence structure and the range of structural options available that fit particular combinations of the key variables. Towards the end of the chapter we explore an organizational form that we believe can enable a firm to deliver high levels of perceived use value at low cost.

ORGANIZATIONAL STRUCTURE: SOME BASIC CONCEPTS

The strategy–structure relationship addresses two issues:
1. Having decided the strategy, how should we divide the overall task into discrete activities and how should we allocate them to individuals and groups? In essence, how should we specialize?
2. Having divided the task into manageable chunks of activity, how do we make sure that all of it gets done so that the strategy is achieved and coordinate the separate activities?

The first issue, specialization, is reflected in the organizational structure of the firm: the departments or divisions that focus on particular activities. This is horizontal specialization, with the different levels of management being vertical specialization. We can obtain a picture of the way the firm has chosen to specialize by inspecting the organization chart (see Figure 7.1). The most basic

116

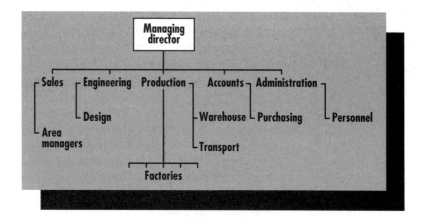

form of specialization is by function, which is explored in the next section. Staff can also be grouped in other ways: by product or product group, by type of customer, by market or geography, by project. There are advantages to grouping in particular ways as it helps to focus the development of expertise, and it facilitates the sharing of knowledge. However, specializing and grouping people around, for example, a project can lead to a gradual reduction in particular functional competences that are combined to deliver the project. This can happen because specialist engineers spend little time with other engineers, which reduces the flow of ideas and experience between these specialists. So, each way of specializing has advantages and disadvantages.

The second issue, coordination, is achieved through organizational processes, which are designed to ensure that the separate activities are linked together in such a way that the overall mission of the firm is achieved. Six basic ways of achieving coordination can be identified (see Mintzberg, 1979 and 1983 for a full explanation of this approach):

- **Direct, face-to-face discussion and communication** between those engaged in different activities – this has been called **mutual adjustment**. This can be a purely informal activity assisted by locating people in close proximity or it can be facilitated by setting up formal meetings, project teams or task forces. The advantages of this coordinating mechanism are that it can help to achieve rapid changes to the way things are done and it can encourage creativity by bringing together different specialists to work on a problem. The disadvantages are that it might be an ad hoc process leading to poor coordination, it can be time consuming if extensive consultations are required, and it is not appropriate if large numbers of people are involved.
- **Direct supervision:** here, instructions about how to do parts of the overall task are issued by the manager to subordinates and, so long as the staff carry out their instructions, the overall task is accomplished. This coordinating mechanism requires the manager to be able to understand the task, break it down into separate activities and issue clear instructions to subordinates. Therefore, this mechanism is only really appropriate when fairly

simple, easily understood tasks are being tackled. There is a limit to the number of subordinates that can be supervised in this management-intensive way, so the size of the organization and/or the size of each unit may be constrained if this is the predominant coordinating mechanism to be employed. The main advantage of the approach is that rapid changes in activity can be achieved by the manager issuing different instructions.

■ **Standardizing the way the activities are performed**: if an activity is to be repeated many times, it is worth finding out the best way of doing it. This is what method study tries to do. By standardizing the way the work is done, and by ensuring that one activity dovetails into the next step in the process, highly specialized activities can be effectively coordinated. This mechanism is only really applicable if the firm is facing a sufficiently predictable workload to justify the investment in standardization. Its advantage is that the work can be routinized to the point where semi-skilled or unskilled people can do it. Its disadvantages emerge from the intrinsically boring and unchallenging work that may be an outcome of standardization, and the lack of organizational flexibility that may result. The organization is really good at doing only a limited range of tasks very efficiently.

■ **Standardization of outputs**: coordination between different activities can be achieved if, at each stage of the process, the activity produces a standardized output. This then becomes a standardized input for the next stage of production. Using tight specifications to set output standards can permit different activities to be performed in different locations, for example in Airbus Industries, or even in different organizations through subcontracting.

■ **Standardization of skills**: here, the people carrying out the activity have standardized skills. If they exercise their skills in the appropriate ways their activities will mesh with the work of other specialists to enable the whole task to be accomplished. Organizations that use this mechanism extensively are accountancy firms, hospitals and universities.

■ **Standardization of values**: this might seem a strange way of bringing about coordination. It refers to groups of people who subscribe to a set of shared values that help to ensure they behave in predictable and appropriate ways. This form of coordination is particularly appropriate where the work of the organization is fragmented, where staff inculcated with the 'right' values can be trusted to perform in the 'correct' way, such as in police work or at McDonald's. Standardization of values is made easier through selection processes that identify people with attitudes and beliefs that are similar to those required. However, the processes whereby people acquire and change their values are not well understood, and it may be extremely difficult to encourage a significant shift in the values held by a group of people. This is considered further in the next chapter.

Coordination within a particular organization can be achieved by using one or a number of these mechanisms. However, one of the six mechanisms often tends to dominate, *e.g.*, direct supervision, and can have a strong influence on the type of organization that emerges. For example, where there is extensive use of work process standardization the organization tends to look like a **machine bureaucracy**, with a mass-production type of operations system; a large number of technical staff, production engineers, and cost estimators; extensive procurement, production scheduling, control andwork measurement; and usually a rather heavy management presence, with many levels in the hierarchy, managing in a fairly autocratic style.

As organizations grow, the predominant coordinating mechanism may change. For example, in a newly established small business, coordination is likely to be achieved either by direct supervision in that the entrepreneur directs the activities of a few staff, or by face-to-face communication. As the business grows, these informal mechanisms are likely to be less effective; there are now too many people to supervise directly and informal communications are not sufficient to keep everyone in the picture. If the organization settles down into providing a limited range of products or services, it may be worth trying to standardize the way the products are made to improve productivity and quality. If the organization subsequently diversifies into several lines of business, *e.g.*, through acquisition, the corporate centre may choose to manage each business unit by setting profit targets, a form of output standardization.

Mintzberg argues that an organization can be subdivided into five different parts:

1. **The strategic apex:** this controls the organization and is held accountable for its performance.
2. **The operating core:** these people deliver the basic mission or task of the organization.
3. **The middle line:** these are the managers and supervisors in direct line authority from the strategic apex to the operating core.
4. **The technostructure:** these are staff analysts that help to bring about coordination through standardising processes, outputs, skills or values.
5. **The support staff:** these are staff whose activities support the main work of the organization. For instance, in a manufacturing firm support staff would provide building maintenance, restaurant facilities, public relations, office cleaning *etc*.

ORGANIZATIONAL PROCESSES

This chapter is concerned with the links between strategy, organizational structures and organizational processes. Included in organizational processes are decision making, delegation, formal and informal communication, training, indoctrination, quality control, operations planning and control, leadership, formal and informal power relationships, management information systems, budgetary control, target setting, incentive systems and disciplinary procedures. The aim of these processes is either specialization, *e.g.*, training, or coordination, *e.g.*, quality control, planning, delegation, target setting.

Certain types of structure make extensive use of particular processes. For example, operations planning and control, training, quality assurance and disciplinary processes are features of the large mass-production firm, the **machine organization**. In contrast, informal communication networks, incentive systems and decentralized decision making might be typically found in a software development company, the **innovative organization**. Therefore, it is important to understand the role that organizational processes are playing in bringing about specialization or coordination within a particular organizational configuration, and not to view them as separate dimensions that can be changed or manipulated independently. Hence, programmes that concentrate on changing quality systems or improving communications need to be tackled with a full appreciation of the role these processes play in the wider organization. Other aspects of formal and informal organizational processes are explored in more depth in the next chapter.

LINKING STRATEGY, STRUCTURE AND PROCESS

We shall now look at the links between strategy change and structure. As most business units adopt some form of functional structure it is worth looking at the strategy–structure relationship within a functional structure first. We will then explore other strategy–structure relationships.

THE FUNCTIONAL STRUCTURE

Most firms solve the first problem of organization by adopting a functional structure, which groups people according to the type of activity in which they are engaged. An engineering organization might have the following functions: production, engineering, sales, accounts, administration, personnel, warehouse/transport (see Figure 7.1).

As a firm grows, the number of functional specializations tends to increase, and they may emerge in a typical order. For example, the very small one- or two-person firm concentrates initially on some form of production, *e.g.*, making novelty candles. Growth in orders means they have to think about how to manage the production activity, so more staff are taken on and some further specialization takes place within the production function: mould making, dying, finishing, packing. Managing the finances and accounts soon becomes an issue. Handled initially by a subcontractor, the firm's accountant, the volume of work now requires the employment of a full-time specialist management accountant. Initially, orders came in without the need for a great deal of marketing effort, but there may now be a need to employ sales people. The amount of paperwork increases, and the loss of a valuable order through poor administration leads to the development of systems to handle orders, cash flow, scheduling and so on.

Thus, as the firm grows, activities that initially formed just part of the founder's responsibility emerge as specializations in their own right, and within functions, further specialization takes place.

Coordination within the operational area in a larger firm is generally achieved through standardization of work processes. The way the work is done is decided by, for example, work study engineers or production engineers. Coordination across the functions is probably achieved through a combination of direct supervision, *e.g.*, decisions and interventions by the managing director, standardization, the setting of budgets and targets for each function, ad hoc discussion or formalized meetings between managers from different functions, and mutual adjustment.

Functional specialization has the advantage of encouraging the development of expertise, but the downside is that it can lead to parochialism and poor coordination of activities across the organization. It is probable that some form of functional specialization is essential in most organizations, otherwise the organization would not be able to fulfill its basic tasks, *e.g.*, patients treated, newspapers printed, cars designed and manufactured. These basic tasks are likely to be common to all firms in a particular industry.

121

However, competitive advantage stems from the ability to outperform competitors in these tasks. Therefore, merely performing the basic tasks of the industry is not enough; this just lets you into the game. To have some chance of winning you must perform the tasks in an extraordinary way. We pick this issue up later in the chapter.

Most organizations display some form of functional specialization. However, the extent and type of specialization varies between organizations, and the predominant coordination mechanisms vary as well. We now set out a contingency approach to the strategy structure relationship that can be used to explore these variations in structural form.

A CONTINGENCY APPROACH TO STRATEGY AND STRUCTURE

Nowadays, few writers would subscribe to the classic rules of good organization, *e.g.*, unity of command and limited span of control, favouring instead a contingency approach. There is no one best way to organize; it all depends on the situation. The most thorough exposition of the contingency approach is probably Mintzberg's synthesis of prior studies in organization set out in his *Structuring of Organizations* (1979). He argues that the appropriate organizational form is contingent upon the states of certain variables: the age of the organization; its size, environmental dynamism and complexity; its external power relationships; and the technical system employed by the organization, *e.g.*, small-batch production, continuous-flow processes. This contingency approach has been further explored by Miller (1986).

Particular combinations of these contingent variables would indicate that some organizational forms are more appropriate than others. For example, a machine bureaucracy structure would fit the following set of contingency conditions: a stable environment, a simple task, powerful external influences, and the old and large organization.

Strategy, as such, is not referred to explicitly in Mintzberg's contingency approach. We could infer, however, that insofar as a strategy determines through a firm's target markets how it is to address its environment, *i.e.* to compete on price and become the lowest-cost producer, the contingent variables identified by Mintzberg would, *inter alia*, be determined by the strategy. That is, we are aiming to serve an essentially stable environment and to be the lowest-cost producer, so we must achieve large volumes; the chosen technology is a regulating mass-production system and so on. This relationship could be set out as follows:

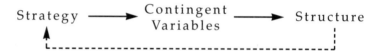

Mintzberg suggests that, although in theory there is a potentially huge array of organizational forms, in reality just a few configurations account for most types of organization. Mintzberg identifies the machine organization, the professional organization, the entrepreneurial organization, the diversified organization, the innovative organization, and the missionary organization (Mintzberg, 1983). It should be noted that structure also has a strong role in constraining strategy, so the process is iterative.

CHANGES IN THE CONTINGENT VARIABLES

If the strategy of the organization leads to significant changes in the contingent variables, substantial structural changes may be required. These may result in the firm moving from one configuration to another, *e.g.*, from a machine organization to a divisionalized structure. Such inter-structural changes may be required when:

■ Substantial changes in product/market scope have been introduced – new markets, exporting, launching different types of product in existing markets, diversification, new products and new markets.

- There have been significant shifts in the tasks facing the firm – tasks may have become increasingly complex, or technical or procedural developments may have simplified the task.
- There have been significant changes in the dynamism of the environment – an increased pace of change in the unpredictability of the environment requires the firm to be much more flexible and adaptable.
- The rules of the game have been changed—increasing competitive pressures lead to more emphasis being given to, for example, the pace of new product introductions; greater emphasis on the tight control of costs; moves towards vertical integration, either forwards into distribution or retail, or backwards into component manufacture; and increasing use of subcontractors for core activities.

Changes of this nature and scope are likely to put the existing structure under considerable pressure. There is evidence to suggest that structural reorganization often lags well behind the change in strategy. There is an inertia in many organizations, compounded by a reluctance on the part of top management to grasp the nettle of structural change, which results in damaging mismatches being perpetuated between the new strategic position of the firm and the former, now inappropriate, structure. Unfortunately, it is often only when a crisis of some sort is reached that the necessary structural changes are introduced. The crisis may take the form of, for example, a dramatic downturn in performance, a takeover threat or replacing the chief executive officer.

123

Strategy changes, which may or may not have resulted from deliberate attempts to shape the future direction of the firm, that result in significant changes in the contingency variables will require shifts in structure to achieve a better strategy–structure alignment. To explore the structural implications of changes in the contingent variables resulting from the strategy change, we can refer to Figure 7.2. Here, three of the more important contingent variables are presented in the form of continuums:

1. **Environmental dynamism.** At one extreme, the firm is facing a very stable and predictable environment; at the other extreme the environment is unpredictable and undergoing rapid change.
2. **Task complexity.** The basic tasks of the firm can be either simple or complex, or somewhere in between these extremes. Simple tasks are tasks that can be comprehended easily, and can be broken down into a number of simple steps. In contrast, complex tasks can not be tackled easily with well-understood procedures or routines; they require the application of specialized knowledge, and a degree of creativity may be involved. In this sense, designing a new car is a complex task but making it is essentially a simple task as it is possible to break down the manufacture of the car into a large set of straightforward, easily understood sub-tasks. Put another way, it is the difference between washing dishes, a task that can be

Figure 7.2
Three main contingent
variables.

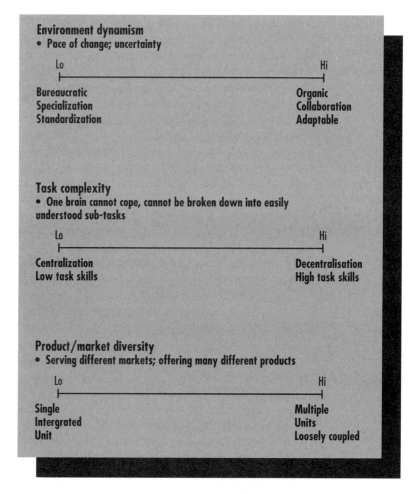

simplified to the point where a machine can do it, and raising happy, well-adjusted children, a task so complex that even basic cause–effect relationships are hard to identify.

3. **Product/market diversity.** Low diversity means the firm is offering a limited range of products to one market; high diversity involves the marketing of a diverse set of products in many different markets.

ORGANIZATIONAL IMPLICATIONS OF THE CONTINGENT VARIABLES

The organizational implications of each of these three contingent variables are expected to be as follows:

1. **Environmental dynamism.** When the organization is facing a relatively stable and predictable environment, the four standardizing processes – work processes, skills, outputs, and values – are viable coordinating mechanisms. These mechanisms are likely to lead to a high degree of specialization and the emergence of staff groups involved in effecting standardization, *e.g.,* those staff concerned with production

engineering, organization and methods, budgeting and standard costing, training and induction, and operations planning and control. Standardization becomes less viable when the organization is facing a rapidly changing and unpredictable environment. Increasing environmental dynamism can be coped with through flexible organization structures that encourage informal communication matrix structures and project teams.

2. **Task complexity.** When the basic tasks of the organization are straightforward, those tasks can be broken down into easily understood activities. Simple tasks mean that decisions can be made centrally using direct supervision as the coordinating mechanism and, when they are broken down into separate, simple steps, relatively unskilled people can carry them out. Complex tasks cannot be broken down into easily-understood steps and usually require highly skilled specialists to execute them. With complex tasks, decision making tends to be located at the level of experts with the required specialist knowledge: task complexity then tends to be associated with decentralized decision making.

3. **Product/market diversity.** Firms trading in one market with a limited range of products can manage effectively with a single, integrated unit. As the markets served and/or the range of products offered become more diverse the single unit is placed under strain. The requirements of different products and markets tend to pull the organization in different directions, leading to conflicting demands and priorities. If no structural change takes place, the resulting performance of the firm is likely to deteriorate. Increasing diversity is best dealt with by allowing parts of the organization to tailor their activities to match the particular requirements of the product/markets they serve, leading ultimately to a multi-divisional structure. One interim solution is the matrix structure, which usually involves overlaying the existing functional specializations with a product/market or project organization.

Combinations of these contingent variables lead to pressure to adopt particular types of structure. Four different combinations of task complexity and environment dynamism are represented in Figure 7.3. Firms tackling simple tasks in stable environments are likely to evolve structures that are centralized and use extensive work-process standardization. As the environment becomes more dynamic, standardization becomes less viable as the firm needs to be much more responsive to unpredictable changes. Because of the basic nature of the tasks, coordination can be effected through direction from the top.

Complex tasks in stable environments mean that it is worthwhile investing time in developing specialist skills to tackle the complexities involved, *e.g.*, surgery. Each specialist can work almost independently if the environment remains stable and predictable. The anaesthetist and the surgeon need not even speak to each other in the operating theatre. However, increasing dynamism and

125

Figure 7.3
Task, environment and
structure.

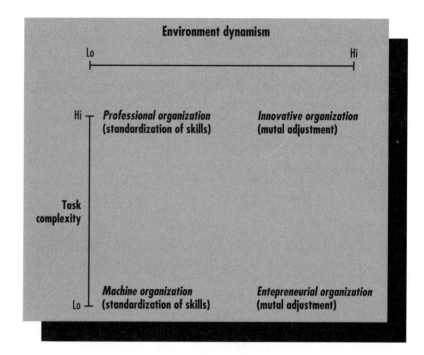

unpredictability mean that new problems emerge, and new creative solutions are required. Now the experts must collaborate in multi-disciplinary teams that form and reform according to changing task demands.

126

STRUCTURAL RESPONSES TO CHANGES IN STRATEGY AND ENVIRONMENT

Changes in the environment, *e.g.*, from stable to dynamic, can be regarded as passive strategic decisions insofar as the firm's management choose to continue to operate in the changing environment. They could, conceivably, consider withdrawing from increasingly hostile environments. However, changes in task complexity and product market diversity are more clearly the stuff of strategic decisions.

If the strategy change involves a shift along just one of the three main contingent variables, it should be fairly clear what the required structural changes are likely to be. Moreover, coherent structures can be achieved with the four combinations of environmental dynamism and task complexity set out in Figure 7.3. Mintzberg (1983) identifies the four structure types as follows:

1. **Simple task/stable environment = the machine organization.** This has a centralized bureaucracy with formalized procedures, sharp divisions of labour, functional groupings and an elaborate hierarchy; an extensive group of staff analysts are concerned with effecting work standardization, and a large support staff reduce uncertainty.
2. **Simple task/dynamic environment = the entrepreneurial organization.** This is a simple structure, with few staff roles

and few middle managers; activities revolve around the founding entrepreneur, who coordinates through direct supervision.

3. **Complex task/stable environment = the professional organization.** This is a large and powerful operating core consisting of highly specialized professionals, *e.g.*, lawyers, surgeons, professors; there is a large support staff and shallow hierarchy, with coordination being effected by standardization of skills.

4. **Complex task/dynamic environment = the innovative organization.** This typically has a fluid, organic and decentralized structure, with experts deployed in multi-disciplinary teams, with coordination through mutual adjustment and perhaps a matrix structure.

Each of these four configurations is an internally consistent combinations of structure and organization processes that is suited to the tasks and environments facing it. However, because the systems, structures and processes are mutually consistent and reinforcing, changing from one configuration to another is very difficult. Each configuration exhibits its own self-preserving dynamics or momentum, which leads to the structure continuing long after the strategy or environment has changed. As suggested earlier, it is often only when the mismatch between the new strategy and the old structural arrangements becomes so great that performance dramatically deteriorates, that a structural reorganization is attempted.

The problems involved in shifting from one configuration to another are immense, particularly if the change challenges existing values and power structures. The move from one configuration to another is likely to be evolutionary in nature, and may even be perceptible only in hindsight.

Structural transformations that involve a shift in just one contingent variable are likely to be less challenging than those requiring shifts in two or three variables. For example, if the entrepreneurial organization is successful, growth in orders may reduce the unpredictability of the environment. The essentially simple nature of the tasks, coupled with increasing stability and an increasing volume of work, should lead to the firm effecting a smooth transition into the machine organization, as more parts of the task are standardized and made routine. This change would probably not seriously challenge the centralization of decision making. However, the values of those who were involved in the early entrepreneurial years, resulting from shared experiences in overcoming the challenges of starting a new business, may well be quite different from the values of new employees, who may have a more calculative involvement in the firm. They are there for the money.

If task complexity and environmental dynamism change, then the required shift from one configuration may be quite traumatic. Take, for example, a small management consultancy with complex tasks in a dynamic environment (= innovative organization) that grows on the strength of a particular approach to payment systems. The firm begins to use fewer skilled staff, using a proceduralized approach, increasing task simplification and environment stability (= the machine organization). The reasons why the founders started the venture – the pursuit of variety and autonomy, and the challenge of tackling complex problems – are replaced by the need to manage an increasingly centralized, bureaucratic organization.

Consider also the case of the manufacturing firm facing increasing foreign competition. Predictability in the environment is undermined, and in order to keep pace with competitive threats the firm needs to rapidly improve its products. So, the comfortable and stable situation that encouraged the emergence of a machine organization is replaced by an increasingly hostile and unpredictable environment and increasing task complexity as the pace of new product introductions is stepped up. These changes in contingent conditions could drive the firm organization towards the innovative organization, but this configuration is almost the polar opposite of the machine organization. Structures, processes, styles and values appropriate to one configuration are entirely inappropriate in the other, hence the challenge of managing such an organizational transformation is immense.

COPING WITH DIVERSITY

The strategic logic underpinning a move to increase product/market diversity must be considered when determining the appropriate structural response. For example, if the increasingly diverse product/market portfolio is the result of attempts to reduce the business risk of the corporation, then it would be appropriate to manage the activities involved in serving these product/markets in autonomous business units. However, if the increasing diversity is the outcome of a strategy built on the notion that the firm possesses some core capabilities, then structures and processes will be required that enable the corporation to utilize these skills across a widening scope of activities. Similarly, if the increasing diversity is the result of attempts to achieve synergy by bringing two businesses together – the whole is greater than the sum of the parts – then systems and structures will be required to foster the transfer of expertise, shared procurement, research and development, and so on.

So, the strategic logic of the move towards increased product/market diversity is central to decisions about the appropriate structural form to adopt. Here, the tensions and conflicts in strategy/structure relationships become apparent. Product/market diversity is best managed where subunits are allowed to develop activities that are tailored to particular product/markets. However, leveraging core skills across different subunits, sharing resources and centralising certain activities, e.g., bulk purchasing, operate against the logic of the decentralized multi-unit structure.

The benefits of fostering inter-relationships between units and sharing resources need to be weighed against the advantages of subunit autonomy – tailoring activities and management account-ability. Compromise solutions are possible where certain activities are managed centrally in order to gain the advantage of scale and scope economies, *e.g.*, procurement of standard inputs and basic research, whilst preserving the essential autonomy and bottom-line accountability of each business unit. We explore these issues in more depth in Part II.

CHANGES IN CONTINGENT VARIABLES

A year after Mintzberg's book on structure appeared, Michael Porter published *Competitive Strategy* (Porter, 1980), introducing the **generic strategy** concepts, which, for all their simplistic nature, have proved to be hugely influential in the strategic management field. Porter argued that, in order to achieve sustainable competitive advantage, the firm must adopt one of three alternative generic strategies – cost leadership, differentiation, or focus – which involves applying one or the other strategies to a narrow market segment. He suggested that failure to do so, or attempting to achieve both cost leadership and differentiation simultaneously, may lead to the firm becoming stuck in the middle.

It was not part of Mintzberg's intention to relate his work on structures to the problems of delivering competitive strategies. Porter similarly devotes very little space in his books (Porter, 1980, 1985) to questions of structure. However, a notable attempt to bring these two contributions together was made by Miller (1986). He suggested that cost leadership is best achieved through the machine bureaucratic structure, and that innovative differentiation requires an operating adhocracy. In other words, the strategy/structure question could be resolved by selecting one of Porter's generic strategies. Once this choice has been made, there are extant and well understood congruent structural forms that fit this particular choice of strategy.

However, a firm needs to be continually developing new sources of advantage, and this needs to be done at low cost. We have also highlighted the importance of know-how, and the need to foster its continual development. Moreover, our exploration of the customer matrix emphasizes the need for firms to be very clear about their target customers, and to tailor their product offerings to meet their needs precisely. Thus, the rather straightforward Porter choice of either being low cost or differentiated is replaced by a much more complex challenge. Therefore, the neat matching of Porter's generic strategies with Mintzberg's structural configurations needs to be re-examined.

The current competitive environment has certainly become more hostile than in the 1980s. Increasing competition from rapidly developing nations, globalization of markets and, more recently, the effects of recession have combined to make life more difficult for most firms. Instability in many markets due to political, economic and social upheaval, *e.g.*, in Eastern Europe, coupled with the pace of change and shortening product life cycles has increased uncertainty and dynamism in the environment. Niches that were once safely protected by brand or other entry barriers are being increasingly penetrated. Now, no firm seems immune from price competition. Note the experiences of Mercedes and BMW in the luxury car market under threat from Japanese competition. Being customer focused and delivering excellent value, as defined and perceived by the customer, are becoming order-qualifying, rather than order-winning capabilities.

These developments can be expressed as changes in two of the contingency variables facing firms. Specifically:

1. **The environment.** It has become more hostile, more unpredictable, and more dynamic.
2. **Tasks.** The need for fast-paced innovation, coupled with the need to offer high value at low cost, but not necessarily low prices, has increased the task complexity of the firm.

Structures have also been undergoing significant changes. Traditional, hierarchical, functional organization structures have been subject to challenge and change. Delayering and downsizing (or rightsizing) are banners under which firms have reduced staff numbers. This is usually in response to deteriorating performance, either through the firm's inability to deliver value to customers, *e.g.*, service or new products, or because of pressures to reduce costs. Delayering involves stripping out levels of management, *i.e.*, the middle line has been truncated, whereas downsizing attempts to take out activities previously done within the organization. Downsizing initially impacted upon support staff, particularly those staff whose activities were loosely coupled to the main tasks of the organization.

In the early 1980s, many firms subcontracted activities such as office cleaning, restaurants and payroll, in line with strategies concerned with focusing on the core of the business. More recently, some firms have taken this philosophy into the technostructure and into the operating core, effecting radical reductions in staff numbers. Indeed, some have had to help create new supplying firms through management buy-outs because no firm existed previously that could deliver the required activities.

Due in part to delayering, and encouraged by ideas popularized by management writers like Tom Peters (1988), **empowerment** of junior levels of staff has gathered momentum. Self-organizing, autonomous teams supported by excellent information systems have challenged the traditional roles of the middle line managers, particularly their role as coordinators through direct supervision. There are also pressures on staff in the operating core to become more flexible, both in terms of their capabilities and their employment contracts.

Empowerment combined with delayering could be regarded as an attempt to eliminate activities that destroy total value. The supervisory and control aspects of managerial work destroy value if the same results can be achieved by self-controlling empowered employees in the operating core.

Business process redesign or re-engineering (BPR) requires firms to challenge existing organizational arrangements, particularly functional organization. Because business processes tend to span existing organizational sub-divisions, adopting BPR has usually resulted in a substantial reorganization around more logical groupings of staff. Flexible manufacturing and the introduction of just-in-time (JIT) systems have led to major restructuring in the operating cores of businesses. The limitations of functional structures, particularly with regard to new product development, have been exposed, and cross-functional teams are increasingly required to improve cooperation and coordination in the process of new product development.

These changes can be expressed in terms of Mintzberg's contingency variables as follows:

■ **Size:** firms are becoming leaner, and smaller.
■ **Technical system:** past ways of organizing the operating core are being challenged (by downsizing, and the introduction of BPR and cross-functional team working).
■ **Power:** the decentralization of decision-making to staff in the operating core, but a shift away from traditional employment contracts.

Clearly, all firms would not experience all these changes in the contingent conditions facing them, but it is worth exploring their implications. There appears to be a congruence, or fit, between Porter's generic strategies and Mintzberg's configurations (Miller, 1986 and 1990). The cost leader adopts the machine form of organization, and the innovative differentiator becomes an operating adhocracy. However, if in order to achieve advantage the firm needs to combine these two strategies in an increasingly hostile environment, what configuration is appropriate?

131

THE MACHINE ADHOCRACY

Mintzberg (1979) argued that the machine organization is adapted to tackling simple tasks in stable environments, and the adhocracy form is appropriate for firms dealing with complex tasks in dynamic environments. We believe that there is evidence of a new configuration of strategy and structure which we have called the **machine adhocracy** (see Bowman and Carter, 1995 for a fuller exposition of this form based on a case example). This structure enables a firm to gain the advantages of efficient product/service delivery, at low cost and with high levels of conformance quality (which is a feature of the machine organization), without the stultifying and disabling inflexibility which seems to accompany the machine form. The machine adhocracy has the ability to adapt more readily to a changing task environment, as does the pure adhocracy form, but the pure adhocracy can be an expensive structural solution if it has the potential to tackle much higher levels of change and task complexity than are required by the extant circumstances facing the firm.

Figure 7.4
The machine adhocracy.

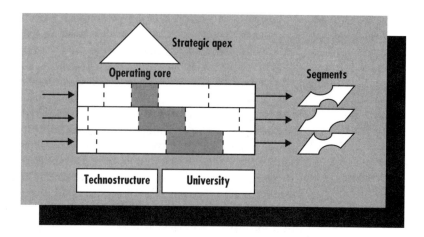

The machine adhocracy delivers continual incremental improvements in the efficiency and effectiveness of the operating core. But, from a day-by-day, short-term perspective, there is *stability* in the operating core. This is necessary to achieve the required levels of efficiency. However, either through an ongoing series of small adjustments, or through periodic larger scale changes, the operating core is evolving and not stagnating. A new staff grouping, labelled the **university** is the key to this evolutionary process, through its research role and its ability to facilitate learning within the core.

We have used Mintzberg's diagrammatic conventions to depict this new form (see Mintzberg, 1983). The machine adhocracy comprises four basic parts (see Figure 7.4):

1. The **strategic apex**.
2. The **operating core**.
3. The **technostructure**.
4. The **university**.

The first three groupings correspond to Mintzberg's categories, but their roles and responsibilities have been developed and refined. The fourth category, the university, is a new type of staff grouping. We now explain the roles and characteristics of each grouping.

The Strategic Apex

The strategic apex has a dual responsibility: first, it is required to ensure the efficient management of the current mission of the firm, and second, it is responsible for the strategic development of the business. Too often, management at the top of the firm focuses too much on the day-to-day running of the business at the expense of its strategic development. Specifically, the apex is required:

- To decide what is legitimate activity for the firm – deciding scope, domain, make or buy, diversification.
- To fund the operations – financing.
- To set the culture and climate.

■ To coordinate and control linkages within the firm, and between the firm and suppliers, alliance partners, customers, and distribution channels.

The Operating Core

The operating core is the heart of the business. All other staff groups serve the core. People in the operating core are responsible for the efficient delivery of valued products and services to customers. They are concerned with producing high quality products or services in terms of conformance quality, at lowest costs. In order to deliver valued products, members of the operating core need to understand what it is the customer values, and they need to organize in ways that can most efficiently deliver that value. The operating core consists of a series of linked activities, and it should undertake only those activities in which it can demonstrate competence relative to competitors, or potential suppliers. Thus, the operating core of a machine adhocracy focuses on a severely limited range of activities. If there is no strategic advantage in the firm carrying out the activity itself, then it should be subcontracted.

In order to cope with an unpredictable and changing task environment, operatives in the core will need to demonstrate flexibility, either through individuals mastering a wider set of skills, which is feasible where the tasks are relatively straightforward, or through teams of specialists forming and reforming into teams to tackle varying task requirements. Teams will largely be self-managing, and they are grouped into sets of activities that clearly link together to deliver value to an identifiable customer group, adopting a **strategic business unit** (SBU) structure within the operating core. Therefore, the machine adhocracy also resembles the divisionalized form of organization. But here the distinctions between SBU groupings tend to be more fine-grained than in a typical corporation, which may have within it SBUs with substantially different product/market scopes. There is also more permeability in the boundaries between SBUs, with a considerable degree of cooperation between them. Where activities are common across SBU value chains, informal coordination processes operate to assist the spreading of expertise and information.

133

The Technostructure

The technostructure consists of staff whose job is to standardize activities taking place in the operating core. These staff may be standardize the way the work is performed, *e.g.* through production engineering, operations planning and scheduling; they may standardize output, *e.g.*, through quality assurance, budgeting and costing; or they may standardize skills, *e.g.*, through job training and selection. Alongside the operating core, staff in the technostructure are responsible for the efficient delivery of high-conformance quality.

The University

In contrast to the rather tenuous position of support staff in the machine organization, the staff in the university are absolutely key to the future strategic development of the business.

Traditional universities carry out three basic functions for society at large:

1. They engage in research (both fundamental and applied).
2. They teach people new knowledge and skills.
3. They provide a store of knowledge.

The university within the firm also carries out these three functions: research into new products, or new processes; helping staff to develop new skills and knowledge; providing valuable information on customers, competitors, markets *etc*. University staff cannot impose their solutions on the operating core; they act as facilitators, supporting the direct value creators in the core. The university is vital because its primary focus is on the future. Whereas the operating core and the technostructure concern themselves primarily with the efficient delivery of the current set of products/services, the university is focused on change and development. Its role is to stimulate the continuous transformation of activities in the operating core.

THE UNIVERSITY AND COMPETENCE DEVELOPMENT

We can usefully explore the role that the university can play in developing the firm's competences. Using our classification of the elements of a competence, we can examine how the machine adhocracy functions. To recap, competences can be viewed as comprising combinations of: resources, *e.g.* people, machines, buildings, brands and cash; systems, *e.g.*, quality, JIT systems and MRP II; and know-how, *e.g.*, special, unique expertise.

Systems are used to deploy resources. Know-how is special knowledge, often implicit or tacit, which enables a firm to operate its systems more effectively than competitors. As we argued in Chapter 3, this special know-how is difficult for competitors to access, so it can form the basis of advantage. But, over time, this know-how itself may become systematized, *i.e.*, it is made explicit, codified, and proceduralized, and is amenable to being taught to others. Once this process develops, the special know-how degrades into an imitable system, which can no longer provide any competitive advantage, because it becomes the norm or the standard practice in the industry.

This suggests that, in order to sustain advantage, firms must continually develop unique, not easily imitable know-how. The university is the *engine* of know-how development. Hence, the university continually seeks to top up the firm's reservoir of know-how (see Figure 7.5). As we explained in Chapter 3, know-how

Figure 7.5
The university's role as the
engine of know-how
development.

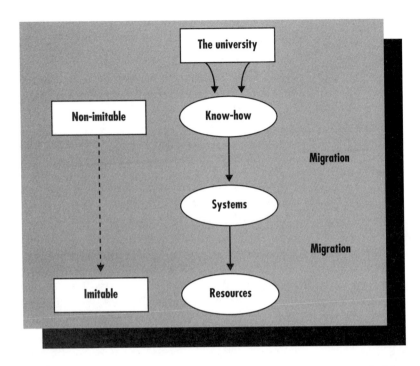

migrates or degrades into systems as it becomes teachable, proceduralized and hence more imitable. Unless know-how is either protected or, more realistically, continually enhanced, the firm will be forced into becoming a 'me-too' player. Know-how, as a source of sustainable advantage, must be explicitly and deliberately managed. The university plays a key part in this process. This does not mean, however, that the university is the sole source of expertise in the organization. A major role for university staff is to facilitate the development and dissemination of expertise within the operating core, as well as to learn from others outside the organization.

The university has different roles and relationships with the other parts of the machine adhocracy. It supports the operating core; it cannot dictate to or impose solutions on the core. It helps core staff to continually update and improve products and processes, and it also facilitates the sharing of experience and knowledge within the core.

The university's relationship with the strategic apex is essentially to provide timely strategic information, and to conduct strategic analyses to support strategy debate within the apex. Its relationship with the technostructure is similarly supportive, but it also helps the technostructure support the operating core, through assistance with training or with managing the introduction of new systems. It can help all parts of the organization to avoid being overly constrained by beliefs and assumptions about, for instance, what we think we're good at, or what we believe customers value. It can also help avoid routine ways of thinking, by introducing new information and ideas from outside the organization which may challenge these taken-for-granted beliefs.

The roles undertaken by the university may be filled by staff from other parts of the organization, either as part of their normal workload, or while on secondment for a period of time. The movement of staff from the operating core and technostructure in and out of university roles would also facilitate the fostering of a learning orientation throughout the structure.

A HYBRID OR A NEW CONFIGURATION?

Whether the machine adhocracy can be regarded as a hybrid form, or a new and stable configuration depends largely on the degree to which this structure differs from other configurations. In each of Mintzberg's configurations there is a predominant coordination mechanism, *e.g.*, mutual adjustment in the adhocracy or innovative organization, and there is a staff grouping which is seen to be critical, *e.g.*, the technostructure in the machine organization. What is the primary coordinating mechanism in the machine adhocracy? And which is the critical staff grouping?

In Figure 7.6, for each combination of task (simple/complex) and environment (stable/dynamic) the appropriate coordinating mechanism and the corresponding configuration is displayed (Mintzberg's original version is Figure 7.3). We have argued that the machine adhocracy faces a more dynamic environment than the traditional machine structure, and that the complexity of the task facing the organization has increased. The machine adhocracy therefore occupies the centre of Figure 7.6. The main issue facing this organization is the need to continually adapt to a changing

136

Figure 7.6
Combinations of task,
environment, and
coordinating mechanisms.

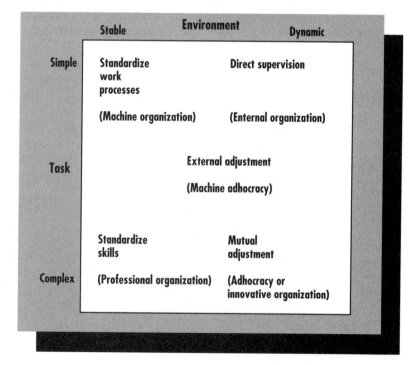

	Environment	
	Stable	**Dynamic**
Simple	Standardize work processes	Direct supervision
	(Machine organization)	(Enternal organization)
Task	External adjustment	
	(Machine adhocracy)	
	Standardize skills	Mutual adjustment
Complex	(Professional organization)	(Adhocracy or innovative organization)

competitive environment, whilst still maintaining efficient operations. They must be low cost, and this is achieved through processes of continual adjustment and learning, throughout the organization. The challenge is not only to coordinate work efficiently inside the organization, it is to do this and coordinate the whole organization with its market place. This external coordination requires excellent information, which is then used to continually adapt the way the firm works. This coordination process could be labelled **external adjustment**, and the grouping that has primary responsibility for effecting external adjustment is the university.

Mintzberg also identifies a number of pulls (Mintzberg, 1979), *e.g.*, a pull from the technostructure to standardize activities. We can see in the machine adhocracy evidence of four pulls operating simultaneously in response to the contingent circumstances facing the organization:

1. The pull from the operating core to professionalize their work through processes of empowerment, decentralization and the reduction of the middle line.
2. The pull to divisionalize the organization into quasi-autonomous SBUs; these are a response to the increasing need to focus on different segments of the market and to tailor what the firm does to meet the demands of specific segments.
3. The pull to collaborate, to share ideas and expertise across specialisms in order to cope with the demands of the dynamic and increasingly complex task environment.
4. The pull to standardize, as the technostructure staff and operating core seek to improve operating efficiency.

In other configurations, one of these pulls tends to dominate, 'pulling' the organization to adopt the corresponding configuration, *e.g.*, the pull to divisionalize leading to the divisionalized form. However, it seems that in the case of the machine adhocracy, these pulls are all strong features of the structure, which suggests that this is a different type of configuration.

Hence, we would argue that there is sufficient evidence here for us to regard the machine adhocracy as new configuration. It faces a different combination of task and environment from Mintzberg's other configurations; it has a new, key-staff grouping – the university; and it displays a new coordinating mechanism – external adjustment.

We further believe that the machine adhocracy will flourish only if there is a strong commitment from the strategic apex to nurture this form of organization. The activities of the university are vulnerable to short-term pressures to cut costs and, if these university activities are reduced significantly, the organization could easily revert or convert to a machine bureaucracy. So, although the university is the key part of the structure it has little formal power. The operating core, who own the processes, can reject advice and help from the university, as can the apex, and the technostructure. The university must *earn* the right to influence these groups by demonstrating how it can add value to the work of these groups.

137

SUMMARY

There is evidence to suggest that business organizations have been undergoing significant changes to their structures. We believe that something interesting is occurring and that our machine adhocracy ideal type is a useful 'straw man' to encourage debate and further research. There also may be other configurations at business unit and corporate levels that are viable responses to increasingly hostile competitive conditions. In this way, the machine adhocracy may be vying with, for example, virtual organizations, alliance networks and forms of learning organization. Darwinian processes may shake out less viable solutions, and they may encourage the further refinement and adaptation of those new configurations.

chapter 8

Strategy and Culture

In the strategy literature a great deal of attention has been focused on the culture of organizations. In large part, this can be explained by the failure of the more rational approaches to strategy that were developed and propounded in the 1960s and 1970s. Corporate planning did not appear to be delivering the required strategic results. Organizational culture, and the need to take account of it in strategic management, formed part of the explanation of the problems of strategy implementation.

Unfortunately, the term 'culture' has been used to refer to almost every aspect of the organization, to the point where it might cease to be a useful concept. Probably the most accessible view of culture is summed up in the phrase 'the way we do things around here'. An early contributor to the field defined culture as:

> ...a customary and traditional way of thinking and doing things, which is shared to a greater or lesser degree by all of [the firm's] members, and which new members must learn and at least partially accept in order to be accepted into service in the firm .
> (Jacques, 1951)

139

Organizations are likely to evolve different ways of tackling essentially the same tasks. One can probably identify fairly readily with this view if one has experience of moving between different organizations in the same industry. More obviously, in contrasting a small consultancy firm with a large multinational corporation, one would undoubtedly identify many ways which are quite different in how things get done. For example, employees in a regional accountancy firm that was taken over by one of the majors experienced substantial changes in the way they carried out essentially the same auditing tasks: the process was more formalized, senior staff were involved in planning the audit, set procedures had to be followed, and reports and analyses had to be presented to the client in a standardized format.

Although, intuitively, this view of culture probably makes sense, we need to delve a little deeper into this important aspect of organizations if we are to understand the role culture plays in strategy. To assist in this exploration we will first set out an overview of the role of culture in the strategy process. Then, the more important dimensions of culture will be explained. Finally, the implications of culture for the strategic decision processes and on the processes of strategic change will be explored.

CULTURE AND STRATEGY

Figure 8.1 indicates a way in which the culture of the organization affects realized strategy. Processes within and outside the organization affect individual perceptions and cognitions. Internal organizational processes include the power relationships between individuals and groups, both formal and informal, the control and reward systems, management style, and organization symbols *e.g.,* status symbols, and symbols of the past. **External influences** is a catch-all term for all the sources of life experiences that shape an individual's view of the world. This includes socialization processes experienced by the individual, including education, family, local, regional and national cultural influences and the individual's past work experiences. These complex influences combine to affect the way individuals think, which we have called the cognitive process.

Included in cognitive processes are the values, beliefs, attitudes and assumptions an individual holds. These are formed through past experiences. A key issue in strategy is the extent to which values, beliefs and assumptions are held in common by the members of an organization. This is because values and beliefs held by individuals influence their behaviour. If there is a large degree of agreement among the members of the organization, then it is likely that they will behave and respond in similar ways. This can be enormously powerful and beneficial if the shared beliefs and values

140

Figure 8.1
Culture and strategy.

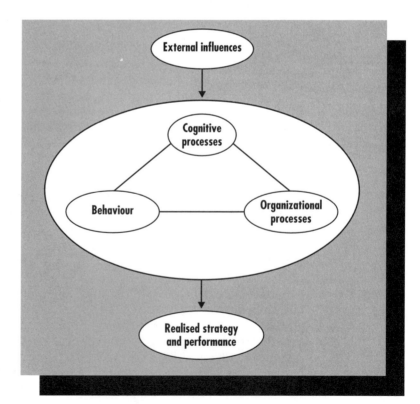

are in line with the intended strategy of the organization and if the intended strategy is appropriate. However, if the intended strategy requires certain behaviours that run counter to the prevailing beliefs, then this represents a major blockage to strategy implementation.

The result of the actions of all the individuals affects the emerging strategy of the organization. We argue, therefore, that organizational processes influence the way individuals see the world, *e.g.*, their values and beliefs, but that these influences operate along with the wider experiences of the individual listed above. The way individuals see the world affects the way they behave, *i.e.*, the decisions they make, the actions they take. Collectively, these actions result in the organization's **realized strategy**.

So the way we see the world affects the way we behave, and the collective behaviours of all the individuals in the organization determines the way things get done.

Although this is a necessarily simplified representation of much more complex processes, this model will enable us to explore some important issues in the strategy–culture area. First, we will set out the more important organizational processes within the organization.

ORGANIZATIONAL PROCESSES

Organizational processes influence, and to some extent are, the culture of the organization. These processes can be grouped into six categories. These categories are not totally distinct, and there are strong interrelationships between them. However, to assist our understanding of culture we shall consider each category in turn.

Organizational processes can be deliberate or emergent. Deliberate processes are those that are intended by top management; emergent processes evolve organically within the organization and may or may not be supportive of top management intentions.

GROUPING

The way the organization specializes is a key dimension of culture. Functional specialization can encourage parochial attitudes and values which may impede cooperation across the organization. Typically unhelpful outcomes of parochialism are 'not invented here – therefore it can't be any good' and 'it's not our fault/problem – it must be that of marketing/engineering/operations'. More subtle manifestations of the problem are differences in beliefs that can emerge if individuals have experience of working only in one function. For example, someone with sales experience is likely to spot the firm's lack of competitiveness earlier than most: they may well see that the reason for the poor performance is the limited product range. Another manager with operations experience may come to a quite different view, seeing the problem as one of high production costs compounded by the proliferation of products in the range.

In some organizations, the position of chief executive officer has tended to be occupied by a representative of the same function over the years. For example, the chief executive is always an accountant, or the top jobs always go to engineers. This can be partly explained by the tendency of people to appoint those with whom they are most comfortable. This could mean that an engineer in the top position may well feel most at ease with like-minded managers – those with whom he has many points of contact through shared or similar past experiences. The problem here for strategy making is that a very similar way of viewing the world is perpetuated at the very top of the organization. This can seriously impede the decision-making processes, reducing the quality of debate and the challenge to received and shared wisdom.

The bases of specialization play a crucial role in signalling to members of the organization what is important. So, a strong functional specialization indicates that the development of particular skills and expertise is important. In contrast, if staff are grouped according to customer types, markets or products, different priorities are being signalled.

Informal groupings evolve spontaneously, a process that is facilitated by people being located together. Even though the formal structure may not require certain staff to interact, if they are located together informal groups *will* emerge. For example, managers may prefer to interact informally with their peers, rather than their subordinates. It is through interactions with others that opinions can be formed. If these interactions are managed formally, *e.g.*, in a planned meeting or presentation, then the process of attitude formation may, to some extent, be under the control of top management. However, attitudes formed through informal interactions may run counter to the management's desired outcomes. Informal opinion leaders can powerfully affect the way certain management actions and pronouncements are received.

POWER TO MAKE DECISIONS

The power to make decisions or to block the implementation of decisions is an important dimension in the strategy–culture relationship. In some organizations, decision making is very decentralized, and staff at lower levels are allowed to make quite important operational decisions. In other organizations, the power to decide even quite trivial matters is centralized at the apex of the structure. This extreme form of centralization can emerge when, for example, the organization is in crisis; more routinely, it can result from strong pressure on the chief executive from corporate headquarters.

Where decision making is seen to be excessively centralized it is likely that the management at lower levels will be either frustrated, with the more able leaving, or may develop behaviours that are passive and dependent, with no initiative being exercised. Attempts to change this, to empower managers, may well founder if the managers feel threatened. Their past experiences may not have given them the confidence to make decisions.

Formal power or authority is vested in management positions in the structure. In recent years there have been attempts to reduce the number of hierarchical levels, both for cost reduction reasons and, more symbolically, to improve relationships and communication between the top and the bottom of the structure.

Informal power is power that individuals or groups may have that lies outside the formal hierarchy. Informal power can derive from several sources:

■ High dependence of the organization on the individual or group. This is a particular issue in professional organizations, *e.g.*, a hospital's dependence on consultants, but it may also emerge when particular groups have the ability to significantly affect the organization's activity, *e.g.*, a high dependence on sales staff, or maintenance or computer operations.

■ Control of information. Information is power, and provision or withholding of information can give individuals influence.

CONTROLS AND REWARDS

'What gets measured gets done' – the control systems of the organization signal priorities. Typically, control systems are based on activities and outputs that lend themselves to quantitative measurement: cost, budgets, sales targets, utilization, overheads and so on. This can lead to a distortion of effort towards those activities that are measured, which may not be in line with the intended strategy. For example, if the intended strategy stresses customer service priorities, but the control systems continue to emphasize cost containment, then the realized strategy may well reflect the control systems rather than the intended strategy.

Similarly, people take notice of which behaviours are rewarded. The desire to be recognized and to be given approval through rewards, which need not be purely monetary, appears to be a core need in individuals. Status, praise and public recognition may all be powerful motivators. Behaviours that are rewarded are likely to be imitated, so, as with the control systems, rewards should reinforce the intended strategy.

MANAGEMENT STYLES

Management or leadership style has been a focus of interest for many years. Management style has been variously categorized, but most approaches recognize differences between autocratic and participative or consultative styles. Attempts have been made to identify more effective management styles, culminating in a contingency approach that suggests that there is no one best way to manage – it all depends on the situation.

Running alongside the more formal, academic exploration of the effects of style, there has been a stream of more populist management literature, including the 'great man' books based on acknowledged leadership success stories, *e.g.*, Iacocca, and Harvey-Jones, and the 'excellence' books, notably Peters and Waterman's *In Search of Excellence* (1982) and its progeny. An important difference between these approaches and the contingency theories is that the great man and excellence schools advocate that managers adopt 'excellence' behaviours regardless of their situation. There is, then, according to these writers, one best way to manage which involves managers listening to staff, empowering them and setting out broad, inspiring visions to guide their decisions.

In contrast, Mintzberg (1989) suggests that certain types of organization encourage, or even *require*, management styles that are quite different. For example, the machine organization is highly centralized with an autocratic management obsessed with control and discipline, whereas an organic adhocracy may require a consultative and informal management style.

As argued earlier, the organizational processes identified are not watertight compartments. For example, management style is influenced by the formal power structure, and the extent and degree of specialization. Writers such as Mintzberg and Miller use the terms **configuration** and **gestalt** to refer to particular combinations of structure and processes that seem to fit together. The machine organization would be one configuration. The organizational structures and processes are mutually reinforcing. If this is the case, then it may be extremely difficult to try to change the dimension of one process without concurrently trying to change other dimensions in order to create a new, mutually reinforcing set of structures and processes – a move from one configuration to another.

To cite a common instance of this problem, it may be questioned whether a technique such as quality circles can be introduced successfully in a machine organization, that is autocratic, centralized and obsessed with control. For quality circles to work, shopfloor employees need to be trusted by management, and to be credited with the ability to analyse quality problems and recommend solutions. If the prevailing beliefs and attitudes of management are that employees cannot be trusted because they cannot exercise initiative, and that they must be continually supervised and controlled, then quality circles will never work.

This is currently being debated in relation to Japanese corporations that have been established successfully in the US and the UK. Are these machine organizations different from those of UK and US corporations? If it is possible to establish a mass-production organization that embodies excellence values, then the configuration approach must be challenged. Or it could be argued that these organizations are essentially the same, and that there are only differences at the margin.

One possible explanation for the differences between Japanese and US or UK firms may be to do with the recruiting processes. For example, Nissan's greenfield plant in Sunderland in the north of England could take advantage of the high levels of local unemployment and the absence of rival car manufacturers to recruit staff whose attitudes and values are more likely to be in line with Nissan's objectives. In a greenfield situation, where a relatively young and inexperienced workforce is being developed, it is more possible to inculcate the required values. If the supervisors and staff have no experience of the way things are done in car plants, there is an opportunity to establish quite different norms and behaviours from those established in older, traditional, car manufacturing regions, *e.g.*, Detroit in the US, or the West Midlands in the UK. In the case of Nissan, key supervisors were taken to plants in Japan for training.

The prevailing style of management in a firm is clearly an important aspect of culture. The behaviour of individual senior managers assumes critical importance in signalling to staff what is important, and what is appropriate behaviour. Subordinates watch their bosses very carefully. If they detect differences between the espoused strategy, *e.g.*,the customer is number one, and top management behaviour, *e.g.*, the chief executive is number one, then it is the latter behaviour that is most likely to shape opinions. The actions of the chief executive assume symbolic importance. For example, the way chief executives use their time signals their priorities. This time could be spent meeting important customers, holding senior management meetings, attending committees at corporate HQ, addressing each and every quality assurance training course or walking around the factory discussing problems with shopfloor workers. The choices chief executives make in allocating their time can have a profound influence in shaping the attitudes and values of subordinates. If chief executives bother to learn the names of every member of the organization, this clearly signals to even the most junior staff that they are a valued part of the organization. The headmaster who knows the names of all 2000 children in the school is an example of this.

145

ROUTINES

Routines are essentially the way things get done in the organization. They can be tightly specified procedures, deliberately established to deal with predictable activities, *e.g.*, ordering components, or evaluating a capital expenditure proposal. They can also be highly emergent in nature, taking the form of generally accepted and understood ways of working that have never been explicitly agreed or even discussed, *e.g.*, new product ideas always start in the research department.

Because routines are so embedded in the organization, they can prove to be major obstacles to change. Formalized routines and procedures at least have the merit of being explicit, so they can be challenged and replaced. It is implicit routines that can exercise an insidious and profound influence on behaviour. Because they are implied, accepted and understood, they can be ways of working that are so obvious that individuals in the organization could not conceive of other ways in which things could be done. As a result, these informal routines can be extremely difficult to identify, let alone change, and it requires a great deal of challenging reflection to uncover such embedded behaviours.

The importance of the part routines play in any organization cannot be overstated: routines are the very fabric of an organization. Without them, people would have to recreate the organization every day. Routines provide an essential rhythm and stability to day-to-day activity. However, the downside is that, if the intended strategy requires a shift in the way the organization is behaving, the taken-for-granted routines must be changed. It is at this very mundane but fundamental level of activity that many of the problems of strategic change lie.

In Chapter 3, we highlighted the importance of organizational know-how in delivering advantage. This shared expertise clearly has a cultural dimension. Know-how is embedded in the routine ways things get done in the organization. So, although some routines may be inefficient and be holding the firm back, others may be the very essence of advantage. This poses a serious problem when attempts are made to change the organization. Some change programmes may destroy know-how inadvertently, *e.g.*, in delayering, business process re-engineering. To avoid this outcome, the management need to develop a sophisticated insight into the unique sources of know-how in the firm, and to ensure that these are nurtured, not destroyed.

STORIES AND SYMBOLS

Stories recounted by members of the organization play a central role in preserving and perpetuating the culture. They help to link the present with the past, they act to bind people together, when, for example, people gather in the bar to recount past successes or failures, and they can operate as a kind of cultural shorthand to communicate quite complex values and beliefs. Thus, stories of heroes and villains help to signal values and behaviours. In contrast, stories about mavericks who buck the system help us to understand what the unstated norms of the organization are.

Symbols are organizational activities or artefacts that convey meaning. We are familiar with symbols of status, *e.g.*, cars, desk size, personal assistants, dining facilities, but more subtle symbols can play an important part in preserving shared values and beliefs. For example, the location of a corporate headquarters can help to convey the values of the business. Is it in the heart of the City of London, or next door to one of the manufacturing sites? Corporate logos and the changing of them have assumed a level of importance recently, largely due to an awareness that they signify what the organization stands for; changing the logo signifies a break with the past.

Language also acts symbolically: If customers are referred to as 'punters' or 'bums on seats' this conveys a certain set of attitudes. Contrast this language with 'guests' or 'delegates'. Actions can have a powerful symbolic influence: the chief executive takes a pay cut, a director of quality is appointed, a shop steward is sacked. No doubt the change in language by British Rail in referring to its passengers as customers is significant symbolically.

Some firms use stage-managed events to signal change or enthuse staff. Motivational sales conferences are highly symbolic events. The prestigious venue, the celebrity speaker and the use of music, video images and staging for dramatic effect combine to elevate the conference into a cultural event.

We have suggested that these and other organizational processes, both deliberate and emergent in nature, influence the way members of the organization see the world. We shall now look at these cognitive processes in a little more detail.

COGNITIVE PROCESSES

Here, we are referring to the beliefs, assumptions, attitudes and values held by individuals. These are formed by past experiences, which may or may not be strongly associated with the organization. For example, some firms have policies that encourage staff to stay with the firm for their entire careers. We would expect, in these firms, the influence of the organization to loom very large in the cognitions of members. In contrast, in a newly established firm, or in one in which there has been a considerable amount of staff turnover, members will not have undergone the same experiences and are therefore less likely to hold the same set of beliefs and values. In these organizations, the range of past experiences is likely to be great, and consequently the ability of organizational processes to inculcate a shared set of values and beliefs is reduced.

Some organizations address this problem explicitly with extensive periods of training and indoctrination. The army and some large multinationals operate in this way. These indoctrination processes are obviously more effective if the new members have reasonably congruent beliefs and values to start with, so selection becomes critical. If this is not possible, perhaps if the army has conscription, then elaborate processes are used to strip out the values and beliefs that new entrants come in with, so that the required values can be introduced. The advantage of recruiting school and college leavers into the organization is that it is easier to inculcate required values and beliefs if someone else has not got there first: there is more of a clean sheet to fill in. Emergent processes can, however, undermine deliberate attempts to shape beliefs and values. The hard work of the training and induction staff can be rapidly undermined by the influence of a cynical informal leader.

Shared beliefs and values can be a source of competitive advantage, so long as they are in line with an appropriate strategy.

However, if the firms in an industry are staffed largely by people with little experience of working in any other industry, then, a shared set of beliefs and assumptions is likely to emerge across the industry. There can be problems of an industry 'recipe' where there are shared beliefs about how to compete, what the customers value and so on, and there may be advantages that could be gained by a firm successfully challenging the accepted rules of the game. In order to mount such a challenge, the management of a firm already inside the industry has to free itself from those unstated, implicit beliefs which, by definition, is not easily done. Therefore, it is often the outsider to the industry who successfully challenges these widely held assumptions. The outsider either comes in to take control of an incumbent firm or is a new entrant. Interestingly, often the successful new entrant simply applies a recipe that brought success in another industry.

Recipes operate at the level of the organization as well. Johnson (1987) has called the organization's recipe the **paradigm**. The paradigm consists of the beliefs and assumptions that are held in common and taken for granted in the organization. As we have seen above, the influence of organizational processes on individual cognitions is greatest when members have shared the same past experiences. Strong paradigms are likely to exist, then, in firms that recruit school and college leavers who stay in the firm for most of their careers, and where policies support internal promotions. The shared past experiences are likely to lead to shared world views.

Strong paradigms can make it extremely difficult for organizations to change strategic direction. Even when the members of the top management try to construct strategies based on analysis and hard facts, their interpretation of the analysis is coloured by their shared beliefs and assumptions. They will tend to place emphasis on analysis that supports their world view, and to discount or even ignore results that challenge these firmly-held assumptions. The real problem, however, is the 'taken-for-grantedness' of these beliefs and assumptions. They operate in a similar way on individual cognitions as routines operate at the level of the organization. They guide thought and shape interpretations of events. They are so understood that they are never discussed, and if they are not brought to the surface in some way they can never be openly challenged.

BEHAVIOUR

Behaviour is what people in the organization actually do, including the actions they take and the decisions they make. We have already discussed the routine nature of most organizational activity. Behaviour that is routinized, whether deliberately or through custom and practice, is very difficult to change.

Routines that are deeply embedded can be a source of great stability in times of turmoil and uncertainty. For example, a building society underwent a succession of major strategic shifts over a period of three years: takeover by a rival society, branch closures and rationalization, the introduction of more banking services, and the stripping out of two layers of management. During this period, the staff at branch level were confused and demoralized, and they relied on embedded routines to provide some much needed stability and security during this time of turbulence. One senior manager observed that the branches, falling back on tried and accepted ways of behaving, actually kept the society functioning, and that if they had not behaved in this way then the society may well not have survived. So, embedded routines can provide stability. Problems emerge, however, when these routines hold back the organization. Their very embeddedness can act as a major barrier to change.

People's behaviour is obviously influenced by their perceptions of what is important. What they perceive to be the priorities in the organization will be influenced by the internal and external processes we have been exploring in this chapter. In some professional organizations, such as law firms and hospitals, individual professionals may well be influenced strongly by external, non-organizational sources. They owe their allegiance to their profession first and the organization second. Hence, their behaviour may, in certain circumstances, not be in line with the intentions of senior management.

If a high degree of value congruence is achieved in the organization, staff can be expected to behave in appropriate ways without the need for formal control and supervision. Such an organization is capable of operating in predictable ways even when the staff are geographically dispersed. If the recruiting processes help to select people whose values are already in line with those the organization requires, so much the better.

At one extreme, there may be organizations whose members have values and beliefs that are very similar; at the other extreme the organization may bring together people with quite diverse beliefs and values, born out of their different experiences. Diversity of beliefs and values can be helpful. Decisions should be informed by a wide range of views and experience, and the organization should be capable of adapting and changing its activity.

The advantages of homogeneity in values and beliefs are that staff are more likely to be committed to the aims of the organization and staff can be expected to act in required ways without close supervision.

The disadvantages of homogeneity of beliefs and values are that decision making processes are not likely to have critical and challenging perspectives introduced into them. Also, the organization will find it difficult to act outside the accepted and routine ways of behaving.

REALIZED STRATEGY AND PERFORMANCE

The collective behaviour of the members of the organization that emerges from the processes and influences outlined above determines the realized strategy, which may or may not be in line with the intended strategy. Intended strategies are implemented through the organizational processes discussed in this chapter. If there is a failure in implementation, the organizational processes have failed to affect behaviour in the desired ways. These issues are explored further in the next chapter.

If there is no clear, intended strategy, then the realized strategy emerges in an unplanned, incremental fashion. This may lead to acceptable performance as the organization adjusts in an organic way to changes in its environment. However, cultural processes can impede the process of adjustment and adaptation to a changing environment, which is likely to lead to poor performance. Routines embedded in the organization that were appropriate in the past are now major barriers to change; systems, styles and structures preserve the *status quo*. Often, the decline in performance that results from an increasing lack of alignment between the organization and its environment acts as a trigger for change, forcing the top management explicitly to address the strategy and to set in motion actions to change the organization.

INTERACTIONS

The categorization of the organization into organizational processes, cognitive processes and behaviour is a convenient way to explore these important dimensions of culture. However, clearly these three categories are inextricably interconnected. In Figure 8.2 we indicate some of these connections.

Connection 1 refers to the interactions between the organization and its external environment. External events impact on the organization if they are perceived and recognized by people inside the firm. There may well be substantial changes in the environment which do not impinge on managers' perceptions or, if they do, they are interpreted in such a way as to lead to little change in behaviour. Managers interpret the environment. They pay attention selectively, and they construct meaning and understanding of external events based on their beliefs and past experiences. So, for example, a competitor may launch a new product. This may be interpreted as a major threat to our business, or it could be explained in other ways. Some managers may construe that the product is not really a close substitute for our products, therefore there is no need to overreact.

Taking this view further Smircich and Stubbart (1985) argue that managers *enact* their environments. In other words, managers construct a view of the environment which suits them, defining competitors, customers and other influences in their own idiosyncratic ways. Hence, changes in the environment will impact on what happens in the firm through processes of interpretation and sensemaking by managers. They construct their environmental 'reality'. Connection 2 implies that organizational processes affect cognitions, and that cognitions affect behaviour. Thus, if the control systems are

Figure 8.2
Interconnections in the
culture model.

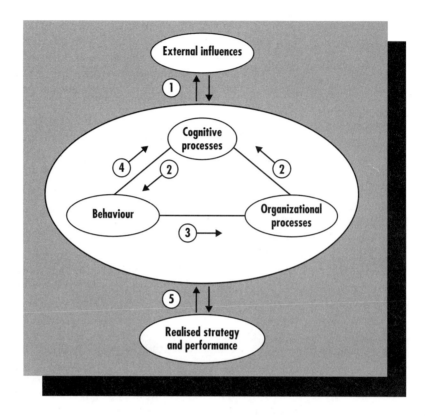

changed from measuring costs to measuring profit contribution, this affects managers' perceptions of what is seen to be important in the organization, which in turn affect the decisions they take in their department and the way they manage their subordinate staff. This straightforward causal linkage would suggest that if top managers wish to change behaviour, they need to change processes and cognitions.

But connection 3 implies that organizational processes and structures are produced and reproduced through people's behaviour. These processes do not stand outside, as immutable 'givens'. They are actively created and recreated through the daily actions of organization members. This imparts an important dynamic into the model, one which we pick up on in the next chapter.

Connection 4 suggests that behaviour influences attitudes and beliefs. An unattributable quote rather cynically sums up this argument: "If you've got them by the throat, their hearts and minds will follow". A more subtle explanation would be that if people are manoeuvred to behave in new ways, they will construct a way of making sense of what they do, and thereby rationalize their behaviour. This has important implications for the management of change. It suggests that a more direct way of bringing about lasting change is not to try to persuade people to change their attitudes through communication and training processes as in connection 2, but rather to engineer changes in behaviour directly. This can be done by, for example, regrouping staff into multi-functional teams, or by having production staff deal with customer complaints.

Realized strategy, in the context of the firm's environment, determines relative performance. Connection 5 implies that performance will impact on the cultural processes. The most direct influence would be on managers' cognitions. There is evidence to suggest that declining performance can trigger substantial change, particularly if it precipitates a crisis. But equally, there is some support for the view that declining performance strengthens commitment to past strategies. We consider the effects of performance on change further in the next chapter.

A REQUIRED CULTURE?

We subscribe to a contingency view of organizations. That is, there is no one best way to do things – it all depends on the situation facing the firm. However, it is tempting to construct an ideal organization, based on our arguments about competitive strategy advanced earlier, that would demonstrate some important aspects of culture, and might act as a notional benchmark when assessing a given firm. We explored the idea of a machine adhocracy in the previous chapter. This might serve our purpose as an ideal.

Using the model set out in Figure 6.1, we have derived a culture for the machine adhocracy – one that embodies the desired features of an organization that is well positioned to compete successfully.

ORGANIZATIONAL PROCESSES

Under this heading we include formal strategy processes, staff grouping, power structures, control and reward systems, management style and routines, stories and symbols. A successful machine adhocracy might display some of these organization processes:
- Strategy is explicit, concise, and well understood.
- Implementation plans are clear, actions are specified, responsibility is understood.
- Staff are grouped together logically to address particular market segments.
- There is clear accountability for key customers, or customer groups.
- Decision making is decentralized, to allow staff to respond rapidly to their markets.
- There are visible rewards for customer-orientated behaviours.
- There is continual monitoring of markets.
- Financial reporting systems focus around product line contribution.
- Marketing expenditures are amortized.

COGNITIVE PROCESSES

We included values, beliefs, assumptions and attitudes under this heading. The following might be commonly found in the machine adhocracy:

- There is a genuine belief that customers pay our salaries.
- Marketing expenditures are perceived as investments not costs.
- Change is an opportunity.
- All staff are valued and respected.
- Learning is continual.
- We are all customer focused, not just sales staff.
- It is OK to try things, and take initiatives.

BEHAVIOUR

We argued that organizational processes affect the way people see the world via their cognitive processes, and this in turn influences their behaviour. These might be behaviours encountered in the machine adhocracy:

- People are willing to accept change.
- Top managers act in line with their espoused strategies and values.
- There is open and honest communication across the organization.
- Managers and non-core staff actively support the operating core.
- People demonstrate their flexibility.
- Non-marketing staff get exposed to customers.

153

REALIZED STRATEGY

The outcome of these behaviours is an organization that is demonstrably market orientated, where continual change and adaptation keeps the firm ahead of the competition.

It would be difficult to point to even one firm that has all these desired features. The point of this exercise was to set out a more rounded view of how a successful organization might look, and might feel if one were a member of it. We have had some experiences of working with and in organizations that have some of these qualities. There is a 'buzz' about the place. People feel positive, they feel that they are able to change things and problems are viewed as challenges. These cultures may well not have ideal structures, or the best resources, but people are willing to work with what there is, and to operate around structural and other shortcomings. The critical intangible here is staff morale, but this is a delicate flower which can be destroyed easily, and which can be very difficult to grow.

Morale is substantially influenced by leadership, particularly the behaviour of the people at the top of the structure. Inspirational leaders can encourage extraordinary performance from staff. They can make each person feel valued, and they can inspire confidence. For staff to believe in their leaders they need to have respect for them, and for their ability to perform as strategic leaders. The self-confidence required to perform comfortably in the role of a strategic leader comes from a combination of successful past experiences in similar exposed roles and from a clear vision of where the organization should be heading. There is little that we can do to help individuals accumulate successful past experiences; what we can help with is the vision or strategic direction that the firm should be heading in. The arguments, techniques and analytical frameworks set out in the book should help top team members form strategic visions which are grounded in sound thinking, open debate and thorough analysis. Strategies formed on these foundations should be robust, realistic and believable.

SUMMARY

The chapter set out to examine the links between strategy and culture. Culture is increasingly of interest to strategists because it influences both the formulation and the implementation of strategy. Using a simple model, we initially disaggregated cultural processes into distinct categories. Organizational processes included grouping, informal and formal power relationships, control and reward systems, management style, stories and symbols. We highlighted the importance of routines in preserving stability and we linked the concept of routines back to our arguments concerning know-how as a source of inimitable advantage advanced in Chapter 3.

The category of cognitive processes captured important contributions to our understanding of strategy processes, particularly the notions of industry recipe, and organizational paradigms. Having considered different aspects of culture in this rather piecemeal fashion, we then looked at some important connections and interactions between these categories of culture. We concluded with a speculative look at the culture of a machine adhocracy.

Managing Strategic Change

> *The new system was accepted in discussion and debates, but not in practice. Managers agreed with what the consultants and change agents presented to them, but they behaved in accordance with the old way of doing things.*

This quote came from a senior manager of a large petroleum corporation. The system referred to was for strategic planning and control, which was designed by one of the major international strategy consultants after an extensive period of analysis and discussion.

Obviously this organization is having a problem with implementing a strategic change. Even though there is a clear statement of intent resulting from the consultant's extensive analysis of the firm's situation, and even though the managers agree with the recommendations, they are still behaving in the old ways. *Why?*

There does not appear to be a problem with the recommendations themselves – the managers agree with what is being suggested, or at least no one seems to be prepared to criticize the recommendations in public. And, objectively, the intended strategy may well be exactly the right course of action for this firm at this time. However, unless the managers start to behave in ways that are in line with the intended strategy, the strategic management process will stall at the point of implementation.

We argued in the previous chapter that culture plays a central role in the strategy process. Therefore, in order to understand some of the issues in managing strategic change, it is appropriate to use the cultural perspective developed in the last chapter (see Figure 8.1). We shall use this approach to help us understand the implementation problems referred to in the above quotation.

CULTURE AND STRATEGIC CHANGE

The implementation problem seems to be that managers are behaving in the old ways. Our model suggests that behaviour is influenced by managers' cognitions, which are in turn influenced by their experiences, both inside and outside the organization. So, problems must exist somewhere in this chain. It would appear that routines – the old ways of doing things – are exerting a powerful influence. Even though there is intellectual agreement and understanding of the need for change, routine ways of behaving predominate. This is probably because the routines are embedded in an organizational structure that supports behaviour in line with the routines, and makes behaviour outside the routines quite difficult. For example, the functional structure, the power relationships, the way people relate and interact, and the control systems are congruent with the old routines, not the new intended strategy.

Miller and Friesen (1980) note that an elaborate set of programmes, goals and expectations grows up around the organization's *modus operandi*. Momentum tends to be pervasive. Organizational change is likely to be characterized by periods of dramatic revolution, when there are reversals in the direction of change across a large number of variables of strategy and structure. Strategic change has been characterized as involving one of more or the following (Asch, 1993):

■ A change of chief executive.
■ A new product/market strategy.
■ A significant change in organizational interactions, *e.g.*, due to revised working methods, new/different facilities.
■ A change in the organizational structure.
■ A change in information/control systems.
■ A significant change in the external environment.

Most research on strategic change (for example Mintzberg and Waters, 1982; Johnson, 1987) finds that, on average, major shifts take place only once every 10 years. Other work, however, demonstrates that the gap between revolutions may be quite short – only 3–4 years. The consequences of incremental change are often the reinforcement of complacency, coupled with decreased flexibility and an unwillingness to learn (Tushman and Romanelli, 1985).

There is, then, overwhelming pressure to retain existing ways of behaving. To change behaviour will probably require more than an intellectual agreement to change. The structures and processes in which the old routines are embedded must be changed as well. This would suggest that:

■ Real strategic change can only be achieved through changes in cultural processes.
■ Such changes will have to be tackled on a broad front in which the many interlocking dimensions of culture are addressed – structures, systems, symbols and so on.

A further implication of this line of reasoning is that if implementation is attempted through existing structures and processes, it is likely that the culture will absorb, dilute and dissipate the intended strategy.

If the influence of culture in preserving routines is strong, the management team trying to effect change will need not only to understand and agree with the strategy, but they must be highly committed to it and believe that change is essential. If we refer back to our quote above, the process whereby the intended strategy was formed was not one that generated the levels of commitment to change that were required to drive the management to overcome their cultural barriers to change.

The strategy was drawn up by external strategy consultants, and although the emerging shape of the strategy was presented to the executives at various stages in its development, it was nevertheless perceived by the executives as the consultants' strategy.

Although the executives could not fault the logic of the strategy, and indeed did not wish to as the consultancy exercise was very expensive, the process of strategy formulation did not generate the required levels of belief and commitment. There was a shared understanding, the strategy was quite explicit and well communicated, but emotional commitment was lacking. This is by no means an isolated example. There is ample evidence of problems of strategy implementation in the literature (*e.g.*, Johnson, 1987).

Commitment is usually generated through involvement. If the members of the executive team feel that the strategy is really theirs, that they own the strategy, then the required changes are much more likely to be driven through even though they may be painful and difficult. So, it is vital that the process of strategy making is one that generates commitment to change. This suggests that the strategy must be decided by those executives who will be responsible for its implementation. However, we noted in the last chapter that the members of a management team may be constrained by a paradigm. They may hold a set of beliefs and assumptions about, for example, their strengths, customer needs and competitors' capabilities, that are implicit and never discussed. If strategy making is left entirely to this group, there is a danger that the quality of debate and the challenging of assumptions that are required to produce high quality strategic thinking will not take place. The resulting strategy is most likely to be some incremental adjustment to existing patterns of activity. Even if analytical processes are used, there is a danger that the results of analysis will be used selectively to justify the strategy that has emerged from past ad hoc, incremental decisions.

So we have a dilemma. If the strategy is left to objective outsiders, such as the staff in the strategic planning department, the quality of the strategy may be high, but the chances of it being implemented may be low. However, if the members of the executive team construct the strategy, there is a danger that they may generate a large degree of commitment to the wrong strategy. What is required are processes that mitigate the dangers of paradigm-dominated thinking, but that capitalize on the benefits of involvement. Such processes should lead to high levels of commitment towards a sound strategic direction.

CONTENT QUALITY VERSUS PROCESS QUALITY

Increasingly, strategy consultants are seeking to establish longer-term relationships with their clients. In the past, the task of the strategy consultant was believed to be to come in as an objective outsider, conduct an extensive analysis of the firm's strategic situation, and then make strategy recommendations. At this point, the report would be handed over to the firm's management and the consultants would leave the scene.

Now, more consultants are working with their clients, helping them to think through the strategic situation they are facing, and facilitating the process of strategy formulation and implementation. The emphasis has shifted away from the content of the strategy towards improving the quality of the strategy process. By helping the members of the top management team in their strategy deliberations, the consultants can generate the necessary commitment to the emerging strategy, but at the same time they can act as devil's advocates, challenging and evaluating the assumptions held by the team. They are also able to provide more objective data on which to base decisions.

The techniques and frameworks we have set out in this book can be used to expose the taken-for-granted assumptions of the team, and in so doing the influence of the paradigm in shaping perceptions and understanding can be reduced.

TRIGGERING CHANGE

We can refer to our culture model set out in Chapter 7 to explore some issues in the change process. We have reproduced the model in Figure 9.1.

Figure 9.1
Culture and change
relationships.

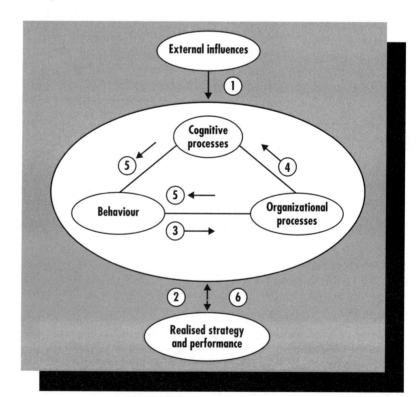

Relationship 1, between the external environment and the organization, is most keenly felt by boundary-spanning staff such as sales people. Often, early signals of the need for change are picked up by this type of staff. They sense that the existing products and services are becoming uncompetitive, or they encounter a new player in the market. However, these signals often fail to reach top managers early enough or the messages contained within them lose some of their impact as they are reinterpreted to justify the current ways of doing things.

It is often only when a crisis is precipitated, usually in the form of a serious deterioration in performance (relationship 2), that senior executives grasp the nettle of change; this may be too late to save the firm. The usual action that flows from this realization is cost cutting in all its various forms. Thus, the crisis leads to staff lay-offs, delayering, downsizing, drastic trimming of the softer budgets like training and research and development, or even to plant closures.

These cuts are easy to understand and relatively straightforward to implement, although they can be painful for those adversely affected. At this stage in the change process, there is no sense of a new strategy or vision informing these actions. The management are seen as merely destroying parts of the past (relationship 3).

In order to embark upon a new phase of development, there needs to be some sense of a new future, a vision or strategy that builds rather than destroys the organization. Relationship 4 suggests that, for this to happen, there may need to be structural and process changes first. The most obvious is the arrival of a new CEO with ways of thinking new to the organization.

159

If a new strategy is to be realized it has to affect routine behaviours. Successful implementation of the new strategy would manifest itself through new routines being embedded in the organization (relationship 5), leading to the emergence of the new realized strategy (relationship 6). If it is the right strategy for the firm, it should lead to more sustained performance improvements than just those stemming from cost cutting.

In the rest of this chapter, we consider a range of process interventions that can help bring about significant change in the organization. We refer to our culture model to assess the role and contribution of each prescription. We begin with mission statements, which seem to have a very mixed press. When working with executives, there appear two contrasting opinions about the usefulness of missions. Most executives view them rather cynically. However, a minority value them, and perceive them to be hugely influential in their organizations. We rarely encounter executives with moderate views about mission statements. They either love them or hate them.

Clearly, there must be some contextual or process factors that are causing these extreme reactions. We shall return to these following a brief summary of mission statements.

THE ROLE OF THE MISSION STATEMENT

Mission statements are supposed to capture the essence of the firm's strategy in a concise statement of intent. However, like many management fads, the quality of most missions statements is very poor. Many organizations have them, but few managers, even those in senior positions, could tell you what is in the statement. Those who can remember them may not believe in the statements made. This is a pity, because a good mission statement can play a powerful part in strategic change.

If the statement is to play this role it needs to be carefully crafted. Some useful guidelines in drawing up a mission statement are set out below. An example of a statement can be found in Figure 9.2.

MISSION STATEMENT: SOME GUIDELINES

The purpose of the mission statement is to communicate to those inside the organization the broad ground rules that the organization has set itself in conducting its business:
- It should be a broadly framed and enduring statement of intent.
- It is essentially an internal working document.
- It should set out as clearly as possible the essence of the competitive strategy.

The essence of the competitive strategy can be considered as:
- The target markets (and segments).
- How competitive advantage will be gained in those markets.
- How competitive advantage will be translated into superior profitability, including cost management.
- It may be appropriate to summarize the required competences to achieve the competitive strategy (see Figure 9.2).
- How success will be measured.
- Attitudes to growth and to financing.

It may also be appropriate to include statements of intent towards various stakeholders, staff, society and the local community.

The statement needs to be concise, but at the same time it must provide unambiguous guidance. This last requirement is what makes mission statements so difficult to get right. Although brevity is desirable, if it results in ambiguity, or worse still a set of bland and generalized 'motherhood' clichés, the statement will not be a living document. It will be viewed cynically and seen as irrelevant.

Although it may be desirable to include value statements about concern for employees or the environment, this should be done only if the team members believe in them sufficiently to back them up with visible actions. If the team puts in pious statements for public and/or employee relations purposes that it has no real intention of

Figure 9.2
Example of a mission
statement.

MISSION STATEMENT

Our business is the marketing of [   ] and
related aftermarket products.

Our market is Europe, Africa, Middle East, C.I.S. and the Indian Subcontinent.

Our aim is to achieve significant market share growth and to generate a
financial performance which will justify the continuing investment of resources
in our business.

Our success will be measured by our performance against the following
objectives.

A [   ] market share growth of 1% p.a.
Hitting out annual targets for
  • Cash Flow
  • Profit volume
  • Asset utilisation

We will meet these objectives by succeeding in the following critical tasks:

Clear identification of our customers' needs and the continuous monitoring of our performance in satisfying those needs.	Engineering Manager
Achievement of 100% uptime for our customers coupled to the lowest cost of ownership.	Engineering Director and Parts Logistics
Provision of a modern competitive product range.	Training & Development Manager (on Corporate NDP Committee)
Achieving the lowest possible delivered cost to the market place.	Manufacturing Director
Working in partnership with our dealers to achieve the distribution of our product and aftermath support in a manner which consistently meets or exceeds agreed standards of performance.	Managing Director
Maximising the business opportunities offered by the aftermarket.	Aftermarket Manager
Full involvement of our employees, supplies and dealers in our drive towards total quality.	QA Manager

Success in achieving our objectives will enable us to grow profitably and to
provide increasing opportunities and rewards for everyone involved in our
business.

161

implementing, then as soon as one piece of evidence is found that
demonstrates a lack of commitment to the espoused values, the
mission statement as a whole will fall into disrepute.

The mission statement should be treated as a working document for managers and should be as tough and clear as possible. If a statement is required for PR purposes, one should be drawn up that meets those requirements. The trap of trying to construct one statement to satisfy two requirements should be avoided. The usual result is a bland wish list that satisfies neither need well.

In order to draw up such a statement, the management team needs to engage in a full-scale strategic analysis. When setting the guidelines for the medium-term strategy of the firm, markets must be analysed, trends in customers needs understood, and the relative performance of competitors and the threat of entrants assessed. Choices must be made to move into or out of particular markets or segments of markets. The key competences to deliver the strategy must be identified and target levels of attainment should be set, *e.g.*, the fastest new product development cycle in the industry, or 100% right first time.

In summarizing the essence of the competitive strategy, it is sometimes useful to focus attention on those product/service dimensions that are valued by customers and can be made better than those offered by the competitors, *i.e.* motivator dimensions, and on those dimensions where the aim is to be as good as the competitors, *i.e.* hygiene dimensions.

One way of judging how good the statement is, is to ask the following questions of it:

- Would a new manager have a clear view of what the firm is trying to achieve just by reading the mission statement?
- Does each phrase and sentence clarify the firm's intentions? If one does not, why is it in there? Could it be taken out?
- Does the top team really believe in the statement in its totality and detail? If not, it should be torn up and redrafted.
- Is it obvious how a whole set of actions must be set in motion if the intentions in the statement are to be realized?

If there are major differences in the product markets that the firm intends to trade in, and if the capabilities required to gain advantage in these markets are very different, it will probably be necessary to draw up more than one mission statement. If the firm prefers to have one overarching document at corporate level, this can be supplemented by a strategy statement for each substantial market or segment grouping.

STRATEGY STATEMENTS FOR FIRMS SERVING MANY SEGMENTS

Most firms serve several segments of demand that may have quite different needs. Ideally, each segment, defined as a group of buyers with similar needs, should be addressed by a strategic business unit dedicated to meeting those needs more effectively than other firms. In practice, firms are rarely able to dedicate parts of the organization to service just one segment. Compromises between segment focus and other imperatives such as economies of scale have to be made.

If a clear view of the various segments of demand the firm is targeting has been established, then the following analysis can be undertaken.

■ For each segment, the needs of the buyers should be identified and rated in importance.

■ The segments should then be compared to establish the extent to which there are common needs that span across segments. These core needs should then be identified.

■ If the core needs are rated highly by all segments, then a competitive strategy can be developed around these needs. Decisions will then need to be taken about which needs the firm intends to address in ways that are superior to those of competitors. Needs that are rated as less important and that are different between segments will then have to be addressed by specific actions, *e.g.*, tailoring some products to meet a particular segment's needs, or using different channels or advertising approaches to address different segments.

■ If there are important differences between the needs of the segments targeted, and if the capabilities required to deliver those needs are fundamentally different, then organizational subunits will have to be created to focus on each segment. Strategy statements will be required for each of these distinct subunits (Figure 9.3).

As a rough guide, mission statements should have an effective life of at least two years. Bringing the organization into line with the

163

Figure 9.3
Subunit mission statements.

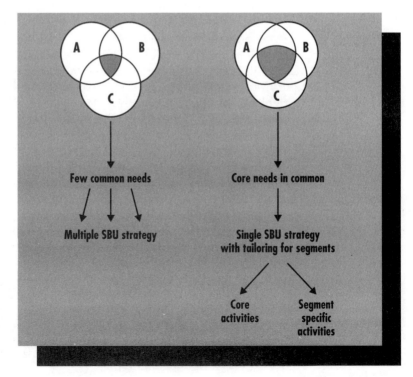

intentions set out in the statement will take time, and people in the organization will need to see some stability in the direction the firm is taking if they are to commit themselves to make the required changes. If the mission statement changes continually it will not be seen as a credible document.

Looked at in this light, it is clear that the mission statement summarizes the output of an extensive process of strategic thinking. It should not therefore be drawn up at the start of such a process. If the mission statement captures the essence of the strategy, it can then be used as *the* key strategic document. A whole set of actions should then be driven by the mission statement.

THE ROLE OF MISSION STATEMENTS IN STRATEGIC CHANGE

Referring to Figure 9.1, we can assess the way in which a mission statement may assist in the process of cultural change. If the team that drafts the statement has not engaged in a challenging debate about strategy, the chances are that the statement will merely confirm past realized strategy. The cognitive processes of the group responsible for the mission may restrict and constrain the emerging vision to the extent that no real change is required to organization processes or behaviours. We should not underestimate the attractions of such an outcome to existing executives. A mission that confirms, broadly, the legitimacy of the *status quo* also confirms the practices, routines and priorities of the past and it justifies the existing structures and power relationships. A mission statement like this is likely to be warmly and actively supported by all those who benefit from the *status quo*.

Mission statements that require significant shifts in the way things are done in the firm can come about in a variety of ways. They can be drawn up by outside consultants, who, being in a more objective position, may be able to set out dispassionately the nature and the extent of the changes required. The chances of this statement impacting on the organization will depend upon the power relationships within the structure, particularly the extent to which the CEO backs the strategy set out by the consultants. Whether change is wholeheartedly adopted by other top team members will depend on the extent to which they are dissatisfied personally with their current situations. A crisis precipitated by a serious deterioration in performance may persuade these executives that there is no option but to change. More positively, there may be attractions in pursuing the change of direction if the executive perceives positive outcomes for him- or herself.

For a top team themselves to construct and be committed to a strategy of change requires them to engage in new ways of thinking. Again, the impetus to explore new strategies may be encouraged by outside events, *e.g.*, performance problems, a new entrant into the market, or pressure from the corporate centre. The ability to conceive of new ways of doing things can be facilitated by outsiders. These may take the form of consultant facilitators, who are able to inject new ways of analysing and can import a wider base of experience or, in some cases, a new CEO or other significant top team member injects the new thinking. Often, though, the new CEO may be simply bringing a familiar and successful recipe from his previous organization. The CEO may have the advantage of past success which instils self-confidence, and can inspire the rest of the team to take on the personal risks of changing.

We have had some involvement as facilitators with top teams who are genuinely searching for a clearer sense of strategic direction. Where these teams come to some agreement about the broad thrust of their firm's strategy, and where they have been able to summarize this into a concise statement of strategic intent, the teams appear to be empowered. The clarification of the firm's strategy gives them confidence in making day-to-day operational decisions, which may previously have been made on a more ad hoc basis. Thus, when confronted by a reporting manager requesting more staff, or capital expenditure, the executive can refer to the strategy in making a judgement. If the manager's request is in line with the intended direction, then the request wins the executive's full support; if it does not support the strategy, the request is denied. This feeds down through the structure, empowering managers at lower levels. There is a sense of direction. Middle managers might not agree with all of it, but at least there is a consistent line coming down from the top.

FROM MISSION STATEMENT INTO ACTION

If the mission statement is to be a live document it must be translated into action. There is no obvious and foolproof way of doing this, but perhaps the least useful approach is to pass on the statement to the executives of each of the existing functions and have them interpret what it means to them. If the statement does not merely endorse the strategy of the past, it will include statements of intent that will require changes to the current ways of doing things. If the statement is passed on to the existing function holders, it is likely to be absorbed and interpreted into functional routines. As illustrated in Figure 9.1, the intended strategy as an organizational process should lead to changes in cognitions which would lead in turn into changes in behaviour, but the intentions can get reinterpreted and comfortably absorbed into existing routines leading to no change.

USING THE *STATUS QUO* TO CHANGE THE *STATUS QUO*

The existing structures and processes in the organization support the current ways of doing things. If the strategy indicates that the organization needs to behave in different ways, a problem is likely to arise if the existing structures are the primary vehicle for implementing the changes. Current structures and processes may well distort and dilute the intended strategy to the point where no discernible change takes place.

If the strategy is implemented through the existing functional structure of the firm, the intended strategy will be interpreted by functional managers in terms that make sense to them and in ways that reflect the types of activity for which the function has previously been responsible. However, it may be that critical actions are required that fall outside the traditional functional division of tasks. If the strategy is translated only into behaviours that reflect the past functional specialization, then actions that lie outside the existing functions or, more typically, actions that cut across several existing functions are not going to be picked up.

It may therefore be necessary to employ other structures and processes if significant changes to routine behaviour are required. If structures and processes that lie outside the *status quo* are used, then this should reduce the possibility that the intended strategy will become assimilated into existing routines.

In order to avoid some of those pitfalls, it is helpful to use the mission statement as a medium to drive actions. Below is an example of how one firm has tried to translate its mission statement into action without working directly through the existing functional structure.

DELIVERING THE AIMS OF THE MISSION STATEMENT

The functional structure may be appropriate for performing the basic tasks of the firm, but as this organizational form is probably common to all firms in a given industry it cannot explain or deliver extra-ordinary task performance to achieve lowest costs, best quality, or both. Processes other than structural specialization must be involved in delivering competitive advantage.

The Wilshire Reporter Group is a regional newspaper company. It has six titles, including an evening paper and weekly local papers. The top management team members have developed a competitive strategy for the business. They have tried to capture the essence of the strategy in a mission statement (Figure 9.4). This is not a wonderful mission statement, but the team likes it and it means something to them. They are excited by it, and feel that in drawing it up they have clarified a lot of issues and provided a sense of direction for the business. The next stage in the process is to identify the actions required – the actions that will help to move the organization from where it is, towards where it needs to be to achieve the strategy.

The team has brainstormed a long list of actions (Figure 9.5). Again, this is not peppered with startling insights or major break-throughs, but the team believes that if action can be started in these areas it will help to move things in the right direction. The current organizational structure is set out in Figure 9.6; this functional structure is typical of the industry. The only moderately unusual

Figure 9.4
Mission statement for the
Wilshire Reporter Group.

MISSION STATEMENT

- We aim to provide a profitable package of publications to meet the needs of advertisers, via our readers

- Our target markets are: (defined by geography)

- We intend to dominate all trade and private advertising within these areas

- We will also maximize advertising opportunities outside these areas

- The needs of existing and potential readers and advertisers in our target markets will be identified and profitably met

- We will grow profitably by expanding our primary market west into the area of...

- We aim to have an organization that all our people are proud to be associated with

Figure 9.5
Action to achieve mission.

ACTIONS TO ACHIEVE MISSION

- Analyse competitors' strategies
- Research advertisers' needs
- Research readers' needs
- Communicate mission statement to all staff
- Get ideas from all staff
- Produce staff handbook
- Monitor profit by publication
- Set profit targets for each publication
- Establish profit centres
- Appoint profit centre managers
- Evaluate current training activities
- Implement customer care programmes
- Evaluate all products re: meeting customer needs
- Encourage open discussion
- Improve lateral communication
- Develop profitable new products that meet unfulfilled needs
- Use low price, efficient press capacity
- Stay abreast of new technology
- Eliminate all print errors
- Clearly define our target markets
- Have motivated staff
- Have visible management
- Print on time
- Review selling methods
- Reward excellence
- Monitor costs
- Control costs across the organization
- Reduce working capital
- Challenge existing products
- Establish missions for each department
- Conduct creative executive meetings
- Measure management performance
- Improve promotional activity
- Find out what motivates staff
- Achieve lowest costs
- Turn everyone into a salesperson
- Set up focus groups
- All managers to see a customer every day
- Achieve dynamic induction processes
- Promote cost awareness
- Make people proud to work here
- Set up job swaps
- Reward efficiency
- Set up suggestion boxes that work
- Monitor product quality
- Find out competitors' costs

167

Figure 9.6
*Management structure of a
regional newspaper:
structure A.*

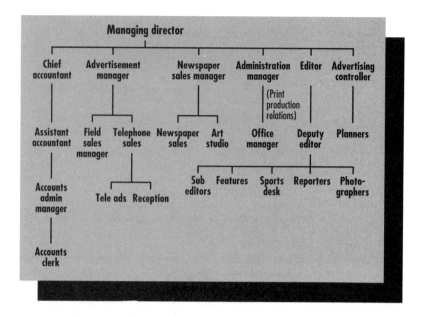

feature of this firm is the absence of a printing press. The newspapers are printed by another company in the group.

If one inspects the actions that have been derived from the brainstorming (Figure 9.5), one can note one striking feature. Most of them do not fall neatly within the typical range of responsibilities assumed by the existing functional departments. They either span several or indeed all departments, or they are not captured by any.

This means that, routinely, these activities will not be picked up. It probably also means that if the management team had not brainstormed the actions required to deliver the mission, but had instead decided that each department should now come up with a functional plan to support the mission, many of these activities would not have been identified. In this sense, then, the existing structure can deliver only the existing strategy. The *status quo* structure cannot easily manage a transition to a new, more competitive strategic posture.

The activities in Figure 9.5 can be grouped into four main areas:
1. Understanding the market place.
2. Delivering profitable valued products.
3. Achieving lowest cost.
4. Motivating people.

These could be viewed as the broad capabilities required to deliver the mission (Figure 9.7). How can these required capabilities be developed within the existing functional structure?

One approach might be to view the capabilities as one dimension of a two-dimensional matrix organization. Most matrix forms involve the overlaying of a project or product orientation onto a functional structure, but in Figure 9.8 we are proposing that the required capabilities assume a cross-functional aspect. They could be headed by capability champions who assume responsibility for initiating actions and projects to achieve the required capabilities.

Figure 9.7
Achieving the mission.

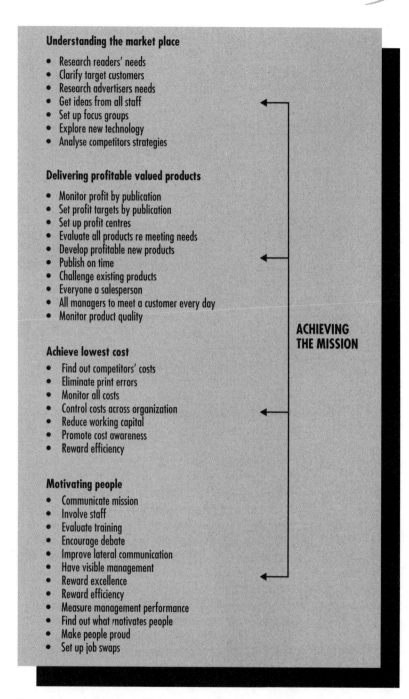

Understanding the market place

- Research readers' needs
- Clarify target customers
- Research advertisers needs
- Get ideas from all staff
- Set up focus groups
- Explore new technology
- Analyse competitors strategies

Delivering profitable valued products

- Monitor profit by publication
- Set profit targets by publication
- Set up profit centres
- Evaluate all products re meeting needs
- Develop profitable new products
- Publish on time
- Challenge existing products
- Everyone a salesperson
- All managers to meet a customer every day
- Monitor product quality

Achieve lowest cost

- Find out competitors' costs
- Eliminate print errors
- Monitor all costs
- Control costs across organization
- Reduce working capital
- Promote cost awareness
- Reward efficiency

Motivating people

- Communicate mission
- Involve staff
- Evaluate training
- Encourage debate
- Improve lateral communication
- Have visible management
- Reward excellence
- Reward efficiency
- Measure management performance
- Find out what motivates people
- Make people proud
- Set up job swaps

ACHIEVING THE MISSION

169

They nevertheless still have functional aspects. This is a small organization, after all.

Thus, the existing structure enables routine activities to be performed that deliver the basic product/service. Processes overlying and intertwining with the functional structure help to deliver competitive advantage. We shall refer to these activities as **transcending activities**. The transcending activities are managed outside the functional structure, but their objective is to operate on

Figure 9.8
A regional newspaper:
structure B.

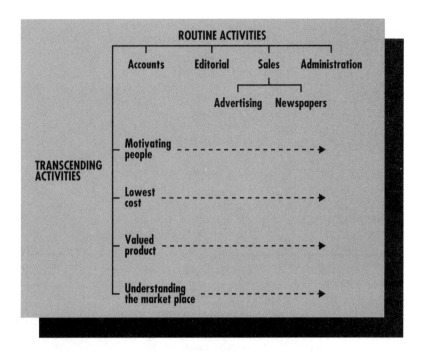

the functional activities in order to develop and embed new routines that help to deliver competitive advantage. In this way the firm transcends the average performance level in the market place and achieves advantage. These transcending activities are managed more formally by the university staff grouping identified in Chapter 6. They are part of the machine adhocracy.

At some point in this transcending process, the logic of the existing functional structure may have to yield to more appropriate bases for specializing and grouping activities. For example the structure may evolve into that depicted in Figure 9.9. Here, there are product groups for each title, supported by shared core activities, *e.g.,* sports, features, photography. In the staff areas there are people specialists concentrating on building a highly skilled and motivated team of people, and there are people focusing exclusively on cost control. Market information and research is a separate activity, allowing staff to specialize and develop skills in gathering and interpreting this crucial information. So, the past functional structure has undergone a transition which now recognizes some new specializations that are required to deliver competitive advantage, *e.g.,* cost control and market information. In this way, the structure may move towards the machine adhocracy configuration that we described in Chapter 6.

If this approach has indeed resulted in the firm achieving competitive advantage, its rivals may try to imitate the strategy or find other ways of achieving an advantage. If the transcending activities implant the appropriate new routines successfully, other firms might find this difficult to imitate. However, over time the industry's standards are likely to be ratcheted up through com-

Figure 9.9
A regional newspaper:
structure C.

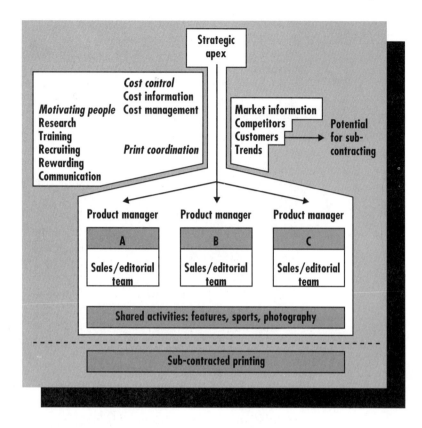

petitive imitation, which may mean that new activities may be required to move the firm further ahead. In time, other structural reorganizations may be required, leading to a continuous process of strategy/structure evolution.

We have encountered a number of other ways in which organizations have used processes outside the existing structures to effect strategic change. Four popular approaches are:
■ Capability champions (used by the Wilshire Reporter Group above).
■ Project management.
■ Cross-functional teams.
■ Reorganizing the structure.

CAPABILITY CHAMPIONS

The actions that are required to move the organization towards the intended strategy are grouped into broad **required capabilities** or **competences**. Examples of required capabilities might be:
■ To achieve lowest delivered cost.
■ To attract and retain well-motivated, well-qualified staff.
■ To achieve rapid new product introductions.

■ To maximize the profitable business opportunities available in the aftermarket.

None of these required capabilities is particularly unusual, but the problem lies in the fact that the existing functions are not delivering these capabilities. It is the role of the capability champion to drive forward the agreed sets of actions that are required to achieve each capability, and to be held accountable by the chief executive and the top team for progress towards improving this capability. The actions usually involve staff from several different functions working together in small teams, which means that, if the capability champions are to influence staff from other departments, they must have power. This can be achieved in one of two ways:

1. The capability champions are selected or volunteer from the group of top managers, bringing with them the formal and informal authority of their functional positions.
2. The capability champions are selected from a pool of high-flying middle/senior managers so they have their own skills and abilities to influence people who may be senior to them, but they are visibly empowered by the chief executive officer to whom they have a direct reporting line.

PROJECT MANAGEMENT

Project management is a well-established discipline that has evolved from the problems of managing large-scale, one-off projects such as dam building or sending a man to the moon. It requires the clear separation of the role of the client from that of project manager. The client sets the objectives of the project and is the ultimate judge of its success; the client can terminate the project at any time. Usually, the project manager is assigned a multi-disciplinary team to carry out the project, and the composition of the team may change as the project moves through its various stages. The project must have a tangible and measurable outcome, and it must be broken down into a sequence of tasks that can be scheduled and controlled.

The advantages of the technique in strategy implementation derive from the disciplines and procedures that have been developed, its multi-disciplinary approach, and the measurability of the outputs. Not all the changes that are required to implement a strategy successfully can be managed in this way but, if the basic disciplines of project management can be introduced into the organization, then the more that can be managed through those processes the greater the likelihood that significant strategic changes can be effected (see Pellegrinelli and Bowman, 1993).

CROSS-FUNCTIONAL TEAMS

Every structure is a compromise. If you specialize by function you reap the advantages of expertise at the cost of a client, product or market focus. Cross-functional teams can be used to overcome some of the disadvantages of functional structures. However, if they are to work they must be managed in the right way:

- They need clear, broad, stable but challenging goals or missions.
- They need to be left alone by functional managers.
- They must have heavyweight leaders with influence.
- The work of teams may need to be coordinated.
- It is important that the members of the team are able to deliver the function they represent, that is, they must be powerful enough to make decisions that commit their function.
- Team contributions must be recognized and rewarded by functional bosses.
- Each team must be stable to allow its members to establish good working relationships and develop a team spirit.

REORGANIZATION

If any one of the three processes described above is used, there may well come a point where the old functional groupings and specializations increasingly become recognised as inappropriate for the changing direction of the organization. At some point, the logic of the old structure becomes untenable as more and more activity is driven by projects and cross-functional teams in pursuit of the required capabilities. The opportunity may present itself to acknowledge the fundamental shift in the focus of the organization by bringing the formal structure more into line with the actual work of the organization.

173

We can see this happening in small ways with the development of new specializations, such as quality assurance, innovation, technology development, and project and programme management. It may be advantageous to anticipate the evolution of new bases of specialization by proactively reshaping the organization. It is clear that, in order to gain sustainable advantage, the firm must develop outstanding capabilities in:

- New product introductions.
- Achieving lowest delivered costs.
- Delivering right-first-time quality.

It might be advantageous to recognize this formally by establishing groups that have the achievement of these capabilities as their primary responsibility. This is a structure that the Wilshire Reporter Group may adopt in the future. This type of bold initiative can be extremely powerful in signalling a major shift in strategic direction.

IDENTIFYING BARRIERS TO CHANGE

A clear sense of strategic direction set out in a good mission statement can be used to help identify the potential barriers to change in the organization. One way of exploring these barriers is to examine the extent to which the current organization supports or constrains movement towards the aims set out in the mission statement. The required capabilities can be derived from brainstorming and grouping the actions needed to fulfil the aims of the statement. The organizational structures, processes, and types of information required to deliver the required capabilities can be explored. This should highlight the need for new systems and information, and there may be a requirement for new specializations and different groupings. Then, the more intangible aspects of culture can be addressed by focusing on the values and management styles that are supportive of the mission.

Thus, a picture can be developed of the way the organization might need to look if it is going to achieve the mission successfully. This vision of a future organization can then be used to compare and contrast the present situation. To do this a **force-field** approach can be useful. In Figure 9.10, the future organization is represented by the dotted wavy line, and the current situation by the solid wavy line. There are forces acting in the organization that are already moving the firm in the right direction, *e.g.*, it is already engaged in extensive training in quality assurance, and shop-floor attitudes seem to be in favour of some changes.

However, set against these pushing forces are resisting forces, or barriers to change. To expose these, the management team members

Figure 9.10
Force-field analysis.

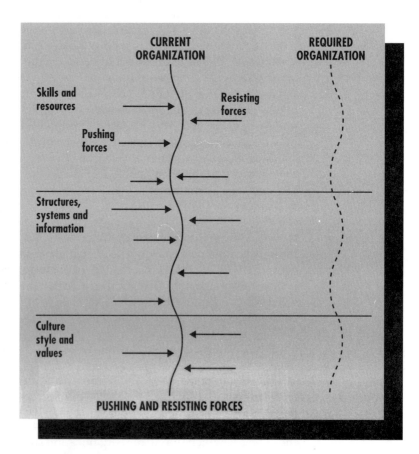

will have to engage in some challenging thinking, and they will need to be very open, honest and explicit. If a major barrier is the cynical attitude of the finance director towards any new initiatives, then this issue must be confronted. If the autocratic chief executive is seen to be stifling initiatives, then this must be brought out into the open and discussed. Not all barriers will be of this sensitive nature, but they may nevertheless be difficult to identify. Routines dominate organizational behaviour. Ways must be found to understand and to evaluate routine ways of doing things.

Some suggestions here might be to take a typical activity and to conduct a type of value engineering exercise on it:

- Why is this being done? Does it contribute to reducing costs or delivering value? If the answer is not clear then perhaps it need not be done at all.
- Should we be doing this ourselves? Could it be subcontracted?
- Why is this done in this way?
- Who else could or should be involved in the activity?
- How else could the activity be performed?
- What other activities does this one affect directly?

Questions such as these may expose some of the taken-for-granted routines that are impediments to change.

Once the major pushing and resisting forces have been identified they can be rated according to their perceived strength or importance. This can be represented on the chart by the length of the arrow.

The pace of movement towards the required organization can be increased by either strengthening the pushing forces, *e.g.*, extending the quality programme to include all staff; adding new pushing forces, *e.g.*, setting up a new product-development task force to explore ways of reducing the time to market; or by reducing the resisting forces, *e.g.*, firing the finance director. In this way, by getting managers to think creatively, tangible actions can be identified which taken together will accelerate progress towards the aims of the mission statement.

175

PRIORITIZING AND OWNERSHIP

If either the force-field technique or the approach driving actions from the mission statement is used, it is likely that a large number of actions will be generated. Senior managers are busy people. Even if they are supposed to be spending time managing the strategy of the organization, they frequently become excessively involved in day-to-day operational activities. The management group has, therefore, a limited capacity to do new things and drive new initiatives. This scarce resource must therefore be deployed to best advantage.

The actions derived from the processes described above must become priority actions. This can be done in a systematic way by identifying which actions impinge on the achievement of more than one capability, and then by rating how well this is currently performed. Alternatively, the managers could agree on a subset of actions to be tackled first. Such a selection should be guided by the following principles:

■ Select actions that can be accomplished fairly easily – early success is vital. If there is visible success in tackling an action this can encourage others to try new ways of doing things, and the momentum of change can be built up.

■ Select an action that has powerful symbolic qualities. Do something that clearly signals to people that things are changing, and that the organization is breaking away from the past.

Each priority action must be owned by an individual, preferably a volunteer. Collective action rarely works. A particular person must feel accountable for delivering the action. This is necessary in order to encourage busy managers to find the time to work on the things that need changing. Without this accountability, the day-to-day demands of the job will drive out the good intentions of the managers. Managers must be accountable, but this does not necessarily mean they are personally responsible for effecting the actions. Instigators of the action may convene small teams from within their departments or from across the organization to implement the required actions.

There must be an agreed timetable of deadlines for the achievement of each action, and managers must be held to account for progress towards the required results. The strategy implementation process should be reviewed periodically. This review should seek to confirm the broad strategic direction set out in the mission statement, and managers should share their experiences of trying to implement the required changes. They may identify some common barriers to change that may require new actions to be initiated. Sharing the experiences of implementation successes can help others to formulate ideas, and should boost morale.

Lastly, it is important that the control and reward systems reflect the intentions of the mission statement. There is little point in having a mission statement that says "We aim to delight our customers" if there is no genuine attempt to measure the firm's performance against this objective. If the control systems still emphasize other variables such as capacity utilization, overhead recover and gross margin, then staff will direct their efforts towards these measures, not towards achieving "delighted customers". To take another example, if the mission statement says "We aim to have an organization that our staff can be proud of", then this must be brought about in some way. First, managers need to know what would make the staff proud to work there. Then they should set about changing things so that the staff become proud of their organization, as well as finding ways, through staff surveys and so on, of measuring how well they are meeting this important aim.

Similarly, rewards must be in tune with the intentions set out in the mission statement. Staff must be recognized and rewarded for behaviour that is clearly in line with the statement. If an employee stays on late to solve a customer's problem, this must be recognized.

If a group of people use their initiative to come up with a way of achieving major savings in material costs they should be appropriately rewarded. If it is important to shift the organization away from a conservative, risk averse culture to one where people are free to experiment, take risks and assume responsibility, it is vital that individuals displaying these qualities are encouraged and promoted.

We have deliberately concentrated our attention in this chapter on the most difficult aspects of managing strategic change. These are changes that require members of an organization to behave in different ways, learn new things, and evolve new attitudes. However, it must be recognized that there is another category of strategic change that is essentially about eliminating or reducing aspects of the business, *e.g.*, closing an inefficient plant; sacking a layer of management; halving the range of products; withdrawing from unprofitable client relationships; eliminating a shift; or closing the research department.

These changes may well be painful for the individuals affected directly, and they are of a quite different nature from changes that are concerned with building new capabilities. There is no doubt that dramatic changes can be effected rapidly by eliminating people or activities from the organization, and that such changes can have a powerful influence on the attitudes and behaviour of those that remain. But when compared with the problems of building capabilities, these draconian changes are fairly straightforward to implement. However, of course, if cutting is easy to implement, it cannot be a source of competitive advantage, because it can be imitated. Moreover, because of the relatively straightforward nature of cutting strategies, they can be regarded as dominant strategies. If building is vague and ambiguous, the clearer cutting strategy will prevail.

A simple model of change, attributed to Gleicher (Beckhard, 1969), helps us understand some of the issues involved. If we take as a starting point that there is usually a degree of inertia in an organization, then what prompts significant change? Gleicher's model can be set out as in Figure 9.11.

The model is multiplicative. This means that no change will occur if any of the items to the left of the inequality is zero. So, before change happens there has to a sufficient critical mass of senior people to be dissatisfied with the way things are at present, to want to do something about it. Second, they need to have some vision of where to take the organization. Third, they need to have some understandable first steps to implement, to start the process of change. Importantly, the total of all of these multiplied together must

Figure 9.11
A model of strategic behaviour.

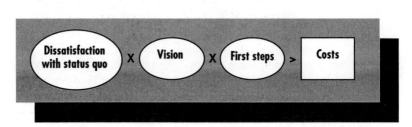

exceed the perceived costs of changing. So, there is little point in having a great strategy, and even setting it out in some detail in an implementation program, if an insufficient critical mass within the company is sufficiently dissatisfied with the way things are at present. In this case, nothing will happen. The level of dissatisfaction can of course be artificially created by manufacturing a crisis, a tactic often adopted by incoming CEOs. This provokes a reaction, which often involves cutting activities, products, people, factories *etc*. Although this can have immense symbolic power, and it can bring about some short-term profit recoveries, it must be followed by a sustained building strategy, concerned with the development of competences that can deliver advantage. In our concluding chapter we adapt Gleicher's model to focus on the individual executive.

SUMMARY

Strategic change needs to be considered from a cultural perspective. Piecemeal changes may be too easily absorbed into the existing culture, and thus lead to no real change. The existing strategy process itself can critically affect the chances of any change occurring, particularly if the process does not generate top-level commitment. We explored a likely sequence in a change process, which is often triggered by a sense of crisis. Prescriptions were proffered that can assist change processes. These included mission statements, capability champions, project management techniques, and the use of cross-functional teams. We showed how blockages to change can be represented using force-field analysis. We concluded with a suggestion that cutting is usually easier to implement than building new capabilities. However, if cutting is easy it cannot be a source of advantage, as it is imitable.

The Nature of Corporate Strategy

Part I of this book has concentrated on **competitive strategy**, since it is our belief that this is the ultimate test of relevance of a business, and hence of its potential in the markets in which it operates. If a corporate strategy is misconceived and destroys corporate value rather than creating it, the remedy may not be difficult to find. Detach the business units from the corporate centre and allow them to function independently. If they have the qualities required for competitive advantage little more need be done. Success will follow, as they are able to deliver what the customers want at prices they find acceptable. The same cannot be said if the competitive strategies are defective, but the corporate strategy is generally sound. In these circumstances, profits will dry up and the corporation will wither away.

This is not to say that **corporate strategy** is unimportant. Collis and Montgomery (1995) state that the Fortune 500 companies which account for about 40% of the GNP of the US are active on average in over ten separate businesses. In organizations with a number of different businesses the distinction between corporate and competitive strategy is most clear. In such circumstances to understand how to achieve **corporate advantage** as well as **competitive advantage** is a very important exercise.

What then is a corporate strategy? It is sometimes defined as a statement answering the questions 'Which businesses should we be in, and how should we run them? There is probably no better short answer than this. However, a fuller statement of a corporate strategy would probably range a little more widely and include the following:

- A vision and/or mission for the corporation, including a set of objectives.
- A portfolio of market sectors and businesses in which the corporation chooses to operate.
- A portfolio of resources, skills and competences in which the corporation aims to be excellent when compared with its rivals.
- Corporate organizational structure, systems and processes with which to coordinate the activities of the corporation.

The major areas of a corporate strategy's domain may be summarized as **selecting**, **resourcing** and **controlling** the businesses within the corporation. The following chapters will describe corporate activities under these three headings.

Above all, the corporate strategy needs to identify clearly how and where the corporate centre will add value, both by what it does well, and by how it is able to assist the business units to achieve a higher performance within the corporation than they could alone. Goold and Campbell (1991) even go so far as to say that the corporate centre must be able to demonstrate it adds more value to its businesses than any other potential parent, otherwise it is legitimately at risk of a take-over on efficiency grounds. In fact, corporations are not quite at this level of risk, since there are considerable costs involved in ownership transfer and reorganization. The benefit of proposed new ownership needs to exceed that of present ownership by a considerable margin before ownership transfer becomes appropriate.

Part II of this book deals exclusively with corporate strategy and the quest for corporate advantage, demonstrated most typically by the creation of value by the centre of the multi-business corporation. Such a corporate strategy is created by the selection of the optimal mission, businesses, competences, structures and systems for the corporation. This chapter sets out to define corporate strategy, and suggests how an appropriate corporate mission can be determined, and corporate competences developed to support it. The following chapters deal with the other major aspects of corporate strategy including selecting the business portfolio, the corporate risk profile, acquiring the necessary resources to succeed, and the control of the corporation. It also addresses these questions in the international theatre and considers how to cope with an increasingly uncertain future. All chapters in this part of the book seek to address the fundamental corporate strategy issues of how a corporation can create value through the configuration and coordination of its multi-market activities.

SELECTING A DIRECTION

A number of frequently used and equally frequently misused tools. including the vision statement, the mission statement, corporate objectives and, ultimately, specific corporate targets, fall under the heading of selecting a direction. There is a tendency for these terms to overlap in usage, and for some of them to descend into banality in content. Read many corporate mission statements and you will hear that the firm aims to give the customer excellent value, and to treat its employees well. A litmus test of a mission statement might be whether a statement of its opposite would still make sense, *e.g.*, give poor customer value and treat employees badly. In this case, such a mission statement is unlikely to be adopted, at least formally, by a company.

These statements tend to be used hierarchically, so that the corporate mission or vision statement provides the umbrella statement within which the more detailed SBU statements must fit. Part I of this book dealt with the concept of mission statement at SBU level. The corporate mission statement needs to perform as an umbrella statement for the corporation as a whole, under which the SBU mission statement can nest relevantly and congruently.

THE VISION STATEMENT

Vision statements tend to be short and pithy and are sometimes referred to as 'bumper stickers'. One of the most famous is that adopted by Komatsu in the 1970s namely 'Encircle Caterpillar'. This has the merit of brevity, memorability, and of encapsulating what the Komatsu top management regarded as the key issue facing the company at the time.

A clear vision defines the rules for acting incrementally and opportunistically. A manager facing an unexpected situation can take a decision after asking himself the question 'Will such an action further the company's vision?' Vision statements often embody the core values of the founding entrepreneur, and say something about the inspiration behind the company that would not be obvious from a reading of its business plans. Steve Jobs, of Apple, set out a vision for his young company: 'One person – one computer'. John Lewis stores capture a vision with their declaration 'Never knowingly undersold'.

Although good vision statements, when read aloud, may sound incredibly simple, this is not the case for firms without a clear vision. In such circumstances, to adopt an advertising copywriter's clever phrase does nothing to create a vision. In the field of politics, George Bush admitted to being uncomfortable with the 'vision thing', and nothing could be done to disguise this. Visions come from within, and the chosen words merely define them. The words cannot create the vision where none exists.

A vision is an image of a better future, however defined; it is a state to which the company aspires, and therefore can, at least logically, be achieved. What happens when Komatsu succeed in encircling Caterpillar? Clearly, a new vision needs to be adopted if the company is not to sink beneath the competitive waves, enthusiastically telling stories of past triumphs. For an ongoing sense of purpose, the mission statement is needed.

181

OBJECTIVES

The process of setting objectives for the corporation, and subsequently for the business units, is the process of translating the corporation's strategies into specific and, if possible, measurable objectives, the achievement of which will signal that the corporation's adopted strategies are working successfully.

Objectives are frequently, but not always, financial. They need not even be measurable, but obviously it helps the monitoring process if they are. The following are typical objectives that a corporation might set for itself, in order to provide behavioural signposts regarding the implementation of strategy as illustrated in Figure 10.1.

Figure 10.1
Measurable corporate
objectives.

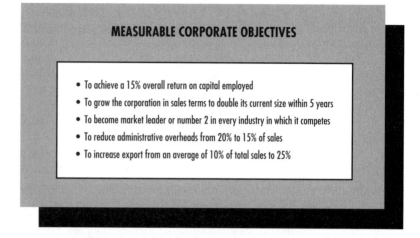

MEASURABLE CORPORATE OBJECTIVES

- To achieve a 15% overall return on capital employed
- To grow the corporation in sales terms to double its current size within 5 years
- To become market leader or number 2 in every industry in which it competes
- To reduce administrative overheads from 20% to 15% of sales
- To increase export from an average of 10% of total sales to 25%

Figure 10.2
Less measurable corporate
objectives.

LESS MEASURABLE OBJECTIVES

- To gain a corporate reputation for product quality
- To improve company morale
- To be more innovative
- To increase commitment throughout the company

Less measurable objectives might be as illustrated in Figure 10.2.

If corporate logic is significantly pitched about leveraging competences and creating synergy, the process of setting corporate objectives should reflect this. Sophisticated objectives would therefore recognize sharing, cooperation and cross-selling, and would monitor the benefits of centralized activities.

Some attempt can be made to measure even the less measurable objectives. For example, the percentage of returns is some measure of product quality, and the level of company morale may be gauged partly by the level of staff turnover, although in times of recession this may not be a very reliable measure. One risk of too great an emphasis on measuring progress towards objectives is that it is a well observed characteristic of organizational life that people concentrate on performing well in areas that they know will be measured, often to the detriment of other sometimes more important, but less easily measured, factors.

One set of objectives might well involve the operationalization of the key statements in the mission statement. For example, an item in Marks and Spencer's mission statement highlights the provision of comfort for customers. This might be translated into an objective to have a certain number of easily accessible seats for customers in every M&S shop as a principle of corporate policy, not at the discretion of the shop manager.

CREATING VALUE FROM THE CENTRE

Part I of this book has discussed in great detail the concepts of key and core competences at a business unit level. However, not all competences within an organization are at this level. The corporate centre may also lay claim to competences, and these may be vital in enabling the firm as a whole to achieve corporate advantage. A key corporate competence of the Hanson group, for example, is the ability to identify undervalued mature industry companies, buy them, and significantly improve their performance, without involving itself in any way in competitive strategy.

Chapter 3 of Part I describes, in its treatment of the producer matrix, how, in order to achieve competitive advantage, the SBU must so develop its core competences that they relate closely to the key competences required for the company to be able to deliver the required PUV at an acceptable price in its chosen markets.

How then do we identify corporate competences that will either help the SBU competences to become stronger, or that will deliver some value to the corporation overall, over and above the SBU competences? The corporate centre can provide value in its direct actions, over and above its primary tasks of selecting, resourcing, and controlling the SBUs. It can carry out activities relevant to the development of the corporation, but in *addition* to those concerned directly with competitive strategy, as illustrated in the triangle below (Figure 10.3).

183

Figure 10.3
The corporate functions triangle.

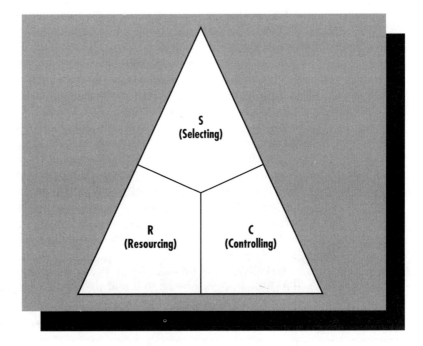

EXERCISING CORPORATE COMPETENCES

The corporate centre can add value in areas of corporate competence distinct from the individual competences found in the SBUs. The corporate centre can carry out two distinct functions:

1. It can identify and develop the core competences that bind the business units together.
2. It can directly exercise certain competences itself.

The nature of competences that bind SBUs together include the characteristics of an SBU that would be expected to be found in the corporation in question, *e.g.*, in a Hanson group SBU – tight cost control; in a 3M SBU – innovation, and in most Japanese multinationals – high quality standards. In a recent strategy workshop carried out by the authors, the SBUs were found individually and differentially to have competitive competences, such as R&D expertise, global distribution and good response times. When the participants considered competences at a corporate level, they identified the following company-wide competences:

- Problem-solving, rather than just selling product.
- Building long-term relationships.
- Sensitive global/local response to market demand.

Such competences are corporation-wide, in that SBUs in the corporation in question are expected to have them in large measure, and their absence in a particular SBU would raise distinct questions regarding the continued presence of that SBU in the group.

However, there are other competences that may be present and be value-enhancing in the corporate centre itself. The Hanson corporate centre has an exceptional ability to identify poorly managed mature industry companies that it can buy at low price:earnings ratios (P:Es), recoup much of the purchase price from asset sales, and then squeeze good profits from the remaining assets. This is a clearly visible corporate competence.

All corporations that are successful in the long term must, of course, have excellent core competences in the prime corporate areas of the selection of appropriate markets in which to operate, resource allocation, and financial and managerial control. As with competitive advantage, the key factors involved in the achievement and maintenance of corporate advantage lie principally in the difficulty other corporations would find in imitating the distinct corporate competences that are in high demand. Thus, a corporate competence that is able to lead to a high level of profit generation, such as Hanson's acquisition skills, and which other companies cannot easily replicate, imitate or appropriate, *e.g.*, by buying key people, or provide equally effective substitute skills for, leads to corporate advantage of a high order.

Ultimately, having a scarce competence that is in such demand that high profits flow from it and that is difficult to imitate, is the essence of the recipe for corporate strategic advantage, as it is with more market-based competences for competitive strategic advantage. Whereas competitive competences relate to the ability to provide high PUV at low cost, the value-adding corporate competences are likely to be more closely related to the corporate functions of perceptive selection of markets, well-judged resource allocation, and effective corporate coordination and control. If these fundamental corporate level tasks are performed well, corporate value will be achieved even in the absence of the more direct tasks of synergy generation and specialist service provision.

SUMMARY

There are three primary tasks that all corporations have, although they carry them out in different ways. These are summarized in the terms **selecting, resourcing** and **control.** The selecting function involves determining an overall purpose and scope for the company reflected in its corporate mission statement and selecting markets and businesses to operate in that represent the best fit between the corporation's core competences and the key competences required for success in these markets. The resourcing function involves ensuring that the corporation's SBUs have the necessary products, competences and resources to make them winners in their chosen markets. This may involve gaining access to such competences by merger, acquisition or alliance, and the leveraging of competences across SBUs. The control function involves managing the corporation so effectively and efficiently that internal inefficiencies are not allowed to develop, particularly in the relationship between the corporate centre and the SBUs.

The corporate centre may add value in ways other than in its primary functions of selecting, resourcing and control. It may carry out distinct corporate activities itself, like value enhancing relations with financial institutions and corporate image development.

185

chapter 11

Selecting:
The Business Portfolio

Which businesses to be in is a fundamental issue for the corporate board. Since the early 1970s the issue has been addressed most commonly by employing one or more of the strategic consultancy company portfolio matrices, the 'box' of the Boston Consulting Group, the Directional Policy Matrix of McKinsey, or the Life-cycle Matrix of Arthur D. Little. None of these matrices explicitly takes into account the resource-based theory of the firm, or makes a rigorous attempt to determine the firm's key or core competences in order to discover the area in which the company is most likely to succeed.

The three most common portfolio matrices are described below, and some of their respective limitations identified. We then develop a modified three-dimensional matrix that deals with some of these limitations by making market selection a critical function of relating the market's required key competences to the corporation's core competences, as well as of the inherent attractiveness of the market.

THE BOSTON BOX

The Boston Box was the earliest of the matrices to be developed, and being perhaps the easiest to understand, is probably still the most popular in the business world. As shown in Figure 11.1, it has four quadrants and two axes: market growth and relative market share.

It is suggested, somewhat simplistically, that the faster the market growth, the more attractive the market. Also, the higher the market share relative to that of the market leader, or the market share relative to the next largest competitor if one *is* the market leader, then the stronger the position of the SBU. This leads to the designation of business units which are market leaders in fast-growth markets as **stars**, market leaders in slow-growth markets as **cash cows**, non-market leaders in fast-growth markets as **question marks** or **problem children**, and non-market leaders in slow-growth markets as **dogs**.

The portfolio philosophy underlying the matrix is of a balanced cash portfolio. Cash cows generate the funds to enable investment to be carried out in the stars and the question marks, whilst not requiring much investment themselves. Question marks require attention in order to help them to gain relative market share and so turn them into stars, and dogs should be divested, though it is not obvious why they should not be developed into cash cows.

Figure 11.1
The Boston Box.

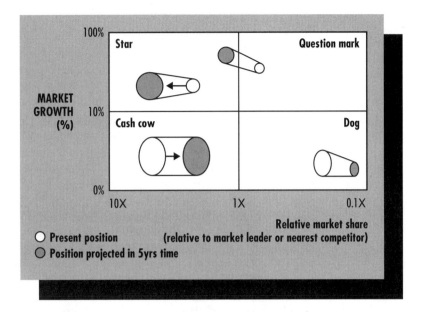

This neat view of the world includes a virtuous sequence, whereby a question mark is developed into a star and, ultimately, with a maturing market declines into a cash cow generating profits to fuel the next generation of stars. As a warning homily, the disastrous sequence is also depicted, in which the star loses market share to become a question mark, and then, with a maturing market, declines into the status of a dog, fit only for divestment.

The theory underlying the concept of the Box is that of the experience curve. This concept, supported empirically by research in a number of industries, holds that unit costs go down as aggregate volume increases. Thus, to gain the market leadership position is to gain a cost advantage over the competition, and hence a potential strategic advantage. PIMS research (Buzzell and Gale, 1987) supports this theory. Clearly then, the faster the market grows and the greater the level of market leadership, the higher the cumulative volume and the greater the reduction in unit cost of production. The horizontal axis measures relative, rather than absolute, market share, since a company with 20% of the market when no other competitor has more than 5% is in a far stronger position than one with 20% but facing three competitors, who each also have around 20%.

The Boston Box has the attraction of its simplicity, but it suffers from a number of weaknesses, and should be used with caution. The two axes attempt to relate the attractiveness of a market to the inherent strength of the business unit. However, market growth rate is only a very approximate surrogate for market attractiveness. Porter's five-forces model described in Chapter 5 illustrates the complexity of the market attractiveness concept, in which market growth has only one part to play in one of the identified key forces affecting market attractiveness. Whether growth is important depends also on whether the business unit concerned has strategic advantage in the key competences that enable the growth to lead to improved results for the company.

Relative market share is also an uncertain surrogate for company strength. Market share can be bought easily by pricing below cost, without the possession of any real internal strength. It also refers to the past, not the future, and could be said to be more the result than the cause of business unit strength. Economic research frequently correlates high market share with high profitability, hence strength, but correlations do not, of course, indicate the direction of causality. Does business strength lead to high market share, or high market share lead to high business strength?

The Boston Box does not allow for declining markets, applies mostly to fast-moving consumer goods companies, and certainly does not fit easily with industrial goods markets, since market shares are often very difficult to ascertain in such highly differentiated markets. It is also difficult to apply with confidence to fragmented industries or to industries in which the experience curve and scale economies give small unit cost advantages. It is also not evident why profitable companies in slow growth industries, who are not market leaders, should be divested. Many may still make good profits without requiring large investment funds. Indeed, in many industries it would not be difficult to find examples for the concept of the 'cash dog' as Hanson is well aware. Furthermore, even slow growth industries exhibit investment opportunities in particular segments or niches, and many well-focused companies in this box may well be acceptably profitable, *e.g.*, Imperial Tobacco. This company is not the market leader, and its industry is in decline; however, it has shown increasing profitability year on year since the Hanson take-over.

THE McKINSEY DIRECTIONAL POLICY MATRIX

The McKinsey matrix attempts to overcome some of the weaknesses of the Boston Box by selecting more realistic multi-dimensional axes to represent industry attractiveness and business strength (as shown in Figure 11.2).

McKinsey is careful not to be over-prescriptive regarding the dimensions of industry attractiveness or of internal business strength. Indeed, McKinsey emphasizes that the relevant factors will vary from industry to industry. However, if the matrix had been developed after the publication of Porter's *Competitive Strategy* and *Competitive Advantage* books it is probable that the five-forces industry attractiveness model would be recommended as a means of assessing the SBU's position on one axis, and the value chain for assessing position on the other axis.

This matrix has its axes in reverse to those of the Boston Box. They are however conceptually similar, in that the box where high industry attractiveness meets high business strength leads to a

Figure 11.2
The directional policy matrix.

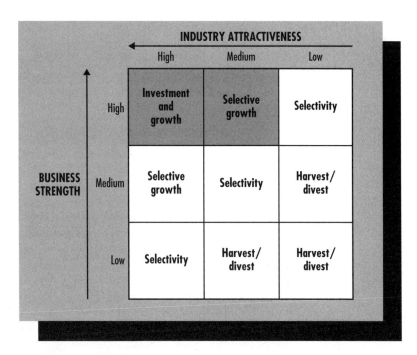

recommendation of investment with the objective of growth, similar to that of the star. Correspondingly, low attractiveness/low strength, as with Boston's dog, leads to the recommendation 'harvest/divest'. The other boxes follow similar logic. Although the McKinsey matrix purports to be an investment matrix in contrast to Boston's cash matrix, the distinction is more a formal difference than a real one, in that the box with the most attractive combination of market position and internal strength is identified as the most attractive one in both matrices. Similarly, the dog on the Boston Matrix lies also in the right-hand corner of the directional policy matrix.

The major weakness of the McKinsey matrix is that there is no easily applied means of establishing the appropriate weightings for the many dimensions of attractiveness and business strength and this enables practitioners or consultants to bias weightings to meet their already established ideas if they are so inclined.

Therefore, in the wrong hands, it can be more of a demonstration tool than an analytical model capable of giving surprising insights. This same criticism can, however, also be levelled against the Porter five-force model.

THE ARTHUR D. LITTLE LIFE-CYCLE MATRIX

A third variant of the portfolio matrix is the Arthur D. Little life-cycle matrix (ADL). Following the customary internal axis, it chooses competitive position as its measure of the firm's strength, not a far

Figure 11.3
The life-cycle portfolio matrix.

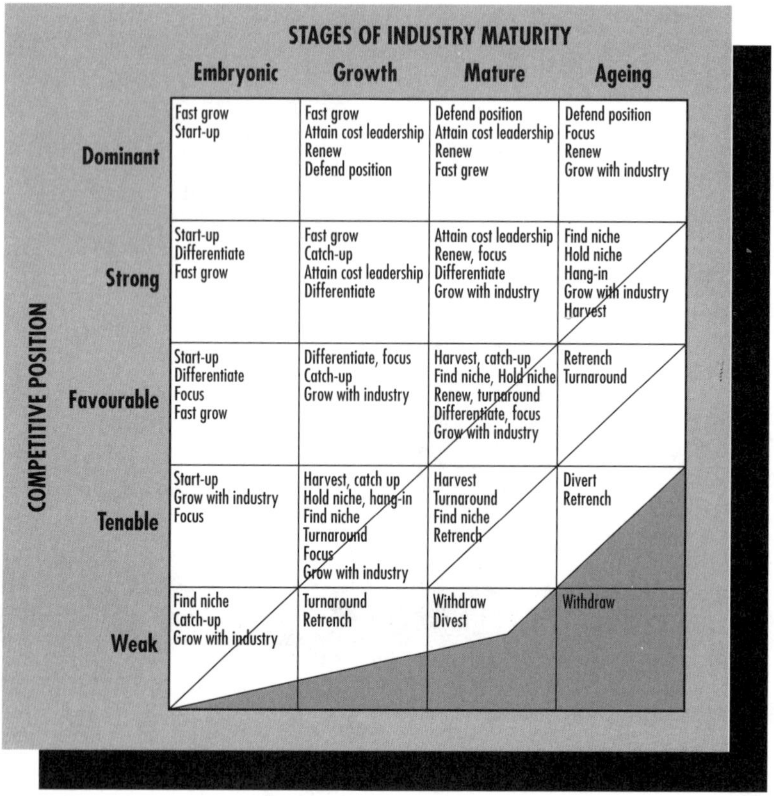

		STAGES OF INDUSTRY MATURITY			
		Embryonic	Growth	Mature	Ageing
COMPETITIVE POSITION	Dominant	Fast grow Start-up	Fast grow Attain cost leadership Renew Defend position	Defend position Attain cost leadership Renew Fast grew	Defend position Focus Renew Grow with industry
	Strong	Start-up Differentiate Fast grow	Fast grow Catch-up Attain cost leadership Differentiate	Attain cost leadership Renew, focus Differentiate Grow with industry	Find niche Hold niche Hang-in Grow with industry Harvest
	Favourable	Start-up Differentiate Focus Fast grow	Differentiate, focus Catch-up Grow with industry	Harvest, catch-up Find niche, Hold niche Renew, turnaround Differentiate, focus Grow with industry	Retrench Turnaround
	Tenable	Start-up Grow with industry Focus	Harvest, catch up Hold niche, hang-in Find niche Turnaround Focus Grow with industry	Harvest Turnaround Find niche Retrench	Divert Retrench
	Weak	Find niche Catch-up Grow with industry	Turnaround Retrench	Withdraw Divest	Withdraw

cry from McKinsey's business strength axis, although measured somewhat differently. Its other axis is quite different however; it selects market maturity as its external measure (see Figure 11.3).

This requires it to aver that there are appropriate strategies for any stage of maturity, and therefore that no particular maturity is good or bad. Indeed, diversified conglomerates seem to prefer that their acquisitions be in mature, rather than growth, markets, since this often means greater stability and lower demand for investment funds.

Very deterministic rules are applied to this matrix for the calculation of competitive position and market maturity, leading to a positioning on the matrix that in turn leads to the recommendation of a very limited range of natural strategic thrusts. A problem exists here, in that if every business unit in a particular matrix position adopts the same strategic thrust in a given market, it is difficult to see how competitive advantage will be gained. In business, as in life generally, the winner is often the competitor who does something unusual, rather than the one who applies rigorously a formula known and available to all.

Other problems attached to this matrix are as follows: it is possible through the use of the ADL methodology to determine the maturity of the market concerned, but it is not possible to determine how quickly the maturation process will take place or, indeed, whether it will take place at all. Some products/markets mature very quickly, *e.g.*, personal computers, but others do not seem to mature at all, *e.g.*, houses, staple foods, or non-fashion clothing. Others, due to fashion, technology breakthroughs or strong marketing activity reverse maturity, *e.g.*, watches or sports shoes. As a predictor of the ageing of markets, the matrix is of little use. Its value for strategy guidance must be similarly limited for the same reasons.

OTHER PROBLEMS

All three matrices have basic flaws, and they also have certain limitations that apply to them generally. All assume that each business unit has no synergistic relationship with any other. Indeed, if this were not the case it would not be possible to regard the positioning of an SBU on a matrix as implying any particular strategic implications without considering carefully any relationship one SBU might have with any other, be it supplier, distributor, joint economy of scope achiever, or whatever. Strictly speaking, therefore, the portfolio matrix approach to corporate resource allocation can be used effectively only where no synergies are sought between the units. Yet one of the major justifications for the existence of a corporation over and above that of separate business units is the belief that such synergies can be realized, and thereby give competitive advantage to the business units benefiting from them. Such matrices are also, by their nature, examples of comparative statics, and do not necessarily enable accurate insights to be gained into enduring future trends. But perhaps this is to expect too much.

191

However, a more fundamental criticism is that in purporting to provide an aid to the corporate chief executive in difficult resource allocation decisions – involving deciding which product/markets to concentrate on – they play little attention, if any, to the growth of risk with increasing unfamiliarity, and to the wisdom of becoming involved only in new businesses whose key factors for success relate closely to the corporation's already demonstrated competences. Indeed, all three matrices can be used to justify totally unrelated acquisitions despite the lack of clearly suitable competences within the corporation. As Collis and Montgomery (1995) point out:

> *The problem with the portfolio matrix was that it did not address how value was being created across the divisions.... The only relation between them was cash. As we have come to learn, the relatedness of businesses is at the heart of value creation in diversified companies.*

Other criticisms of the portfolio matrices are that they assume corporations have to be self-sufficient in capital and should find a use for all internally generated cash. They were silent on the question of the competitive advantage a business received from being owned by a corporation compared with the costs of owning it.

A NEW APPROACH TO RESOURCE ALLOCATION

Resource allocation cannot be carried out using just one tool, the portfolio matrix, even if the three most popular variants are all used as a check on each other. Not enough questions can be posed and answered to determine the most appropriate businesses to be in using this tool. The portfolio matrix does not help clarify the question of how the various SBUs in the corporate portfolio might be expected to help each other to create value.

To overcome some of these problems, a portfolio cube can be constructed that gives a unified picture of the attractiveness of the markets in which the corporation operates, and of the corporation's relative competitive strength in these markets (Figure 11.4). This matrix has an additional axis to the usual two axes which represent market attractiveness and business strength. The third axis illustrates the closeness of the corporation's core competences to each other, and thus suggests where value may be created in the corporation through the relatedness of the corporation's competences in one market to those in another. The matrix therefore answers the following questions:

- Which markets are we in, or should we be in?
- How attractive are they?
- How strong are we in the key competences required for success in these markets compared with our competitors?
- How close are these competences to the core competences of the corporation?

Figure 11.4
The portfolio cube.

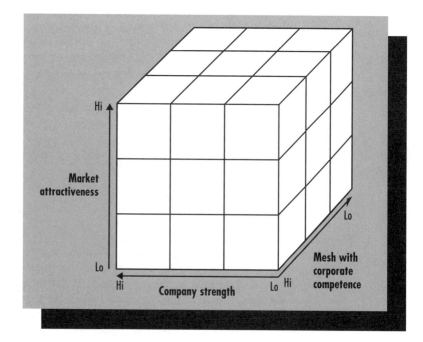

THE PORTFOLIO CUBE

The position of each SBU in the corporation can be assessed on the market attractiveness axis in the following way. First, the Porter five-forces analysis should be used to determine the level of competitive intensity in the market and the key structural forces. The future might then be considered by applying a PEST factor check list, and reviewing the five-forces analysis in the light of this. It is important to define the market appropriate to this analysis. In order to do this, the degree of substitutability of the products concerned with their nearest needs neighbours should be the guiding factor. Thus, a Volkswagen is substitutable for a Ferrari only in exceptional circumstances, and the two cars should therefore not be considered to be members of the same market for analytic purposes.

Two other key factors need to be considered when assessing the attractiveness of particular markets. First, the market size is important. A market may be structurally attractive, but very limited in its size, and therefore not attractive to a broadly-based corporation for that reason. Indeed, when investigating new markets, their potential size is often the first thing a businessman will consider, as only markets of a substantial size will justify investment of time and resources. The second factor is the price elasticity of demand for the product. Thus, if demand is price elastic, firms are limited to the role of price takers, and no differentiation of product is possible, thus eliminating the opportunity for establishing added value, and hence competitive advantage by branding or other similar differentiating methods. However, as the demand elasticity reduces, the opportunity for product differentiation increases, and to that extent the attractiveness of the market to firms with appropriate key competences also increases.

The second axis of the cube, as is consistently the case in portfolio matrices, is a measure of the strength of the firm in relation to its competitors. BCG attempt to evaluate this by measuring relative market share. McKinsey use a range of measures, many of which approximate to value chain analysis (Porter, 1985). ADL estimate the firm's competitive position by means of their own rubric, which includes market share and an evaluation of many internal factors. We believe the appropriate measure of a firm's competitive strength lies in the level of its possession of the key competences required for success in each particular market. Key competences, it will be remembered, are those capabilities in a firm that are measurable in terms of value-adding effectiveness and that are required to succeed in a particular market. They may be contrasted or related to a firm's core competences which are capabilities similarly measured, but are defined purely as the functions in which the firm is most proficient. Thus, for example, Burroughs might have had excellent core competences in mechanical engineering, which might also have been some of the key competences to succeed in the mechanical adding machine market. They ceased to be key competences, however, with

193

the onset of the electronic age. Core competences that were previously aligned closely with the required key competences suddenly ceased to be so, and the firm found itself needing to develop new and sometimes alien competences if it was to survive.

The position on the company strength axis of the cube can be determined by constructing a producer matrix as described in Chapter 3. This will position the firm in terms of its key competences relative to its competitors in each market in which it operates.

The third axis is necessary in order to develop a view on the degree to which the portfolio of SBUs in the corporation's ownership are able to add value to each other by the relatedness of their competences. We can thus estimate the degree to which they may justify their existence within the same corporation, according to the dictates of the resource-based view (RBV) of the firm. This view suggests that firms are unique bundles of physical and intangible assets, capabilities, and organizational cultures. The configuration of the factors determines how well a corporation performs its activities, and how well it is positioned to succeed where these internal factors are the most appropriate ones for particular markets. The RBV therefore combines both the external and the internal aspects of competitive strategy.

The RBV also suggests that investing in resources that are valuable because they are in high demand in particular markets, are scarce and are difficult to imitate, is a good route to corporate success. Some competences may be specific to markets, and hence to competitive strategy. Many of a corporation's competences are, however, likely to apply across the board and thus be linchpins of corporate strategy. Hence, Disney's brand name and its skills in characterization and in animation apply across more than one potential product/market SBU. The corporation's core competences therefore represent the basic high level capabilities that should guide the corporation in determining what businesses it is most likely to succeed in. Some core competences are wide in their application, *e.g.*, Honda's expertise in four-stroke engines, but others are much narrower, *e.g.*, when Xerox tried to use its strong brand name to diversify into a whole range of 'office of the future' products, it discovered that the market saw it principally as a photocopier company. By building outwards from limited core competences, the corporation can, however, deliberately extend its range of capabilities in an incremental fashion. It is this aspect of the portfolio matrix that the third axis aims to capture.

There is an important additional point that cannot be captured even on the three-dimensional portfolio matrix described above, and this involves the existence of key corporate competences. So far, we have advocated a portfolio in which the core competences of the SBUs are sufficiently closely related for value to be created. Thus, the sum of the value of the total portfolio is greater than the sum of its parts. However, in many corporations there exist corporate competences that cannot be shown on the portfolio matrix, but nonetheless are a key value-creating part of the corporation.

In the Tompkins Group, the corporate centre knows how to identify mature companies with well-known brand names that have the potential, with tighter financial control, for being very profitable. It also knows how to negotiate their purchase at a good price, and how to find buyers for those parts of the new purchase that are deemed to be non-core, and hence ripe for divestment. Finally, it knows how to apply financial controls to the acquisition in such a way as to both motivate its managers and squeeze good profits from it. These competences do not show up in the portfolio cube, but they are as important to the success of Tompkins as are the competitive strategies of the SBUs. Where much of the Group's success depends upon corporate strategies of this nature, the need for synergistic core competences in the SBUs is, of course, less strong. It is not true, however, that nothing of this corporate competence gets passed down to the SBUs. What is passed down and pervades the whole Group is the corporate culture of financial stringency, personal incentives, and the drive for profits, even if they are short-term.

Xerox Group

The Xerox Group portfolio (as at 1982) provides a good example of how the portfolio cube works. During the period prior to that date, Xerox had been conscious that its pre-eminence in the plain-paper photocopier market was coming to an end. Its patents were running out and the Japanese, with Canon in the lead, were eating away at its market share. In order to combat this assault, Xerox decided to diversify its product range and attempt to become the leading office-automation company. As the 'office of the future' took longer to become translated from concepts into actual sales volume, Xerox decided that they were credible as a major diversified corporation, with a wide and varied industry portfolio, and bought into the financial services industry through the acquisition of Crum and Forster, the insurance company. Later in the 1980s, having discovered that such diversification did not lead to high corporate performance, Xerox divested themselves of most of their acquisitions unrelated to xerography, and concentrated on fighting the competition in the area of their competitive strength, *i.e.*, reprographics. In this they were successful, but only after billions of dollars of shareholders' funds had been lost on unrelated diversification.

In a three-dimensional form, the Xerox portfolio resembled a construction similar to that which is shown in Figure 11.5.

Xerox's core competences lay in the skills associated with designing, manufacturing, selling and servicing photocopiers. In more detail, they could be said to have understanding of and be operating with, electrostatic processes, particularly the process of xerography. They provided all the necessary services in relation to photocopiers, from design, through manufacture, to after-sales support services, in research and development skills (concentrating in this and related areas), and the marketing and distribution of photocopiers and related paper and chemicals. More general competences were to be found in the financial strength of the company and its strong brand name, although this latter factor

Figure 11.5
Xerox's portfolio.

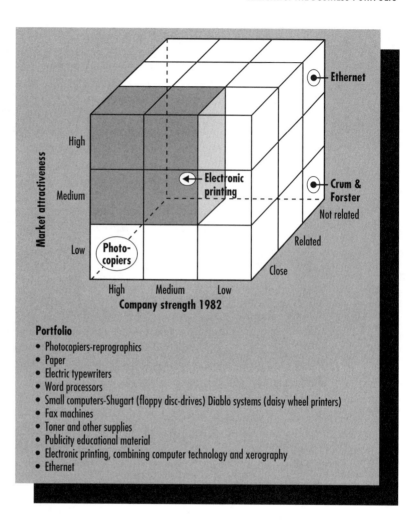

Portfolio
- Photocopiers-reprographics
- Paper
- Electric typewriters
- Word processors
- Small computers-Shugart (floppy disc-drives) Diablo systems (daisy wheel printers)
- Fax machines
- Toner and other supplies
- Publicity educational material
- Electronic printing, combining computer technology and xerography
- Ethernet

proved problematic, since the company believed the name to be instantly transferable to other products, whereas the market identified it only with photocopiers.

The portfolio cube attempts to measure on the vertical axis the attractiveness of the market for each of Xerox's products. Along the horizontal axis it measures company strength, as in the producer matrix, by measuring each SBU's competitive strength in the key competences required for success in each segment, and adds to this its market share in order to determine the degree to which the SBU's competences have been successfully translated into success in the market place. The third axis assesses the mesh between an individual SBU's core competences and the core competences of the corporation, in this case the competences associated with the xerography business. Using the resource-based view of an appropriate portfolio for a corporation, the shaded area of the cube represents the area within which it would be recommended that the majority of the portfolio should fall. It can be seen from the figure that only electronic printers which use electrostatic technology join the core reprographics business within that sub-cube. Ethernet, whilst in an

Figure 11.6
Xerox's portfolio (three
planes).

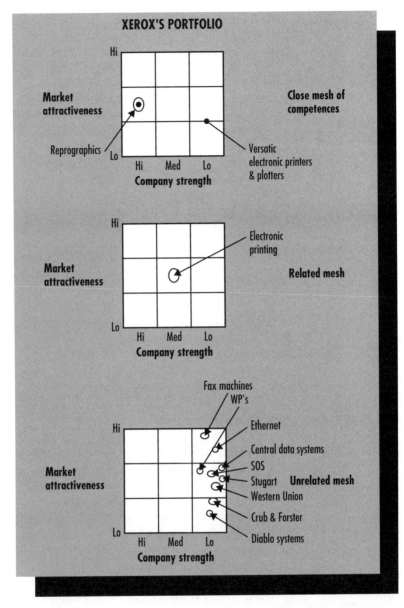

XEROX'S PORTFOLIO

attractive market, is not closely related to reprographic technologies, and Xerox are not strong in this field. While Crum & Forster are not in an attractive market, nor are they particularly strong, they are quite unrelated to Xerox's known competences. It is therefore not surprising, perhaps, that the stock market marked Xerox shares down drastically when news of the intended purchase reached it. In order to carry out this analysis, some agreement is necessary within the company as to what constitutes the core of the business, the corporate heartland as it were. In Xerox's case, this was clearly apparent, but in many cases, *e.g.*, Tompkins or Pearson, the ident-ification of such a core might generate fierce debate.

Figure 11.6 breaks the cube out into its three planes in order to see the individual SBUs of the portfolio more clearly. It can be seen that only the Versatic product range of electrostatic printers and plotters are closely meshed to Xerox technology, and the company is not strong in this market; nor is it a particularly attractive one.

Electronic printing comes within the related mesh plane, but the vast majority of the acquisitions and developments fall within the unrelated plane and suggest, therefore, on the basis of the RBV, a poorly constructed portfolio, with few synergies between the SBUs and an excess of products in areas in which Xerox cannot demonstrate high degrees of core competence.

Despite the disapproval of Wall Street of its acquisition of the insurance company Crum & Forster against all RBV logic, Xerox went on to acquire Furman Selz, an investment bank, and Van Kampen Merritt, a mutual fund business. The remainder of the 1980s saw Xerox working hard to improve the performance of its traditional core business with some success, and devoting an increasing level of resources to its new love, financial services. Indeed, by 1991, financial services operations contributed one third of Xerox revenues, but only 3% of its profits.

In 1991 under a new chairman, Xerox decided to divest itself entirely of its financial services arm. Xerox shareholders have thus had to pay a heavy price for Xerox directors' decision to develop a corporate portfolio without reference to the corporation's core competences.

DIVERSIFICATION AND STRATEGIC-RISK OPTIONS

198

The selection task of the corporation does not stop at the SBU level. It is also of importance when the corporation is deciding whether to go into a new product/market or to develop new competences. This section addresses the problems encountered when a firm assesses that it cannot necessarily expect to achieve its financial and other objectives operating with its current products in its current markets. It must venture beyond known product/market boundaries and possibly develop or acquire new competences. This involves increasing risk.

We set out a model for assessing the varying levels of risk involved in different diversification moves. Whilst it is not suggested that use of the model necessarily describes accurately the relative levels of risk of particular situations, it is claimed that the model can generate useful insights in this regard and lead to the posing of questions that will reveal when the exception that proves the rule has been encountered. Thus there may be situations where an alliance involves more risk than an acquisition, and where internal development is higher risk than a joint venture, but in most cases this will not be the case.

THE RISK CUBE

A firm may not be able to achieve competitive advantage in its current product/market segment, in which case it will need to consider other options, *e.g.*, marketing the same product to a different market. Once product/market options have been listed and researched in relation to the size of the opportunities, the strength of the competition, and the necessary key competences to succeed, each needs to be assessed for relative risk.

Strategic risk of this nature comes in two major types:

1. The risk of losing one's investment or being significantly damaged as a result of the alliance, *i.e.*, vulnerability. This we call **type 1 risk**.
2. The risk of not achieving the objectives set out for the alliance, which is **type 2 risk**.

The option cube only addresses type 1 risk. The aim of the analysis is to identify the option that will achieve acceptable objectives, *i.e.*, low type 2 risk, with the lowest level of type 1 risk.

The risk cube in Figure 11.7 illustrates the options open to the strategist, with the ascending arrow going into the back of the cube representing increasing type 1 risk. Hence, the activity with the lowest type 1 risk option is to continue to operate in the familiar product/market segment using the firm's existing demonstrated competences, and to attempt to grow by internal development.

However, a strategy to continue operating in the existing product/market segment with the existing competences may not get acceptable results, *i.e.*, type 1 risk may be low, but type 2 risk is high. The product/market may be saturated and/or the competences obsolescent, or at least in decline. In this event, the next options to be considered, in ascending type 1 risk terms, are to use new competences, *e.g.*, new technologies, in the present product/market, or to use the existing competences in a new product/market. Only in exceptional circumstances should the excessively high risk option of marketing an unfamiliar competence application in an unfamiliar product/market be considered.

The type 1 risk element of these moves is increased if the firm attempts to make any of the above moves by methods other than by internal development. Joint development involves operating with a partner with whom one is unfamiliar, and over whom one has very limited control. This increases the level of uncertainty, and hence of risk. Development by acquisition increases type 1 risk even further, since it involves purchasing an unfamiliar company which is likely to have been marketed in such a way as to maximize the price the seller is able to achieve. On conclusion of the acquisition, therefore, the purchaser will not only need time to establish the real value of the assets purchased, but may be in control of a top

Figure 11.7
The partners' risk profiles are important in determining strategic choice.

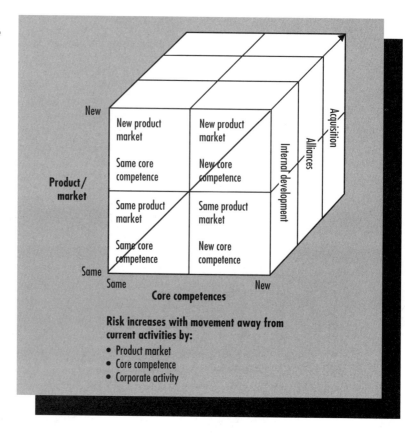

Risk increases with movement away from current activities by:
- Product market
- Core competence
- Corporate activity

management team substantially demotivated or depleted as a result of the ownership transfer. This option is likely to be the highest type 1 risk option, as well as the most expensive one. If the acquired company operates with unfamiliar competences in product/markets unfamiliar to the acquirer, the highest risk option of all has been taken.

Options can be analysed in terms of direction and of method. Both factors involve risk. Thus, under the heading of **direction** we will consider which product/markets to operate in, noting that risk increases the further away the markets, products and competences get from those in which the company is currently active. Under the heading of **method** we will encompass internal development, joint development or alliance, and acquisition: categories, once again, in generally ascending levels of risk. Clearly, it is not rational to adopt a greater level of risk to achieve a desired objective, if that same objective is attainable taking less risk.

The risk cube shown in Figure 11.7 illustrates the options open to the strategist.

So, in general, the lowest type 1 risk option is to continue to operate in the familiar product/market segment using the firm's existing demonstrated competences, and to attempt to grow by internal development. It should be noted that it is not helpful to think of a product as distinct from a market. A product/market combination represents the suggested solution to a particular consumer need. Once a product is targeted at a different market it becomes a different product in the sense that the consumer will analyse it by means of different dimensions of perceived use value (PUV). Thus, a family car targeted at the sports car market may be found defective, since it will be measured by PUV dimensions such as performance, styling and acceleration. Yet, in the family car market, it will be measured by such dimensions as fuel economy, comfort and luggage space, and may well score highly. A product, in empirical terms, is how it is described, a bundle of attributes attempting to meet a need. In the example therefore, description of the product cannot be separated from description of the market it is attempting to serve. In different markets it will also meet different competitors, against which its relative strength will vary. The analysis is therefore most usefully carried out using product/market segments as unique entities for analysis, rather than thinking of products as distinct from markets.

The various moves can be considered first on the face of the cube which resembles an inverted and adapted Ansoff matrix (1965).

SAME PRODUCT/MARKET, SAME COMPETENCES

Within the base quadrant (same product/market and same competences) the possible strategic actions can be classified thus:

- Continue with strategy unchanged.
- Withdraw from product/market.
- Consolidate in core business.
- Penetrate existing product/market further.

All fall within the same box, *i.e.*, the bottom left-hand front box. They are each analysable using the existing perceived use value, competitor positioning, price and competences data as the basis for considering alternative strategic moves.

Continue with Strategy Unchanged

Continuing with strategy unchanged as a strategic option can be an appropriate strategy in some circumstances. In circumstances where an acceptable level of profit is being achieved, where the firm's market share is good, where the firm has a clear competitive advantage sustainable in the medium term, where its product range is still in the growth phase of the product life-cycle and where no imminent turbulence in the market can be discerned, then the continuance of the existing strategy is clearly correct. However, this should not lead to complacency, and a failure to scan the market closely for possible change and to invest in the development of new products could lead to future problems.

Withdraw from Existing Product/Market

Withdrawal from the existing product/market as a strategy is appropriate in a number of circumstances. In a declining product/market when a firm's market share is poor, and shows little possibility of substantial improvement, a timely withdrawal may minimize future losses. Where the firm has no competitive advantage and cannot foresee attaining one, it is better to withdraw early than to incur heavy losses and to be forced out later. Other circumstances in which withdrawal is an appropriate strategy are where the resources can be deployed more profitably elsewhere, but only where exit costs are acceptably low. Where they are high, this must be taken into consideration before adopting a withdrawal strategy.

A further set of circumstances are those where the industry is strongly cyclical, and withdrawal in order to re-enter later at a better point in the cycle shows good judgement. Thus, an astute housing company will build its land bank when prices are at the bottom of the cycle, and sell it off when a boom develops, only to repurchase during the next down swing. Such strategies apply also to foreign exchange, metals, commodities and other speculative industries.

Consolidate in Current Product/Market

A product/market strategy of consolidation involves the reduction of a firm's activities to its profitable core. During the upswing of a business cycle, a firm is likely to consider expanding into new areas of activity, accepting that they will not necessarily be instantly profitable, but given good judgement and investment should become so in the future. Correspondingly, with the onset of recession, it is appropriate for a firm to consolidate its position in the areas where it has its greatest strength, normally its profitable core business. This involves concentrating its investment in the core areas, and withdrawing from low profit or unprofitable activities.

Other activities associated with a consolidation strategy are likely to be severe cost cutting and downsizing, particularly of central overheads, and, for the market leader, acquisition at low prices of smaller competitors in order to push market share from strong to dominant. High capacity utilization is valued in consolidation mode far more than a varied high turnover over a wide range of activities.

Penetrate Existing Product/Market Further

Market penetration of the existing product/market as a strategy is particularly necessary when market growth is slowing, or markets are actually declining. In the event that growth of a given market is strong, competitors can achieve fast growth without increasing their market share. However, when the market matures and growth slows, only a strategy of market penetration can enable a firm to increase its sales. Market penetration can be achieved by any combination of perceived price reduction and increased perceived use value. Thus, the buyer will purchase the firm's product rather than a competitor's, because it is believed to offer better value for money.

SAME COMPETENCES, NEW PRODUCT/MARKET

A new product/market development strategy using the same core competences is the next lowest risk option. This involves conducting a new PUV analysis for the new application for the upper left-hand quadrant on the face of the risk cube, coupled with a new competitor analysis. It may also be necessary to determine whether the firm's core competences are those required in this segment, and whether the firm's relative competitive position with regard to its competences, and those of competitors operating in this segment, are different to those in the base core segment.

A strategy of this kind can be carried out in a variety of ways and particularly by extending market segments. If, for example, Mercedes is primarily targeted at the over 45s, the easiest and lowest risk strategy extension is to develop small variants targeted at the 35-year-old. A second possibility is to extend the marketing to new geographical areas. A product sold purely nationally can be extended to other markets after a little market research to determine acceptable price levels and possible taste differences. A third variant is to discover new uses for existing products, *e.g.*, the extension of the home games computer to the word processing personal computer.

203

NEW COMPETENCES, SAME PRODUCT/MARKET

The strategy of competence development is higher risk than any of the other strategies discussed so far. Whilst overtly only concerned with unfamiliarity in the product area, it is also inevitably operating in a new market area, *i.e.*, one for the new competence application.

The strategy can be carried out in a number of ways with varying risk.
- By competence extension.
- By licensing or franchising a new technology.
- By developing a new competence through R&D.

Competence range extension is the lowest risk of the three strategy variants. The only risk attached to this strategy is of the cannibalization of revenue from the existing competence applications range. This is, of course, possible, and the risk attached to it increases the further the range is extended. It is, however, the natural first resort for a firm wishing to increase its sales without changing a winning formula by more than a marginal amount, and hence with a relatively low risk profile.

The licensing of a new competence, perhaps through technology transfer, has the advantage that the licensed technology has by definition been successful in the product/market of its origin. The risk attached to this strategy is that demand in the prospective licensee's market is different from that in the technology's market of origin, and the possibility that the new competence will not succeed outside its original home country. The benefit to the licensee is that the technology has already been tested and proved successful from an effectiveness viewpoint, and that no expenditure is needed on R&D. The licenser may even be persuaded to support the application with some marketing expenditure to spread the brand name. Many international product recipes including specific competences from Coca-Cola to McDonalds and Body Shop have been licensed or franchised successfully to the benefit of both licenser and licensee.

The riskiest competence development strategy variant is that based on the firm's own R&D. It is reputed that no more than one in a hundred of R&D-developed competences is actually successful in a major way when an attempt is made to convert them into product/market applications. Only companies with a strong financial position, very strong competence in research and particularly development, and a very effective marketing department should risk embarking on totally new competences or technologies. In general, such a strategy is expensive, very risky and potentially unprofitable. The first follower strategy is often the one to pursue here, although it should be noted that there are strong advocates of the 'first in the market' school, as this may be the way to establish a large installed base and thus ensure repeat sales and prescription by purveyors of linked products, *e.g.*, Microsoft in computer software.

NEW COMPETENCES, NEW PRODUCT/MARKET

To embark upon the development of new competences and their application to new product/markets is tantamount to setting up a new company – always a very risky business, especially in unfamiliar territory. Thus, if a traditional watchmaker, seeing the market for coiled spring watches decline, were to launch into microchip technology but, having done so, immediately attempted to establish himself in the fashion Swatch watch segment, he would be taking very grave risks with his business. Not only would his new developing competence in the microchip technology be based on fragile foundations, and hence at increased risk, but his very slight knowledge of the fashion watch market area would compound this risk. New competence, new product/market moves should be made only if there are judged to be no lower risk moves available that will provide acceptable returns.

The risk cube enables strategists to assess the comparative risk of different options involved in selecting a specific product/market competence strategy as a means of pursuing a strategic direction. In general, the risk is higher the greater the unfamiliarity of the firm with the challenges facing it. Strategy options should be considered initially from the viewpoint of risk. The further they require the company to stray from the business area in which it has competence and confidence, the greater the risk in most cases. A riskier strategy should not be adopted if a less risky one would achieve the chosen objectives equally well.

It must be stressed that the model should not be used without careful reflection. There may be situations, for example, where it is much higher risk to remain in the same competence, same product/market quadrant than to move. This will certainly be the case if the existing product/market is in decline (the old buggy whip example) and/or the competence becomes obsolete, *e.g.*, valve radios. The model does no more than pose risk questions that require careful analysis. It does not mechanistically answer them.

A company's initial concern must be to achieve a position that is as strong as possible using its existing, proven competences in existing product/market situations. If this gives inadequate results in terms of company objectives, the firm will need to consider the higher risk options of moving to different product/markets, and/or possibly developing different competences. These moves involve higher risk, since they mean moving into unfamiliar territory.

DEVELOPMENT METHOD

The questions of whether to make the moves by internal development, by alliance or by acquisition also need to be considered, since all but internal development also involve the unfamiliar, and thus involve a raising of the company's risk profile. When the identified options have been analysed and compared, the choice of the preferred option can be made by rating each option against the criteria of suitability, feasibility and acceptability (Johnson and Scholes, 1993). The preferred option needs to rate acceptably high when measured against all three criteria.

The firm needs to decide at this stage how to put together the necessary resources and competences to have a chance of achieving competitive advantage in its selected product/markets. There are only three possible answers to the question 'How?':
1. By internal development.
2. By joint development.
3. By acquisition.
Clearly, internal development generally involves the lowest type 1 risk, as it has the greatest level of control and of familiarity with the firm's existing competences. However, if this option is not possible, perhaps for reasons of resource deficiency or the need for speed in getting a new product/market launched to meet an opportunity without having appropriate internal competences to do this, the riskier options of alliance or acquisition must be considered.

Some form of alliance with a partner overcomes many of the problems of lack of resources and competences. New products from one company can be married to sales forces with spare capacity from another, and the time from product to market can be dramatically shortened. Companies strong on technology can collaborate with partners strong on marketing, to their mutual benefit. The wide variety of joint development forms provides a varied menu of possibilities for partners to select from, to optimize their development possibilities. Joint development is appropriate where sustainable competitive advantage can be achieved together, but not separately. A weak competence can be transformed through an alliance by the addition of the partner's core competences. The ground rules which can be said to obtain in alliances are described in Chapter 14 and those in acquisitions in Chapter 13.

SUMMARY

The strategic risk cube is a device that enables a firm bent upon development by diversification to assess the varying strategic risks involved in different possible moves. Strategic risk includes both type 1 risk, which is the possibility of losing one's investment, and type 2 risk, which is the risk of failing to achieve one's objectives. The cube assesses the level of type 1 risk for a given level of type 2 risk. On the front face of the cube, the firm may assess how it can use its competences, which are directed towards providing the needs of one particular product/market segment, to develop its position without overstretching itself by attempting to cope at the same time with the development of new competences and their direction into unfamiliar product/market segments.

On the side faces of the cube, the question of how the chosen product/market/competence strategy mix is to be achieved is posed in type 1 risk terms. Should the firm grow incrementally relying on its own resources, or should it form alliances or acquire? Both alliances and acquisition strategies are generally pursued by companies in order to strengthen their chances of achieving sustainable competitive advantage, by providing them with stronger competences or access to new product/market segments. The methods are not necessarily mutually exclusive, and in fact the lowest risk approach may well be to form an alliance in order to get to know a partner better, possibly before acquiring it. An alliance for its own sake, and not followed by acquisition is also, however, an appropriate competitive strategy if it strengthens the firm's overall value chain, and thus its overall competitive position in its chosen product/market segments.

Selecting: The Scope of the Corporation

The selection task is also of concern to the corporation at the level of activities. Such questions as 'Should we do our own production, or focus solely on being a marketing company?' are central to the selection task of the corporation, and not only of interest to the SBU. At a simple level of description, economic activity takes place in companies or in markets, or through voluntary cooperative behaviour. Markets operate through the price mechanism, and come about because different economic agents value items or activities differently. If I buy a car for a given price, it is because I value the car more than the money I have to pay for it, and the seller values the money more than the car.

Companies, on the other hand, operate by means of an instruction-giving hierarchy. I carry out a given task because my boss requires me to do so, and this is a condition for receiving my wages. The instruction needs to be very unreasonable before I would consider refusing to obey it. My career progress and even my job depends upon recognizing the power of the hierarchy, and behaving accordingly.

Cooperative behaviour takes place because partners recognize that by working together they can realize valued objectives more readily than they can by working independently. This form of activity involves identifying overlapping agendas, and developing consensus to pursue a jointly determined course of action.

These three fundamental modes of carrying out transactions are rarely totally distinct in economic activity. Markets take place between companies as well as between individuals, and are to be found inside companies where they operate alongside hierarchically-organized activities. Cooperative activities takes place between companies, and within them. Even in cooperative alliances some activities are market based.

The questions critical to an understanding of the boundaries of organizations include the following.

■ When is it most appropriate to organize economic transactions in companies by markets or cooperatively?
■ Within an overall value chain, which activities should a particular company do itself, buy in or do with partners?
■ What determines the optimal size of a company, in terms of its vertical and horizontal scope?

The major concerns of corporate strategy are to add value to the direction of the corporation by selecting the right markets to be in, resourcing them appropriately, and controlling the resources efficiently. The question of which activities the corporation should carry out itself, which ones it should buy in and which it should carry out with partners, addresses the fundamental corporate task in a central way. It is not until we have decided which activities we should buy in, carry out directly or do with partners, that we can address the basic questions of resourcing, and control of those resources. For example, a corporation may be ill-advised to manufacture a piece of undifferentiated hardware from raw materials, when it can buy in a similar quality product at lower costs and with considerably less effort.

TRANSACTION COST ANALYSIS

A body of theory originating with Coase (1920) and revived and developed particularly by Williamson (1975, 1985) suggests that the market or the hierarchy and, therefore, by implication, cooperative hybrids of these two basic forms, will be chosen for particular economic activities according to the respective levels of transaction costs associated with each form. Thus, it is held that stock exchange activity is best carried out through a market, as the price mechanism operates effectively since there are large numbers of buyers, large numbers of sellers, and an abundance of information available on which to base judgements.

On the other hand, the manufacture of some electronic products may be best carried out in a hierarchically controlled organizational form, because in many of the intermediate product areas the price mechanism would not operate easily, due to the presence of only a small number of buyers and sellers. There are also substantial economies of scale, since the technologies allow low unit costs only at high-volume levels, and the process of manufacture is most efficiently coordinated by individuals, who understand the necessary activities, and are trained to issue congruent sets of instructions.

Similarly, firms do well to engage in cooperative activity, if they perceive that due to the complementarity of their assets and cultures, their joint value chains have a better chance of achieving competitive advantage than either value chain separately. Figure 12.1 illustrates a transaction costs schema, setting out some of the major characteristics of situations that make them most appropriately handled by markets, in hierarchies or through alliances.

The transaction cost theorists therefore take a deterministic and an evolutionary approach to answering the question 'How should a particular set of economic activities be organized?'. Their answer is: in the form that minimizes the sum of transaction and production costs. However, certain types of transaction cost are quite impossible to quantify, *e.g.*, no one can put a figure on the costs involved of operating with colleagues who are opportunistic, as it is suggested people are when they have market relationships with each other. Transaction costs theorists would answer this by stating that such costs nonetheless exist, and thus only firms with the most appropriate

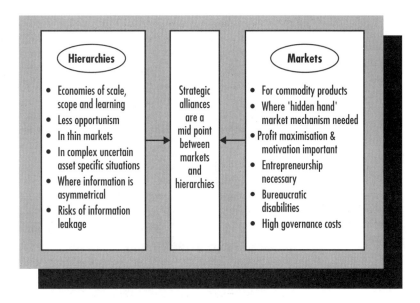

Figure 12.1
Alliances and hybrids
between markets and
hierarchies.

Hierarchies

- Economies of scale, scope and learning
- Less opportunism
- In thin markets
- In complex uncertain asset specific situations
- Where information is asymmetrical
- Risks of information leakage

Strategic alliances are a mid point between markets and hierarchies

Markets

- For commodity products
- Where 'hidden hand' market mechanism needed
- Profit maximisation & motivation important
- Entrepreneurship necessary
- Bureaucratic disabilities
- High governance costs

form for a given set of circumstances will succeed competitively, so natural selection will weed out the inappropriately organized. The arguments that corporate leaders have considerable discretion in the way in which they organize their activities, and that many varied forms may coexist at least in the medium term in the same product/market situation (Child, 1972), sit uneasily with transaction cost analysis, but are more comfortably held by management theorists than by organizational economists.

Transaction cost analysis represents an attempt by organizational economists to bring their discipline closer to the reality of organizations, as found in the world of sizeable companies with brand names and unique cultural characteristics. These qualities are not found in the stylized world of producers with identical production functions, perfect information, infinitely rational decision makers, and no transaction costs.

The transaction cost model assumes that people are 'boundedly rational' and that they frequently display opportunistic behaviour. They operate in an environment that is often uncertain and complex. Also, in many sets of circumstances, there are insufficient transactions of a particular type to enable the price mechanism to work efficiently, *i.e.*, the markets are thin. To illustrate such a situation, consider a boundedly rational chief executive wishing to buy a new piece of technology which, he is informed, will improve his competitive position. He must assume that the sellers of the technology may be opportunistic in presenting a case for the technology slanted more to make the sale rather than to rigorous truthfulness. The technology market is complex, and he is not confident in his ability to distinguish between the merits of alternative technological solutions to his problems. He is also uncertain what the future will bring in terms of demand and prices for his products. The technology application is specially designed for his particular product application, and therefore high in asset specificity. In such circumstances, the chief executive cannot be expected to make a simple market purchase. He will need a contract. He will need to check out the reputation of the technology firm, and to carry out market research to establish the intensity of use he is likely to have for the technology. All these actions represent transaction costs, and have to be taken into account when he attempts to determine whether or not he will be acting sensibly to acquire the technology, over and above validating the production cost benefits it is claimed that the new technology will bring.

If we apply these complicating factors of the real world to the issue of what form a particular set of economic activities should most appropriately have, it can be seen that the following general guidelines may apply. Activities are best carried out in markets when products are relatively homogeneous and are frequently traded by large numbers of buyers and sellers – thus ensuring that the price mechanism operates effectively; when cost reducing economies of scale and scope are largely absent; and when the transactions are neither complex nor uncertain in nature.

Companies are best set up to carry out economic activity in correspondingly complex uncertain situations, where there are significant economies of scale and/or scope, where markets are thin and assets are specific. Cooperative activity may be most appropriate where some of the characteristics appropriate to markets and some to hierarchies apply in particular circumstances, and when operators find difficulty in putting together the necessary resources and competences through the market or internally.

Of course, sets of circumstances tend to be unique in nature, and the difficulty in quantifying many transaction costs makes the theory extremely difficult to apply in a rigorous fashion. How, for example, in attempting to determine the level of transaction costs for a given situation, do you add the cost of the risk of opportunism to the cost of operating in a thin market with high asset specificity? Nonetheless, the principles are valuable when addressing the question of whether or not to carry out particular actions through the market route or in a company, even if precise quantification is impossible.

Transaction cost analysis can therefore provide some general guidelines regarding why it may be appropriate to carry out certain activities by setting up a company rather than bringing about an outcome in a more atomistic market way, *i.e.,* rather than by using the products of self-employed individuals carrying out specific activities and selling their products or services. The answer may be market failure due to thin markets, asset specificity, scale and/or scope economies, or other reasons. Transaction cost analysis at least gives us a language of analysis to evaluate such matters. And it is critically important for a corporation to be able to decide which activities it should develop competences to perform and which it can safely leave to others, whilst it concentrates on the areas in which it believes itself to have superior and differentiated abilities.

THE MAKE–BUY–ALLY MATRIX

Transaction cost analysis provides a useful check-list of factors to consider when deciding whether a product should be organized through the market mechanism, through a corporate hierarchy, or through some form of inter-company collaboration between the two basic forms. In the economist's marginalist language, the boundary of the firm should be determined at the point where the transaction cost of carrying out an extra transaction internally is equal to that of carrying it out in the market.

In reality, however, this point would be very difficult to determine, and it fails to take note of the synergies that may arise from the joint exercise of competences in a firm, which might make it more worthwhile to continue to operate in a firm for a particular activity than to buy it in from a subcontractor.

The attitudes of different managements to risk may also influence where they decide to draw the boundaries of the firm. For example, Tonka Toys is a toy company that subcontracts as many activities as possible outside the marketing function. Its key operating competences are therefore toy selection, buying, negotiation in the Far East, and brand marketing. Mattell is another toy company, but it operates in an integrated manufacturing fashion from primary metal forming through to sales. The two companies' value chains will therefore look radically different – largely for policy reasons – but this will not be evident to the consumer who buys a toy branded Tonka or one branded Mattell. And whilst both make good profits that satisfy shareholders, there is no great pressure to change the method of operation of either company.

The competence of the company in particular activities is therefore a further influence in determining the boundary of a particular company. The make–buy–ally matrix illustrated in Figure 12.2 below

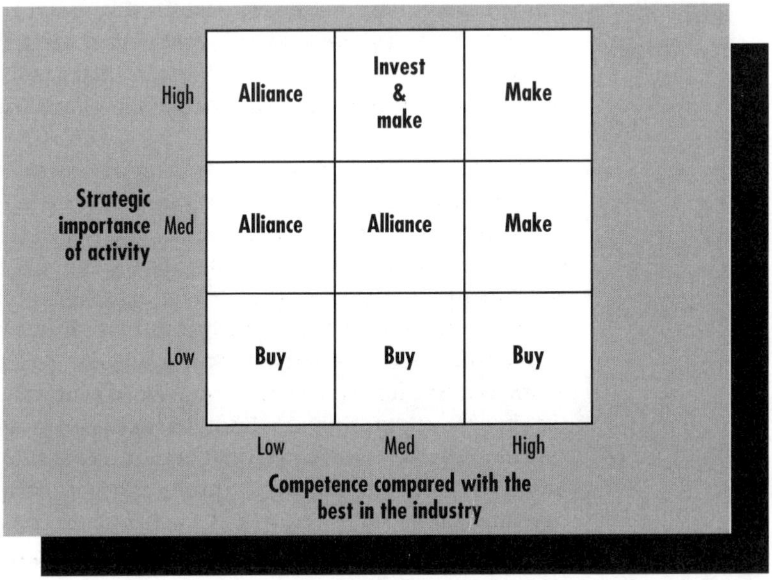

211

Figure 12.2
Make–buy–alliance matrix.

Strategic importance of activity		Low	Med	High
	High	Alliance	Invest & make	Make
	Med	Alliance	Alliance	Make
	Low	Buy	Buy	Buy

Competence compared with the best in the industry

helps a company's management to determine how best it should carry out particular activities. The two axes measure dimensions of the relative competences of firms needing to carry out specific activities, and the strategic importance of particular activities to the competitive success of those firms.

The thinking behind the matrix is as follows. All companies, even the largest, have scarce resources, so it is not the best use of those resources to use them on activities which are not strategically significant. Very few companies make their own travel arrangements for example. They subcontract them to a travel company who can then take advantage of scale economies and the experience curve to provide a better and cheaper service than the company could if it were to carry out the activity itself. It is also doubtful whether it is wise to carry out activities in which the company shows little expertise or skill.

Thus, if the activity is of little strategic significance to the company it should be bought in, even if the company would be very proficient at carrying it out itself – it is not the best use of its scarce resources. If, however, the activity is fairly to very strategically significant, and the company carries it out very well, this activity should be performed internally. If the activity is very strategically significant, and the company performs only fairly well, it should invest to improve its performance in the activity. If, however, the activity is fairly to very strategically significant, and the company performs it moderately to poorly, an alliance may be needed to enable the company to learn the necessary skills to improve its performance in the activity.

This matrix relates closely to the concepts discussed in Chapters 2, 3 and 4 on competitive strategy, where it was suggested that competences tend, over time, to migrate from strategically significant factors to hygiene factors. What was once an order winning factor, like central locking in a car, soon becomes strategically insignificant, and necessary – but not sufficient – to win the order. Thus, activities will migrate down the vertical axis on the matrix and ultimately become candidates for buying in.

The operational value of the above schema depends, of course, on how accurately it is possible to measure strategic significance and efficiency of performance. The latter axis is the easier to measure. The producer matrix (Chapter 3) sets out a method for measuring efficiency and effectiveness of performance in relation to competitors. Measuring strategic significance is, however, more difficult.

Perhaps the key measure is whether the activity is important to the achievement of competitive advantage. Hence, a computer hardware company that subcontracts all its manufacturing is taking a high strategic risk, as it is consigning the production of items upon which its reputation depends to companies it does not control. Where, as with Tonka Toys, the company is basically a product selection and marketing company, the risk is lower, since the competitive advantage lies in the selection of particular toys and their brand marketing.

VERTICAL AND HORIZONTAL INTEGRATION

We have so far identified two tools to help us define the most appropriate boundaries for our firm. Transaction cost analysis enables us to consider the tangible and intangible costs attached to carrying out particular transactions. It gives some general guidance as to whether, in the particular circumstances, these transactions are best carried out within a company environment, or whether they should be acquired through the market. This approach focuses on individual transactions, treats each as identically strategically significant, and ignores the issue of how well the company performs the activities relative to its competitors. It is an efficiency tool. Cost is assessed, but not quality in terms of the excellence or otherwise of the skill in question.

The make–buy–ally matrix remedies these defects, and provides further pointers as to which activities should be performed internally, and which consigned to the market. Neither tool, however, deals with the relationship between competences, and the economies of scale and scope available in the performance of one activity or a range of activities.

If many products are best produced in companies, which activities should the company carry out, and why should there be any limit to the size of a company? A large part of the answer to these questions is to be found in the shape of the firm's cost curve, and the limits to the degree of economies of scale and scope that exist, after which such matters as in the diseconomies of bureaucracy begin to cause the curve to bend upwards. When this point is reached, it becomes more efficient to operate in a smaller company, or to buy in more activities and restrict the company's activities to only those in which it excels, and which give it its competitive advantage.

The arguments in favour of vertical integration are that markets for upstream components with a low level of activity, activities involving proprietorial technologies, and activities requiring high levels of coordination lead to more reliable performance if they are carried out within the firm. As volume grows, the experience curve enables costs to be lowered, and scale and scope economies strengthen the cost reduction movement even further. With integrated manufacture, quality control is also easier to ensure, and the risks of opportunism at the transfer stages are substantially reduced, as indeed transaction costs are lower.

However, there are also arguments against vertical integration. Vertical integration removes the market discipline at each transfer interface, and therefore is likely to lead to X-inefficiency, and the reverse of lean production. Each stage in the production process involves manufacturing sufficient volume only for the end product's requirements. This is likely to mean sub-optimal production volumes from the viewpoint of maximizing scale economies. An integrated firm loses flexibility, and can become locked into old technologies whereas a subcontracting firm can switch subcontractors more easily.

213

Furthermore, firms that buy parts in the market and economize on the use of capital reduce the overall level of risk, and can, if they choose suppliers carefully, take advantage of the production of expert specialist firms without having to go to the time and expense of learning the specialisms.

The arguments for and against vertical integration, then, are finely balanced, and can be resolved only on a case-by-case basis. They have no doubt been strongly debated in both Tonka Toys and Mattell during the evolution of those two firms. The boards of directors in this instance decided upon radically different configuration strategies, thereby demonstrating the element of strategic choice that exists in most strategic decisions. The world is not so determinist as some would have us believe.

The arguments for horizontal integration, *i.e.*, integrating activities with those of a competitor through merger, acquisition or partnership, are easier. Horizontal integration is appropriate if it enables the firm to take optimal advantage of the opportunities presented by the existence of potential economies of scale and scope. Clearly, if buying your competitor involves operating two suboptimally-sized factories and two overlapping sales forces, then the argument for horizontal integration is not made. But if it enables you to achieve maximum economic production size in one factory, the cost argument for doing so is strong.

It is evident then that some firms are successful with an integrationist policy, and others with a market-orientated subcontracting policy. Evolutionary economists will argue that the firms that have made the wrong decision from a transaction-cost viewpoint will fail, and only the fit form will survive. However, as Hannan and Freeman (1989) point out, the drive for the lowest cost organizational form rarely overrides political and institutional considerations, and many organizations survive even though they do not minimize transaction costs. In the real world, four key factors inhibit the move towards an equilibrium in which transaction cost is minimized:

1. **Friction:** where institutional factors prevent immediate adjustment to changed circumstances.
2. **Market immaturity:** where embryonic markets develop and give rise to organizational forms that will not survive in the longer term.
3. **Market imperfections:** that exist in all markets other than pure commodities, and thereby provide barriers to change and instant adjustment.
4. **Time-lags:** that incur costs and make the precise nature of evolution unpredictable. Indeed, before the supposed inexorable forces moving towards equilibrium can take effect, in the modern turbulent world further technological change or distrubances of another sort frequently divert the equilibrating force in yet another direction.

SUMMARY

The conclusion of the issue of the appropriate boundary of the firm must then be a contingency one, *i.e.*, it all depends on the circumstances.

No two sets of circumstances are identical and the appropriate boundaries are likely to vary with the circumstances. One important circumstantial factor is likely to be the attitude of management, *i.e.*, the existence of strategic structural choice. However, this is not to deny the existence of strong forces, the strength and nature of which need to be assessed carefully before decisions are taken on where to integrate, bringing hierarchies, and where to subcontract, bringing markets. In order to make such circumstantial assessments, transaction-cost analysis can provide a useful check-list of factors to consider.

The make–buy–ally matrix can serve to emphasize the strategic significance of certain activities, the importance of competences, and the existence of administrative, technological and production economies and diseconomies. It can provide pointers to viable boundaries to the firm in given circumstances.

Finally, we would argue that it is probable that for all sets of circumstances, there is a range of organizational forms that are viable, but that some will certainly be more effective than others.

Resourcing: The Self-Sufficient Approach

The corporate centre's primary task of deciding which product/ markets it should operate in and within those product/markets which activities it should carry out directly and which it should subcontract or buy in, determines the scope and boundaries of the corporation. Decisions of this nature inevitably add to or reduce the value of the corporation, according to the wisdom of the judgements made.

Equally important, however, is another set of decisions of the corporate centre, which involves deciding how to provide the resources necessary to operate in the chosen segments. This resourcing task involves providing the resources to the existing SBUs for their investment and development, providing some services directly from the centre, identifying and implementing synergies between the SBUs, and developing the corporation through merger, acquisition and the creation of strategic alliances with other companies.

PROVIDING SPECIALIST SERVICES

By the provision of specialist services (*e.g.*, planning, management development, internal consultancy or R&D) the corporate centre can increase the competences of all the SBUs whilst achieving an economically efficient critical mass for the service. It is difficult to decide which services to provide at a corporate level and which to allow SBUs to provide themselves or to obtain independently from third party providers. A list of corporate services intended to add value to SBUs might include: market research, advertising, internal consultancy, strategic planning, corporate communications, information technology, human resources and training. However, opinion has swung in the last decade from the provision of many of these services on an on-demand basis to the authorization of SBUs to contract for them as required.

A logical approach to the question of whether to provide a service from the centre or not would be to assess the proposed service on the basis of its potential effectiveness and efficiency if provided centrally, and compare that on the same basis with a contracted-out service, or one provided at SBU level.

Effectiveness might be measured using the make–buy–ally matrix (MBA) described in Chapter 12. This matrix has axes of:
1. Competence compared with the best in the industry.
2. Strategic significance of the activity.

Using this matrix, a decision would be made to contract out all support services of low strategic significance, no matter how well the corporation is able to perform them. This might, for some companies, include such activities as market research and training.

However, as activities come to be judged to have greater strategic significance, their claims to be carried out within the corporation, or through a partnership with another company, grow. Such activities as internal consultancy, human resources and R&D might come under this category. The greater the degree to which the activity in question is central to the core competences of the corporation, the greater its claim to be managed centrally, even if this means locating it in a lead SBU and then ensuring its availability to the rest of the corporation. In this way, the coordination function from the centre is a potential source of added value.

However, this matrix alone cannot settle the matter. There are other issues to be assessed concerning the efficiency and effectiveness of providing particular services internally. Economies of scale are critical to the cost of most services. Thus, a high quality R&D department cannot be provided by a handful of scientists or engineers. A certain critical mass is needed to cover all the necessary skills required for a high quality research laboratory. It is also unlikely that an internal advertising department will be as high quality as one surviving and prospering with a range of clients in the external market. Similarly, for most companies (other than, perhaps, the very largest), the creation and maintenance of a strategic planning department may not be the most efficient way to handle strategy advice to the CEO and SBUs' general managers. Periodic use of strategic consultancy firms may be both more cost effective and lead to more innovative advice. Before such a decision is made, however the top management team should refer back to the MBA matrix, to ensure that they do not consider strategic advice to be of such high strategic significance for it to be retained within the company for reasons of confidentiality.

Decisions on whether to provide support services from the corporate centre are therefore matters for the judgement of the top management team, and that judgement should be guided by balancing the issues of efficiency and effectiveness, as there may be situations where these two criteria point in different directions. With regard to R&D for example, the firm may doubt the financial advisability of providing the service internally, because of the drain on funds if a department of sufficient size and quality were to be created to be as effective as the best in the industry. However, the function may be regarded as of such critical strategic significance to the corporate and competitive advantage of the firm as to make such internal provision a strong priority.

ACHIEVING SYNERGIES

The corporate centre can identify and help in the achievement of any synergies that may potentially exist between the SBUs, thus aiding in the achievement of economies of scope. The identification and realization of synergies can be an important part of the value-added contribution brought about by the corporate centre. The SBU concept, upon which the multi-divisional form (M-form – Chandler, 1962) of diversified company organizational structure is based, works on the assumption that SBUs are self-contained businesses. This, by definition, drives out synergies. Many corporations using the SBU principle in general are less rigorous in applying it in practice, and breach its pure form, when they recognize the existence of large opportunities for scope economies and other synergistic relationships between SBUs.

In principle, the opportunity to examine potential synergies rises directly with the acquisition by the corporation of new business units. Two units may have a common supplier, a third a common customer, a fourth may allow manufacture with common plant, and so the opportunities increase. It is important, however, that the benefits from the realization of these synergies exceeds by a significant margin the costs involved in achieving them. The use of a value chain analysis for each business unit in the corporation will identify many of the possible areas of synergy.

Synergies may exist in all value-chain activities. Marketing synergies may exist through the spreading of the corporate brand name over a wider range of products, through shared advertising and promotion, through the use of the same distribution network and sales force for a wider range of product, through cross-selling by executives in different SBUs, or through sharing the back-office administration associated with the sales and marketing function.

Procurement synergies may exist through shared purchasing, leading to greater volume discounts; production synergies through shared production facilities, shared quality systems and shared maintenance departments. State-of-the-art technologies may also be valuably spread over a range of business units to corporate advantage. Less tangible synergies may also be realized, *e.g.*, through the use by more than one SBU of a similar strategy, the targeting of similar customers, and the use of valuable corporate contacts of use to a range of business units.

On the negative side, there are of course inevitable costs of both a financial and a motivational nature in attempting to realize synergies between SBUs. On the financial side, there are the costs involved in setting up and maintaining the coordination systems necessary to realize the synergies; this means champions, task forces, management time, committees, and the compromises that are needed when one SBU is measured by its results, and yet required to take actions that may benefit another SBU and not itself in the interest of the corporation as a whole.

Motivational costs may thus be an important consideration in selecting which synergies to go for. The achievement of intra-SBU synergies inevitably leads to a degree of diffused profit responsibility, loss of focus, reduced flexibility, and a blurring of the cause–effect relationship. It is difficult to know whether you are right to sell off

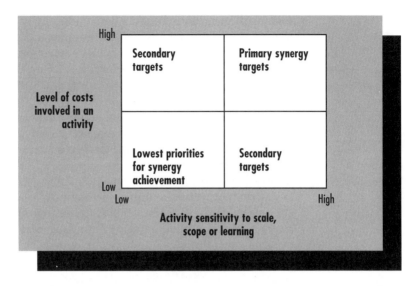

Figure 13.1
Scale, scope and synergy.

a poorly performing business when it is intertwined in a complex way with the rest of the corporation, sharing production plant, sales force and maybe R&D.

It is important, therefore, to attempt to realize only the synergies that are clearly sensitive to economies of scale, scope or learning, and at the same time represent a large amount of operating costs or assets of the corporation (see Figure 13.1).

Putting it the other way around, potential synergies should be ignored if their realization incurs greater costs than benefits; if the benefits would be difficult to realize; if they are small items of expenditure; or if they are not very clearly subject to scale or scope economies.

Only the corporate centre can make the achievement of these synergies possible, as there is an understandable tendency for executives allocated to an SBU to put the interests of that SBU before those of the corporation as a whole. However, optimizing actions within each SBU may lead to sub-optimization of outcomes for the corporation, in that it ignores the potential benefits from inter-SBU synergies. The pursuit of and achievement of appropriate synergies is therefore an important area where the corporate centre can add value.

219

MERGERS AND ACQUISITIONS

An acquisition or merger is an alternative way of providing resources to that of internal development. However, if an acquisition is carried out of a company of which the acquirer knows little prior to the bid, this provides the highest-risk way of providing resources for the corporation. If an acquisition is not pursued after an extended period of close collaboration with the target company as a partner, or by a group whose corporate core competences include identifying and negotiating acquisitions then it is undoubtedly high risk. As a means of effecting a competitive strategy, it is generally pursued to get access to core competences in which the acquiring company feels itself to be deficient, and thereby to enable it to compete successfully in a particular market. The hope is that both companies individually may lack competitive advantage in their chosen market, but together they may achieve it.

Acquisitions may be undertaken for other reasons of corporate strategy, *e.g.*, restructuring the market; achieving a more balanced portfolio of businesses; gaining access to advantageous tax losses; building a bigger empire; or achieving corporate growth targets at times when development through organic growth proves difficult. However, it is the combining of resources and skills in order to achieve strategic advantage that is the primary strategic reason for making an acquisition.

ACQUISITIONS – THE ENIGMA

Acquisitions, particularly those involving major publicly-quoted companies, probably attract more attention in the media than any other aspect of business life, except perhaps scandals involving prominent personalities. In the eyes of the economist, they are mechanisms that ensure that the market remains efficient. Thus, if X-inefficiency develops in a company, financial results begin to slide, and the stock market starts to value the company by a low price: earnings multiple compared with competitors in its sector, a take-over bid ensues and new management is brought in to remove the X-inefficiency and achieve an acceptable return on the assets employed. Yet, there are several enigmas to the real world of acquisitions that suggest that the process described above may not always lead to so beneficial results for all concerned.

First, premiums in excess of 30% are quite commonly found, particularly in the case of contested bids. But, if the takeover target is correctly valued by the stock market, why are such high premiums over that valuation so often paid by the bidder? Clearly, the *prima facie* justification for this must be that the incoming management can recognize ways of adding value through synergies and/or removing the sources of x-inefficiency. This level of premium must be difficult to justify without forsaking efficient market beliefs. If gains are assessed in relation to bidder share price at the point at which the bid is successful, it is possible to determine whether the bidder shareholder can realize a gain. Clearly, at this point no one, let alone the stock exchange, can know whether net synergies will be achieved in the longer term, and it is quite impossible to determine the optimal future point at which such a calculation should be made. However, the share price when the bid is successful is knowable, and since shareholders could realize their gains at this point, it represents a reasonable point of comparison.

At this point, Jensen and Roebach (1983), having analysed a wide range of research, find the bidder shareholders to have gained on

Figure 13.2
The failure rate of
acquisitions in the US is high.

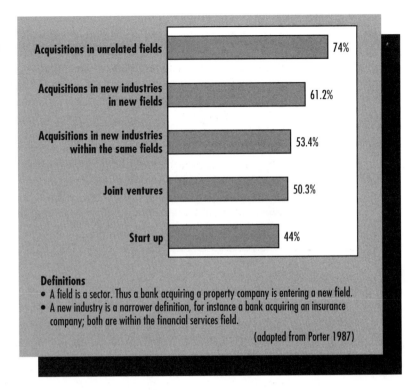

Definitions
- A field is a sector. Thus a bank acquiring a property company is entering a new field.
- A new industry is a narrower definition, for instance a bank acquiring an insurance company; both are within the financial services field.

(adapted from Porter 1987)

average by 4% in the take-overs and by 0% in mergers. The target shareholders, however, are seen to gain by 30% in take-overs and 20% in mergers on average.

Second, if the main justification for acquisitions is the existence of potential synergies between the acquirer and the target, why are these synergies apparently so seldom realized?

Third, if the acquisition is an efficiency enhancing mechanism, then why are there clearly discernible waves of merger/acquisition activity as in the early 1970s and the middle and late 1980s? Would a lemming mentality or fashion explanation not have more apparent credibility than that of an efficiency producing hidden hand?

If acquisitions are generally promoted by the bidding company, and can be seen to lead to gains for at least one party, why do the figures suggest that the gainers are most frequently the shareholders of the victim company and the management of the predator, with the shareholders of the bidder and the management of the victim, frequently the losers. This is a clear illustration of a principal/agent problem.

If buying another company is such a good idea why, according to Porter's research (1987), are a majority of such liaisons unwound within five years? Porter's research into the record of acquisitions made in areas unrelated to the core competences or experience of the acquiring company shows a failure rate between 53% and 74% (see Figure 13.2).

WHY ACQUIRE?

Acquisition has some theoretical advantages over both internal development and alliances which make it a popular strategy for an ambitious company intent on fast growth:

1. It enables a firm to get into new market or product areas rapidly, and if the acquisition is at an attractive price, and the acquired management team is genuinely willing to transfer their allegiance to the acquirer company, it can clearly lead to a new and strengthened, enlarged enterprise.
2. It may enable costs to be reduced through rationalization, and the consequent economies of scale and of scope to be realized.
3. It may bring valuable skills and resources to the acquiring company, thereby strengthening its core and key competences, and improving its competitive position.
4. By acquiring a competitor, the company may improve its market share, and put itself in a stronger market position and restructure the market to its advantage.
5. By acquiring a company either upstream or downstream in its value system (Porter, 1985), a firm may reduce costs at the interface between value-chain activities, improve intra-firm information, reduce the incentive for opportunism to be exercised by suppliers or distributors, and replace the potential wastes incurred by competition in favour of cooperative action.

The above arguments are, however, largely theoretical, and sometimes difficult to substantiate in the case of actual acquisitions. Other arguments are less theoretical. Thus, take-over bids are generally mounted by the management rather than the shareholders of the bidding company, and whatever the results for the shareholders, it is rare that the new managers of the enlarged enterprise do not benefit by a substantial salary increase and, possibly, share options.

A further argument (Jensen, 1986) is that firms with free cash flow, finding organic growth difficult, prefer acquisitions to the alternative of returning the cash to the shareholders. This is a variant on the traditional empire building argument for expansion by acquisition.

Once it is conceded that the stock market is less than a perfect mechanism for valuing companies, as is suggested in Fama's 1980 critique of the efficient market hypothesis, motives for acquisitions become clearer. Thus, if the bidding company has superior information it can recognize a bargain of which the stock market is unaware. It may also, for reasons of fashion, have a very high price:earnings ratio not really justified by the firm's genuine long-term prospects. In this case, to use the high P:E and buy with paper, *i.e.*, its own overvalued shares, represents a rational decision and a certain way of increasing shareholder value, at least in the short term.

A further motive for acquisitions is to diversify risk, or to iron out seasonal variations in cash flow. This may give the company more

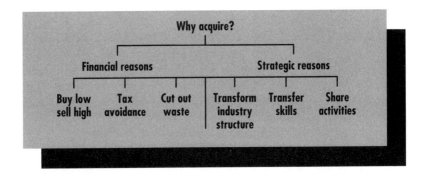

Figure 13.3
Financial and strategic
division of the principal
motives for acquisitions.

stable earnings which, if the effect is substantial, may lower its cost of borrowing by increasing its credit rating. The generally poor performance of conglomerates in the medium-term past has, however, somewhat discredited this argument.

The consultancy firm Braxton Associates divides the principal motives for acquisitions into two streams: financial and strategic (see Figure 13.3). This model covers most of the primary legitimate reasons for adopting an acquisition programme, ignoring the less legitimate reasons, at least from the shareholders' viewpoint, of personal managerial aggrandisement or empire building.

RISKS ATTACHED TO ACQUISITION

However, there are frequently major risks attached to acquisitions, against which the buyer must guard very carefully. Of the four parties involved – the shareholders and the management of the bidding party, and the shareholders and management of the target company – those most at risk in a successful bid are the shareholders of the bidding party and the management of the target company. In most cases, the value of the bidder's shares will not increase in value, and many of the target's top management will be out of a job. Almost regardless of the achievement of the holy grail of long-term synergy however, the management of the bidder will have gained themselves enhanced salaries and status, and the shareholders of the target will have had the opportunity to exchange their shares for cash at a substantial premium price. This argument emphasizes the tenets of agency theory, but does nothing for the economists' arguments that take-overs increase industry efficiency.

Synergy does not automatically arise when two companies are brought together. Once the deal is done, managements frequently lose their taste for the ruthless actions necessary to achieve the synergies so trumpeted during the bid. Indeed, extra costs may be incurred from having to learn to deliver on the success factors that relate to unfamiliar markets and products.

Furthermore, the business equivalent of catch 22 often applies. If the price of the target company is low and represents a discount

223

on asset value, then the company may be a weak one, and would represent a poor purchase, likely to absorb management time and weaken the acquirer. If the company is a good one however, the price is likely to be correspondingly high, which will mean the addition of a large amount of goodwill to the acquirer's balance sheet, and an initial decline in return on capital, until some synergies can be realized and caused to feed through to profits.

A further problem is valuation. A shrewd seller will, of course, dress up the company's accounts, within the bounds of auditing practice, to appear in the most profitable light to achieve the best purchase price. Such profits and asset values may turn out not to be sustainable after the purchase has been completed.

The best of the acquired company's personnel may have left by the time the new owner takes over and, if the acquired company was largely owner managed, the ex-owners may be less highly motivated on becoming employees.

Company cultures may be found to clash, and the process of achieving the promised synergies may prove more difficult than seemed apparent during the acquisition appraisal process. An understanding of the nature of another company's corporate culture takes some time, and is rarely a factor given much attention in the heat of a take-over deal. Yet, when it comes to the job of achieving the synergistic form that combines the skills and resources of the two companies, their respective cultures frequently provide one of the largest barriers to the achievement of the required integration.

THE EVIDENCE

In the recent past, the evidence seems to be that the great conglomerate–merger wave of the 1960s did not generally lead to gains in performance for those involved, and was to a large extent reversed by the selling of unrelated businesses that was carried out in the 1980s. The two arguments behind the 1960s movement were the following:

1. Top management was conceived as being largely about budgeting, financing, procurement and control. These were seen as generic skills, and therefore industry experience was considered to be of secondary importance. Purchases of unrelated businesses were therefore quite in order if they enabled top management to exercise its generic management skills effectively over an enlarged industrial area.
2. Professional managers were believed to be better than investors at directing capital to its best uses, and diversifying risks between businesses. Conglomerates were therefore to be considered as powerful industrial institutions.

Neither argument stood the test of time and performance. The counter-argument soon gained ground that capital holders could achieve their own diversification quite well through market mechanisms, and did not require to have it done for them by agents who might have other interests than those of the capital holder at heart. Furthermore, Wernerfelt and Montgomery (1991) and Rumelt (1974), among others, found that the more focused firms performed better than diversified ones, and notably were perceived to do so by the market, as they had higher values of Tobin's q, *i.e.*, the ratio of the market value of the firm to the replacement value of its assets, seen as a measure of the value being created by the firm. With the growing disenchantment with conglomerates, this corporate species came to be valued at less than its constituent parts, and set in motion the unbundling movement of the late 1970s and early 1980s. This led to a significant decrease in overall diversification in industry, and to the belief that, if acquisitions were to be carried out, they should be of firms of which the key factors for success related closely to the bidder's core competences. Indeed Lichtenberg (cited in Milgrom and Roberts, 1992) determined that, in the 1980s, the shares of firms out-performed the market in years when the firms became more focused, and did worse than the market in years when they became more diversified.

There are then two issues here, the first of which is whether take-overs of unrelated businesses are likely to add value. Here, the wealth of evidence from the last 30 years, with notable exceptions such as the Hanson or the Tompkins groups, seems to suggest fairly conclusively that for a take-over to be successful in the longer term there need to be clearly identifiable and realizable synergies between the companies, and that the likelihood of this happening is highest if the companies operate in the same market sector. The experience of corporations like Xerox as it diversified from photocopiers into, *inter alia*, financial services provide a cautionary tale for entrepreneurs wishing to develop conglomerates.

The second issue is whether acquisitions generally add value at all, given the costs involved in putting them together. In economic terms, society would clearly benefit if take-overs could be shown to represent the taking away of assets from inefficient managers, their replacement by more efficient managers, with the benefit being passed on to consumers. There is, however, little evidence to suggest that this does in fact happen. In the 1960s, the UK Monopolies Commission found no evidence for it, and nor did a succession of academic researchers. The more plausible argument found by Cowling *et al.* (1980) was that each takeover represented a cost–benefit equation for society, in which the potential benefits of the gain in efficiency had to be balanced against the costs of the increase in monopoly power with its capacity to increase profits by raising prices.

Although there is no convincing evidence that the economy gains from take-overs, this does not mean that no one gains. Even if the cake does not necessarily become larger, the relative sizes of the slices generally change in favour of some parties and at the expense of others.

TARGET COMPANY SELECTION

There is more to an acquisition programme than the purely transitory climax of the successful bid with its creation of the potential for realizing gains and its furtherance of one management's careers often at the expense of the other's. Merger and acquisition represent a path to the successful development of a business enterprise, albeit at high risk, coupled with the possibility of disaster if the wrong target company is chosen, the negotiations are poorly carried out, or the implementation plan is ill considered or badly executed.

Good target selection is therefore vital. As Rumelt has shown and Porter's (1987) research confirms, the most successful acquisitions are those of companies in related areas. More specifically, using the resource-based view of the firm, these are acquisitions of companies that can benefit from the bidding firm's core competences. This does not, of course, infallibly predict failure for acquisitions where this asset complementarity is absent. It does, however, suggest that the probability of a successful acquisition in the absence of such relatedness is substantially lower than where it is present.

The selection of candidate target companies should therefore be preceded by careful selection of the industry sectors in which to trawl. This can be done by first assessing the attractiveness of the various sectors that relate fairly closely to that in which the bidding company operates. Attractiveness can be judged as suggested in Chapter 5 by use of Porter's five-forces model, coupled with an assessment of the actual and potential size of the market sector in question, and a consideration using a PEST check-list of likely changes in the market in the plannable future.

The would-be acquiring company should then undertake an internal analysis to determine its own core competences as suggested in Chapter 3, and should then relate those competences to the key competences required for success in the target sector. Where it perceives deficiencies in its competences it may seek to redress them by seeking a target company with the key competences that it feels itself to lack . The consultancy company Arthur D. Little have developed a matrix that helps to assess the appropriateness of a market sector to a company's strengths (Figure 13.4). Clearly, the best sectors to go for are those in the top-left corner of the matrix, where a company's core competences are key to success in the sector and the company's strength in these competences is high. This gives it good mesh with the requirements of the target sector.

For market-sector selection, an attractiveness–mesh matrix can now be prepared (Figure 13.5).

This will enable the would-be acquiring company to choose sectors that appear most attractive to it on the matrix. Clearly, those in the top, right-hand box are the most attractive, and those in the bottom, left-hand box the least attractive. However, selection in any box other than these two requires a judgmental balance to be struck between higher mesh in a relatively less attractive sector, and lower

Figure 13.4
Low mesh means higher risk.

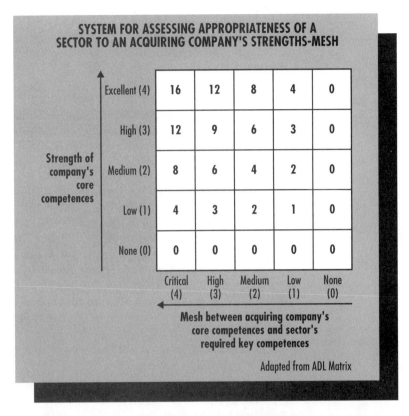

Figure 13.5
System for overall
assessment of sectors.

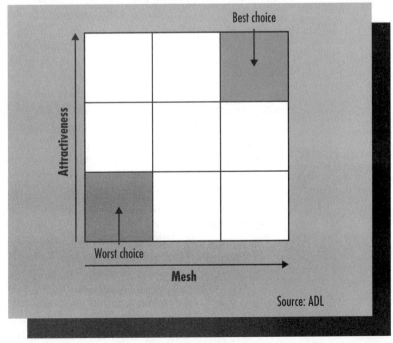

227

mesh in a more attractive sector. The resource-based view of competitive advantage would suggest that more weight should be given to the mesh factor than to the sector-attractiveness factor. After all, what use is there in operating in an attractive sector is you do not possess the key competences to succeed in it? Once the market sectors in which to seek targets have been identified, the process of finding a company to acquire can begin.

A PROPOSED APPROACH

It is important, if an acquisition strategy is to be adopted, to pursue it in a methodical, low risk way, noting certain key factors before proceeding. For example, an acquisition can in general be justified only if it leaves the combined enterprise stronger than the sum of the two individual enterprises. This normally means that both companies should be able to bring something to the party, in the same way that is expected from an alliance. The requirement that the joint value chains of the acquiring and the acquired company be able to achieve competitive advantage not easily attainable by either party separately, applies to acquisitions as well as to alliances. It therefore requires the possession of complementary assets, and of realizable synergies between the two parties. An acquisition made principally to increase the size of a portfolio, and not able to achieve, for example, economies of scale or scope, is therefore of doubtful value as a strategic move.

The following seven step approach is suggested as a route to minimizing acquisition risks:

1. As suggested above, rule out acquisitions in industries and fields unrelated to those with which the acquirer has experience, and which seem to require skills and competences that the acquirer does not have.

2. Conduct an internal appraisal of your own business, including value chain analysis, core competence profiling and a resource audit. Estimate the financial worth of your company, identify the nature and strength of your claim to competitive advantage, and the breadth of product/market segments in which it applies.

3. Within the market sectors selected through use of the mesh–attractiveness matrix, select criteria for acquisition candidates and divide them into 'must haves' and 'nice to haves'. For example a 'must have' criterion might be existing strong and committed management plus key competences that, in combination with the bidder's competences, suggest the possibility of competitive advantage in the chosen market sectors. A 'nice to have' criterion might be a factory geographically close to the operation of the bidding company. This would aid coordination of activities, but is not vital to success. The selection of the criteria depends upon the carefully thought out requirements of the acquiring company, and should be closely adhered to both in the trawling, and the subsequent **due diligence** phases of the acquisition process. A high risk always exists that, in the excitement of the bid, some

key 'must have' criteria will be quietly put on one side as adrenaline takes over from reason.

4. Identify potential candidates that meet the criteria within the selected industry sectors. Having done so, the value chains and competence profiles of the acquiring and would-be acquired companies should be compared to identify potential complementarities and synergies.

5. The candidates should then be investigated further to determine their ownership, track record, potential problems, and possible risk areas, and to validate the existence of the claimed positive qualities identified in the desk research criteria evaluation. Approximate acquisition values should then be assigned to the target companies at this stage.

6. Once an appropriate candidate has been identified and contacted, and has shown interest, a careful and rigorous due diligence process, including the real reason for interest in a possible sale, must be carried out if unpleasant surprises are to be avoided. This will involve company visits if the bid is not a hostile one, and extended time spent with target company management in order to build up an accurate picture of them and their company.

7. Once the negotiations have been brought to a successful conclusion, the acquisition should be integrated with determination, and as fast as possible according to a pre-determined plan, using as the spearhead a project team with membership from both companies. The aim must be to maximize the value of the enlarged enterprise, through the early realization of the anticipated synergies, whilst at the same time minimizing the inevitable impact of culture shock on the acquired company. Since culture shock of some kind is inevitable it should be anticipated, and mechanisms put in place to stimulate and motivate the key members of the acquired company, thereby giving them the personal incentive to deal effectively with their own culture shock in a positive manner.

If the above steps are carried out thoroughly and carefully, the inevitable risks attendant on any acquisition should be minimized.

In general, the acquisition strategy is one that should be employed with great caution. Typically, the more closely related the businesses of the acquisition candidate and the acquirer are, the lower the risk will be, because the new owner will be familiar with the major problems likely to be encountered, and will be experienced in dealing with them. An acquisition of an unfamiliar company in an unrelated area of business both from a market and product viewpoint is, therefore, the highest risk strategy of all, and should be resisted if at all possible.

The major exception to this general rule is when the acquiring company's core competence is in company appraisal, acquisition and financial management, e.g., Hanson. In this case, such a company can legitimately claim to be operating in the area it knows best, *i.e.,* the bottom-left quadrant of the options cube, even if the products and markets of the company to be acquired are not familiar.

SUMMARY

An acquisition strategy is generally pursued by companies in order to strengthen their chances of achieving sustainable competitive advantage, by providing them with a stronger producer matrix position in terms of both effectiveness and efficiency. They hope, thereby, to strengthen their position on the customer matrix, which is the ultimate arbiter of competitive success.

When compared with the other 'How?' strategies of internal development or strategic alliance, an acquisition strategy is a high risk one. To buy a company is always more expensive than to form an alliance with one, and a management selling its company has less incentive to be absolutely truthful in the negotiations than one attempting to set up an alliance. It also has less incentive to stay around and ensure the success of the joint endeavour after the deal has been concluded.

An acquisition strategy is not necessarily bound to fail, however, but it is high risk for all the reasons outlined above.

The lowest risk approach is probably to form an alliance in order to get to know a partner better. A decision on the acquisition of the partner may then be made with the background knowledge that has been gained.

chapter 14

Resourcing:
Joint Development

A key value-adding role of the corporate centre is to provide resources and competences when the corporation does not currently possess them. If acquisition is thought not to be appropriate, joint development or strategic alliances may well be an attractive option. Some form of alliance with a partner overcomes many of the problems of lack of resources and competences. New products from one company can be married to distribution networks from another. Companies strong on technology can collaborate with partners strong on marketing to their mutual benefit. The wide variety of joint development forms provides a varied menu of possibilities for partners to select from, to optimize their development possibilities.

Joint development is appropriate where sustainable competitive advantage can be achieved together, but not separately. A weak position on the producer matrix can be transformed through an alliance by the addition of the partner's core competences. Joint venture, collaboration and consortium are the principal types of alliance to meet differing situational and firm needs. Other, less committing and interdependent forms of joint development include one-off projects, licensing, franchising, relationship contracting and the appointments of exclusive agents. These are often **unilateral** arrangements, implying only limited interdependence between the cooperating firms, and are ultimately crystallized by a financial deal, *e.g.*, 'I will market your product in the UK, and for the right to use the brand name and product specification I will pay you a royalty of 5% on all sales.'

As was suggested in Chapter 12, the make–buy–ally matrix suggests situations in which alliance formation is the most appropriate action to take. Each prospective partner will, of course, face a different matrix, and one of the keys to alliance success is to ensure that the two matrices are congruent. For example, in the Rover–Honda alliance, Rover was poor at production systems which was a very strategically significant activity, but strong on styling, so its needs were in the top left-hand box and its bargaining chips in the top right-hand box. Honda, on the other hand, were good at production systems but poor on the styling required for European sales. Their styling needs were therefore in their top left-hand box, and their bargaining chips, *i.e.*, their production skills, were in their top right-hand box. The two matrices were therefore congruent, and the partners forged a mutually beneficial alliances. The opportunity for **bilateral** arrangements is therefore present.

However, joint development has risks attached. Know-how will inevitably leak intentionally and often unintentionally to a partner, who may become a future competitor. Joint development means working with new people and learning new ways of doing things, which can take time, lead to cultural problems, and incur additional costs of coordination. Finally, in a joint development arrangement, there is an inevitable lack of clarity of authority, which may be a disadvantage when confronted with an internally developed rival with clear lines of decision making.

COOPERATIVE STRATEGY

Cooperative strategy is, however, rapidly becoming the counterpart to competitive strategy as a key strategic management approach. It is perhaps the primary means for companies that are deficient in particular competences or resources to link with others that have complementary skills and resources to give them, jointly, a competitive advantage, particularly in the increasingly globalizing world markets, within a very short time period. This enables them to take advantage of a product/market opportunity that may not last for long. It also has the added advantage of flexibility in a volatile world.

It is probably unhelpful, however, to think of cooperation as the opposite of competition, since firms generally cooperate with each other only in order to harness the resources, skills and power to compete more effectively with others in the market place. The issue, then, is not to compete or to cooperate, but rather how best to organize the appropriate set of resources and competences to become a winner in the competitive market place. Since more market places are becoming global, the critical mass of resources needed to succeed is growing faster than many internally developed companies can cope with alone. Thus, the resource-based approach to strategy development described in Chapter 3 may lead a company to identify the competences it needs if it is to succeed. Cooperation with another company is one way of meeting these needs.

In a growing number of areas, a careful consideration of the appropriate make-or-buy options for particular company activities may lead many manufacturers to opt to become mere assemblers, or even purely brand marketing companies. Medium-sized companies may become global enterprises almost overnight by setting up a wide network of strategic alliances to meet global challenges and opportunities.

The movement of enterprises away from a simple, wholly-owned corporate structure to more federated forms is accentuated by the growth of alliances and other strategic networks, which aid the development of global loyalties and cooperative endeavours. These are quite distinct from those encouraged by the old national and firm boundaries.

In transaction-cost analysis described in Chapter 12, organizational forms are conventionally described on a scale of increasing

Figure 14.1
There are many intermediate organizational forms between markets and hierarchies.

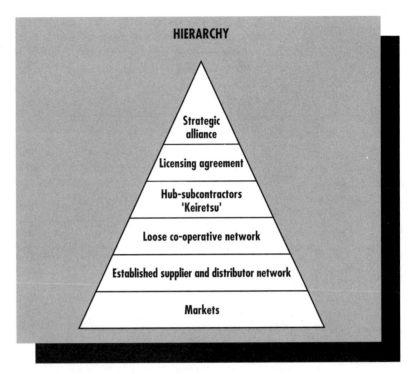

integration, with markets at one end as the absolute of non-integration, to hierarchies or completely integrated companies at the other. It is suggested that the organizations that survive are those that involve the lowest costs to run in the particular circumstances in which they exist. Thus, integrated companies will be the lowest cost in situations when assets are very specific and markets are thin, and where conditions are highly complex and uncertain. Such conditions would make the fully-integrated form of organization the most appropriate one, as it would be very difficult, and therefore costly, to handle transactions in a fragmented, market place way.

At the other extreme, transactions are best carried out in markets where no one deal implies commitment to another, and relationships are completely at arm's length. This is most commonly the case when the product is a frequently traded commodity, assets are not specific, market pricing is needed for efficiency, there are many alternative sources of supply, and the costs of running a company would be very high. Thus, few companies needing filing cabinets occasionally, but without their being critical and in scarce supply, would manufacture them. They buy them in the market from companies who make it their business to produce them in volume at acceptable prices to an efficient design.

Between the extremes of markets and integrated companies, there are a range of inter-organizational forms of increasing levels of integration which have evolved to deal with varying circumstances and, where they survive, may be assumed to do so as a result of their varying appropriateness to the situation (see Figure 14.1). All forms between the extremes of markets and hierarchies exhibit some degree of cooperation in their activities. It is even likely that most hierarchies include internal markets within them in order to create situations where market pricing will improve efficiency, *e.g.*, an SBU may be empowered to use third party marketing advice if it is not satisfied with that available internally.

Hence, arm's length market relationships may develop into those with established suppliers and distributors, and then may integrate further into loose cooperative networks.

Further up the ladder of integration come the hub–subcontractor networks like Marks and Spencer's close interrelationships with its suppliers. Licensing agreements come next, in which the relationship between the licenser and the licensee is integrated from the viewpoint of activities in a defined area, but both retain their separate ownership and identities.

Between licensing agreements and completely integrated companies, where rule by price (markets) is replaced by rule by fiat (companies), comes the most integrated form of rule by cooperation, namely that found in strategic alliances.

Alliances may be preferred organizational forms where sensitive market awareness is required; where the price mechanism remains importan; where risks of information leakage are not considered unacceptably high; where scale economies are available and finance risks are high; and where there is resource limitation and flexibility is important.

In the consideration of cooperative strategy a number of issues need to be addressed:
- What is the motivation for alliances?
- How do alliance firms select their partners?
- What form of cooperation should alliance firms choose?
- How should they manage the alliance?
- What happens to cooperative arrangements in the long-term?

WHAT IS THE MOTIVATION FOR ALLIANCES?

Cooperative relationships develop normally because a firm develops a feeling that it is deficient in certain important competences. Companies with weak positions on the customer matrix, reflecting equally weak positions on the producer matrix seek partners to strengthen their key competences in certain important markets, and thus to improve their competitive position. They may even seek alliances to improve their corporate competences in a more general way. Through its alliance with Honda, for example, Rover was transformed into a genuine **learning organization** – a critical corporate competence. Realization by a firm that it is in a weak position in relation to certain key competences often comes about as a result of the growth in strength of an external force that starts to make it feel vulnerable, often causing its financial or market performance to decline.

External Forces

There are a number of external forces that have stimulated the growth of strategic alliances in recent years. Among the most important are the globalization of tastes and markets, the rapid spread and shortening life-cycle of new technology and its products, the development of opportunities for achieving major economies of scale, scope and learning, increasing turbulence in international economies, a heightened level of uncertainty in all aspects of life, and declining international trade barriers.

Theodore Levitt was credited over 30 years ago with having first drawn attention to the increasing homogenization of tastes, leading to the development of the global village. Since that time, the globalization movement has spread to an increasing number of industries, and as Kenichi Ohmae (1987) points out, it is now possible to travel from New York to Paris and on to Tokyo, and to see very similar articles on display in department stores in all three cities.

After the Second World War, trade barriers between nations placed a limit to the development of a world economy. With the dramatic economic recovery of the major combatant nations, particularly Germany and Japan, the move towards increasing international trade was stimulated by international agreements to reduce trade barriers, and thus increase overall economic welfare by allowing greater specialization on the basis of comparative costs.

GATT, the EU, EFTA and other trading agreements and common markets enabled national firms to develop opportunities internationally, and to grow into multinationals. More recently, the 1992 EU legislation, the reunification of Germany, the establishment of NAFTA, and the break-up of the communist bloc have accelerated this movement and, in so doing, stimulated the growth of strategic alliances between firms in different nations.

However, not only are markets rapidly becoming global, but the most modern technologies – microelectronics, genetic engineering and advanced material sciences – are now all subject to truly global competition. The global technologies involved in the communications revolution have also succeeded in effectively shrinking the world, and have led to the design and manufacture of products with global appeal, due to their pricing, reliability and technical qualities. But, not only is technology becoming global in nature, it is also changing faster than previously, which means a single firm needs correspondingly greater resources to be capable of replacing the old technology with the new on a regular basis. This is often difficult to finance and resource.

The globalization of markets and technologies leads to the need to be able to produce at a sufficiently large volume to realize the maximum economies of scale and scope, and thus compete globally on a unit cost basis. Although one effect of the new technologies is the growth of the ability, through flexible manufacturing systems, to produce small lots economically, the importance of scale and scope economies is still critical to global economic competitiveness in many areas. Alliances are often the only way to achieve such a large scale of operation to generate these economies. The advantages of alliances and networks over integrated firms are in the areas of specialization, entrepreneurship and flexibility of arrangements. These characteristics are particularly appropriate to meet the needs of today's turbulent and changing environment.

The oil crises of 1973 and 1978, the Middle East wars, and the subsequent aggravated economic cycles of boom and recession, coupled with ever shortening product life-cycles has made economic forecasting as hazardous as long-term weather forecasting. Strategic vulnerability due to environmental uncertainty has become a fact of life in most industries. Cooperative strategy helps to reduce that vulnerability by enabling **federated enterprises**, in Handy's term (1992), to grow or decline flexibly, to match the increasing variability of the market situation.

Internal Conditions

A range of external conditions may stimulate the creation of strategic alliances. However, firms will only enter into such arrangements when their internal circumstances make this seem to be the right move. These internal circumstances have most commonly included a feeling of inadequacy in resources and competences, in that an alliance would give a firm access to valuable markets, technologies, special skills or raw materials in which it feels itself to be deficient, and which it could not easily get in any other way. This is sometimes characterized as the **resource dependency perspective** (Pfeffer and Salancik, 1978). This perspective suggests the need to improve the firm's position on the producer matrix by operating on the vertical axis, *i.e.*, that which measures the level of high competences within the firm.

The theory of resource dependency or competence inadequacy suggests that the crucial condition determining the survival of a firm is not its competitive advantage but its access to resources and competences. Thus, if a highly competitive firm overtrades, *i.e.*, runs out of resources, it fails to survive. On the other hand, if a sleepy firm is part of a very large and indulgent conglomerate, it can survive as long as its parent considers it worth supplying the necessary resources.

In conditions of economic turbulence and high uncertainty, access to the necessary resources for many firms becomes a risk, which raises the spectre of potential strategic vulnerability for even the most efficient firm. This leads to the need to reduce that uncertainty, and secure more reliable access to the necessary resources, whether they be supplies, skills or markets. Strategic alliances with firms able to supply the resources may then develop where previously market relationships may have dominated.

For cooperation to be appropriate, both partners should need and be able to provide some resource or competence that the other possesses. If the needs are not reciprocal, then the best course of action is for the partner in need to buy the competence or resource, or, if appropriate, buy the company possessing it. Cooperative arrangements require the satisfaction of complementary needs on the part of both partners, and thereby lead to competitive advantage.

There are many forms of resource dependency:

■ Access to markets is a common form. One firm has a successful product in its home market, but lacks the sales force and perhaps the local knowledge to gain access to other markets. The alliance between Cincinnati Bell Information Systems (CBIS) of the US and Kingston Communications of Hull, England, was set up from CBIS's viewpoint in order to gain market access into the European Community, with the purpose of selling its automated telecommunications equipment. The market motivator is also a strong one in the current spate of Eastern Europe and former USSR alliances with Western firms.

■ Access to technology is another form of resource need. Thus, in forming Cereal Partners to fight Kellogg's domination of the breakfast cereals market, Nestlé has joined forces with General Mills principally to gain access to its breakfast cereals technology.

■ Access to special skills is a similar form of resource need to access to technology. The special skills or competences may be of many types, and include the know-how associated with experience in a particular product area.

■ Access to raw materials is a further form. Thus, for example, Monarch Resources has allied with Cyprus Minerals to gain access to Venezuelan gold mines. Although this motivation was a very common one in past decades when the developed nations sought allies in less developed area, it is currently less common.

Other internal circumstances that have stimulated the search for alliances have included the belief that running an alliance would be cheaper than running and financing an integrated company, or the belief that an alliance, or a series of alliances, would provide strong protection against take-over predators. Others may be that firms believe it is the best way to limit risk, or to achieve a desired market position faster than by any other way. Transaction cost theory encompasses these motivations within its orbit. Although accurate calculation of the costs involved in various organizational forms is very difficult to compute since it involves adding the quantitative and the qualitative costs, the lowest cost concept is still valuable in determining whether a particular activity is best carried out by internal means, by purchasing it in the market, or by collaboration with a partner. This is reflected on the efficiency axis of the producer matrix. So, where the transactions cost perspective is taken as the justification for the development of the alliance, this suggests the priority is to improve the firm's position on the horizontal axis (unit costs) of its producer matrix.

Alliances are also frequently formed as a result of the need to limit *risk*. The nature of the risk may be its sheer size in terms of financial resources. Thus, a £100 million project shared between three alliance partners is a much lower risk for each partner than the same project shouldered alone. The risk may also be portfolio risk. Thus, £100 million invested in alliances in four countries probably represents a lower risk than the same figure invested alone in one project. The trade-off is between higher control and lower risk. An acquisition represents a high level of control but is expensive, and however well the acquirer may have researched the target company before purchase, it may still receive some unexpected surprises after the conclusion of the deal. A strategic alliance involves shared risk, is probably easier to unravel if it proves disappointing, and enables the partners to get to know each other slowly as their relationship develops.

The need to achieve speed is a further internal reason for alliance formation. Many objectives in the business world of the 1990s can be achieved only if the firm acts quickly. In many industries there is a need for almost instantaneous product launches in the retail markets of London, Tokyo and New York if opportunities which may not last for ever are not to be missed. This suggests the need for alliances, which can be activated rapidly to take advantage of such opportunities.

Alliances are not all formed with expansionary aims in mind, however. Many are the result of fear of being taken over. Thus, in the European insurance world, AXA and Groupe Midi of France formed an alliance and eventually merged to avoid being taken over by Generali of Italy. General Electric of the UK has formed an alliance with the its namesake in the US for similar defensive reasons.

HOW DO ALLIANCE FIRMS SELECT A PARTNER?

The creation of a strategic alliance does not, of course, guarantee its long-term survival. Research by the consultancy firms McKinsey and Coopers and Lybrands has shown that there is no better than a 50% survival probability for alliances over a five-year term. This conclusion is, however, put in perspective when considered against Porter's (1987) research into the success of acquisitions, which concluded that the acquisition route to growth was even less likely to be a good one in terms of probable successful outcome.

One of the keys to a successful alliance must be to choose the right partner. This requires the consideration of two basic factors:
1. The synergy or strategic fit between the partners.
2. The cultural fit between them.
The importance of strategic fit and cultural fit are illustrated in Figure 14.2.

Figure 14.2
The best alliances should aim for both strategic and cultural fit.

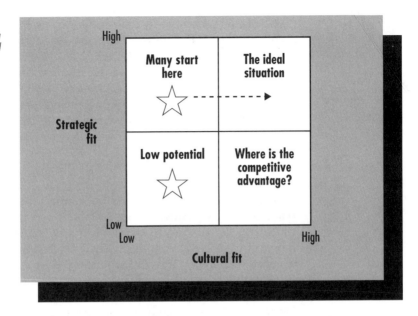

Strategic Fit

A high degree of strategic fit is essential to justify the alliance in the first place. Strategic fit implies that the core competences of the two companies are highly complementary. Whichever partner is sought, it must be one with complementary assets, *i.e.*, to supply some of the resource or competences needed to achieve the alliance objectives. These complementary needs may come about in a number of circumstances:

- **Legal Necessity:** This may be as a result of a legal requirement, particularly in many developing countries, that international companies take a local partner before being granted permission to trade.
- **Reciprocity:** Where the assets of the two partners have a reciprocal strength, *i.e.*, there are synergies such that a newly configured joint value chain leads to greater power than the two companies could hope to exercise separately.
- **Efficiency:** Where an alliance leads to lower joint costs over an important range of areas: scale, scope, transaction, procurement and so forth, then this provides a powerful stimulus to alliance formation.
- **Reputation:** Alliances are set up to create a more prestigious enterprise with a higher profile in the market place, enhanced image, prestige and reputation.

Strategic fit of some form or another is normally the fundamental reason that the alliance has been set up in the first place. It is important both that it is clearly there at the outset, and that it continues to exist for the lifetime of the alliance. Strategic fit implies that the alliance has, or is capable of developing, a clearly identifiable source of sustainable competitive advantage.

239

Whichever partner is sought, it must be one with complementary assets so that it supplies some of the resources or competences needed to achieve the alliance objectives.

If the needs are not reciprocal, then the best course of action is for the partner in need to buy the competence or resource, or if appropriate buy the company possessing it. Cooperative arrangements require the satisfaction of complementary needs on the part of both partners, and thereby lead to competitive advantage.

Cultural Fit

However, for the alliance to endure, cultural adaptation must take place, leading the most successful alliances to graduate to the top right-hand box of Figure 14.2. Cultural fit is an expression that is more difficult to define than strategic fit. In the sense used here, it covers the following factors: the partners have cultural sensitivities sufficiently acute and flexible to be able to work effectively together, and to learn from each other's cultural differences. The partners are balanced in the sense of being of roughly equivalent size, strength and consciousness of need. One is not therefore likely to attempt to dominate the other. Also, their attitude to risk and to ethical considerations is compatible.

It is interesting to note that cultural difficulties are very frequently cited as the reason for the failure of an alliance, but the question of compatible cultures is rarely explicitly addressed when an alliance is being set up. Additionally, it is interesting to note that clearly different cultures, *e.g.*, UK and Japan often make for better alliances than superficially similar ones, *e.g.*, UK and US. Indeed, in support of this point, research (Lu Yuan, 1995) has shown that an ethnically Chinese American national has a far more difficult task running a US–Chinese joint venture in China than an explicitly Caucasian American. Less tolerance is accorded to the ethnically Chinese American for cultural lapses in China.

FORMING THE ALLIANCE

Having found an appropriate partner, the new allies are faced with the question of how to form an alliance in the most appropriate way. Alliances can usefully be classified along three dimensions that define their nature, form and membership:
1. Focused – complex.
2. Joint venture – collaboration.
3. Two partners only – consortium.
Figure 14.3 illustrates the options available from which a choice may be made.

Focused Alliances

The focused alliance is an arrangement between two or more companies, which is set up to meet a clearly defined set of circum-

Figure 14.3
The strategic alliance options.

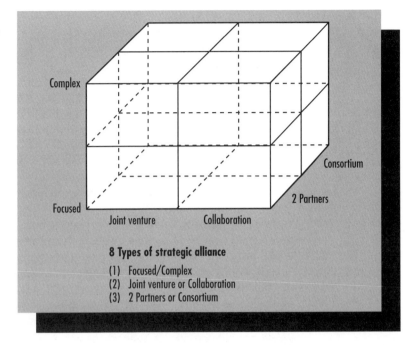

8 Types of strategic alliance
(1) Focused/Complex
(2) Joint venture or Collaboration
(3) 2 Partners or Consortium

stances in a particular way. It normally involves, for each partner, only one major activity or function, or at least is clearly defined and limited in its objectives. Thus, for example, a US company seeking to enter the EU market with a given set of products may form an alliance with a European distribution company as its means of market entry. The US company provides the product, and probably some market and sales literature, and the European company provides the sales force and local know-how. The precise form of arrangement may vary widely, but the nature of the alliance is a focused one with clear remits, and understandings of respective contributions and rewards.

Complex Alliances

Complex alliances may involve the complete activity–cost chains of the partners. The companies recognize that together, they form a potentially far more powerful competitive enterprise than they do apart. Yet they wish to retain their separate identities and overall aspirations, whilst being willing to cooperate with each other over a wide range of activities. Rover–Honda is a good example of a complex alliance. It includes joint R&D, joint manufacturing, joint development and sourcing of parts. It remains separate, however, in the critical marketing and sales areas, and both companies retain clearly distinct images. The alliance involved a 20% share exchange between Rover and Honda's UK manufacturing company. However, since BMW's purchase of Rover, this share exchange has been reversed. It is not, therefore, the justification for the alliance: mutual learning provides this justification. Alliances that begin focused often develop into the complex form if they are successful.

Joint Ventures

Joint ventures involve the creation of a legally separate company from that of the partners. The new company normally starts life with the partners as its shareholders, and with an agreed set of objectives in a specific area of activity. Thus, a US company may set up a joint venture with a UK company to market in the EU. The partners provide finance and other support competences and resources for the joint venture in agreed amounts. The aim of the joint venture is normally that the new company should ultimately become a self-standing entity with its own employees and strategic aims, quite distinct from those of its parent shareholders. Unilever is a good example of a joint venture set up by a Dutch and an English company in the 1920s, and which has grown into a major multi-national enterprise. Joint ventures usually involve non-core activities of the partners, and are characterized by having clear boundaries, specific assets, personnel, and managerial responsibilities. Ultimately, they are divestible by the partners in a way that the non-joint venture form is not. They are the most popular of alliance forms, being responsible for about half of all alliances created in the samples of several alliance researchers.

Collaborations

The collaborative alliance form is employed when partners do not wish to set up a separate joint venture company to provide boundaries to their relationship. This might be because they do not know at the outset where such boundaries should lie, and hence the more flexible collaborative form meets their needs better. Collaborative alliances are also preferred when the partners' core business is the area of the alliances, and therefore assets can not be separated from the core business and allocated to a dedicated joint venture. The collaborative form can be expanded or contracted to meet the partners' needs far more easily than can a joint venture. Rover–Honda is a classic example of the collaboration form of alliance.

The Consortium

The consortium is a distinct form of strategic alliance in that it has a number of partners, and is normally a very large scale activity set up for a very specific purpose, and usually managed in a hands-off fashion from the contributing shareholders. Consortia are particularly common for large scale projects in the defence or aerospace industries where massive funds, and a wide range of specialist competences are required for success. Airbus Industrie is a consortium where a number of European shareholders have set up an aircraft manufacturing company to compete on world markets with Boeing and McDonnell Douglas. The European shareholders, although large themselves, felt the need to create a large enough pool of funds to ensure they reached critical mass in terms of resources for aircraft development, and chose to form an international consortium to do this.

There are, then, eight possible basic configurations of alliance covering the alliance's nature, its form, and the number of partners it has, *i.e.,* focused/two partner/joint venture/complex/consortium venture, and so forth. The alliance type that involves setting up a joint-venture company is currently by far the most popular method. There are also well trodden paths by which alliances evolve. For example, focused alliances that are successful frequently develop into complex alliances, as the partners find other areas for mutual cooperation. Two-partner alliances often recruit further partners, and develop into consortia, as the scale and complexity of opportunities become apparent. Alliances, initially without joint-venture companies, frequently form them subsequently, as they experience difficulty in operating in a partially merged fashion without clear boundaries between the cooperative and the independent parts. It is also quite common for one partner in a joint venture to buy out the other. This need not mean the alliance was a failure. It may have been a considerable success, but the strategic objectives of the two companies may have moved onto different paths.

Other paths of evolution, however, are probably less likely to be followed. Consortia are unlikely to reduce to two-partner alliances. Alliances with joint venture companies are unlikely to revert to a non-joint venture situation, but to keep the alliance in being. Similarly, complex alliances are unlikely to revert to a simple, focused relationship between the partners.

It is not possible to predict definitively which form of cooperative agreement will be adopted in which specific set of circumstances, since certain companies show policy preferences for certain forms rather than others, irrespective of their appropriateness. Most cooperative agreements may be classified into four types:

1. Two-partner joint ventures.
2. Two-partner collaborations.
3. Consortium joint ventures.
4. Collaborative networks.

Firms seeking cooperative arrangements generally choose between these four forms, before moving on to define their relationships in a more specific way.

243

HOW SHOULD THE PARTNERS MANAGE THE ALLIANCE?

The management of an alliance consists of two primary factors:
1. The attitudes of the partners towards each other.
2. The systems and mechanisms chosen to operate the alliance.

Although the mechanisms chosen will obviously vary widely according to the chosen alliance form, the attitudes necessary for success are similar in all forms of alliance. The relationship of the partners, as in a marriage, is a key to the success of the arrangement.

Figure 14.4
The significant management
variables.

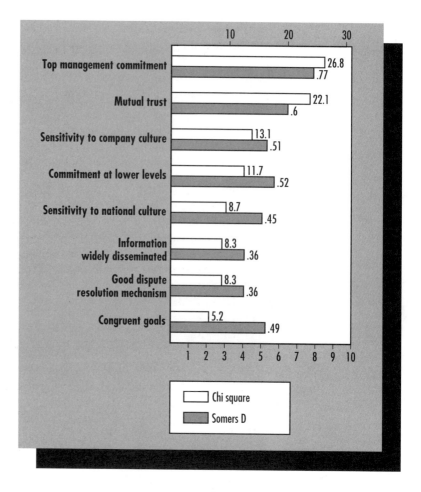

It may not be a sufficient factor by itself, since the successful alliance needs positive quantifiable results, but it is certainly a necessary condition. An appropriate attitude has two major components: commitment and trust.

Lack of commitment can kill an alliance in a very short time. When the Rover–Honda alliance was set up in 1979, commentators were concerned as to whether Rover's commitment to it was matched equally by that of Honda. Rover's economic survival depended upon the alliance and its commitment has been high from the outset. The alliance was less important from Honda's viewpoint. However, the Japanese company has shown an equal degree of commitment throughout, and the alliance has been a very successful one. Other alliances have failed because the partners have not allocated their best people to the project, have placed it low on the priority agenda, or have set up too many alliances, in the hope that at least some would succeed. These attitudes have the seeds of failure within them. Figure 14.4 shows the importance of different factors as revealed from Faulkner's (1994) research into 67 alliances.

Trust is the second key factor for survival. Unless this develops early on in the partnership the alliance soon ceases to be the best

Figure 14.5
AT&T and Olivetti apparently
offer excellent strategic
synergy.

AT&T AND OLIVETTI OFFER EXCELLENT SYNERGY - ON PAPER

1983

AT&T – (=$3–10 billion)	Olivetti – (= $2 billion)
+ Outstanding technology - in the lab, especially in networking	- Weak technology - but excellent market exploitation
+ Massive financial resources and power	- Relatively weak financial position
+ Substantial distribution network in place in USA	- Weak position in USA
- Virtually no distribution in Europe and elsewhere	+ Strong office automation distribution network in Europe. Good distribution elsewhere
- Slow, bureaucratic, paternalistic	+ Fast, market oriented, entrepreneurial
- Accustomed to imposing standards on customers	+ Understanding of the office environment
- No international experience	+ Substantial international experience

Source: Taucher, 1988

organizational arrangement for the partners, as they spend increasing amounts of time and resources monitoring each other's activities as a result of their mutual lack of trust. Trust does not imply naive revelation of company secrets not covered by the alliance agreement. It implies the belief that the partner will act with integrity, and will carry out its commitments. The appropriate attitude must be set from the start. During the negotiation stage, friendliness should be exhibited, and a deal struck that is clearly win–win. These qualities are quite different from those that often characterize takeover negotiations.

Cultural sensitivity can also be the key to alliance success. Many alliances have failed purely as a result of cultural incompatibility. Cultural compatibility does not necessarily imply the existence of similar cultures. Indeed, partners have more to learn from differences than from similarities. It does, however, require a willingness to display cultural sensitivity, and to accept that there is often more than one acceptable way of doing things. A comparison of the partners' cultural profiles will often highlight possible areas of future cultural discord. The major problem between AT&T and Olivetti, as shown in Figure 14.5, probably stemmed from a clash between the contrasting cultures of a bureaucratic US giant corporation in AT&T, and an entrepreneurial Italian marketing company in Olivetti. This may lead to difficulty in working together, to mistrust and ultimately to a growing scepticism as to whether the strategic synergy was there in the first place.

Goal compatibility is vital to the long-term success of a partnership. Of course, the specific goals of the alliance will evolve over

245

time. However, if the goals of the partners at a basic level clash fundamentally, then the alliance cannot but be a short-term opportunistic affair. Compatibility does not necessarily mean the partners' goals must be identical. Rover's current goals are to be an up-market niche player in the automobile industry. Honda has more ambitious goals of global success over a wide product range. There is, however, no fundamental incompatibility in this.

MECHANISMS FOR ALLIANCE MANAGEMENT

The mechanisms for running a joint venture are quite distinct from those of a collaboration. A joint venture, whether two-partner or consortium, involves, by definition, the creation of a separate company distinct from those of the partners. There are therefore two types of relationship to cope with, *i.e.*, the relationship between the partners, and the relationship between each partner and the joint venture company.

In a sense, the most appropriate systems for running a joint venture are also the simplest. The venture should be set up with sufficient resources, guaranteed assistance by the partners whilst it is young, and allowed to get on with the job of realizing its objectives and targets. Involvement by the partners should be limited to board level, except at the request of the venture company. A chief executive should be appointed and given sufficient autonomy to build the joint venture company. Although this seems common sense, it is surprising how many joint ventures falter or fail through the unwillingness of the partners to give them sufficient autonomy and assets, and to realize that the venture will inevitably have objectives that are not fully congruent with those of the partners (Faulkner, 1994). All of the joint ventures researched by Faulkner were deprived of powers that equivalent, competitive, stand-alone companies would certainly have, and were thus handicapped in their pursuit of competitive advantage. Joint venture companies inevitably develop cultures, lives and objectives of their own, and owner–partners frequently find this fact difficult to adjust come to terms with. The retired managing director of the EVC joint venture between ICI and Enichem is on record as claiming that both partners expected him to pursue their interests rather than those of the joint venture company he was employed to run, and both accused him of being biased in favour of the interest of their partner.

The relationship between the partners is different in nature between partners in collaborations. Here, the boundary spanning mechanism is the area crucial for success. The interface between the companies is the area where culture clashes, or conflict of objectives, will probably show themselves first. The establishment of a 'gateway' executive or office, as a channel for all contacts between the partners, at least during the settling-down period of the alliance, is a good way to avoid unnecessary misunderstandings.

In all circumstances, a good mechanism to resolve disputes should be established before the alliance begins to operate. If this

is left to be worked out as necessary, the risk that its absence will lead to a souring of the relationship between the partners at the ultrasensitive early stage of the partnership will be too high.

An effective system for disseminating alliance information widely within the partner companies is a further important factor for ensuring that both, or all partners gain in learning to the greatest degree possible from the cooperative arrangement.

Finally, a procedure in the event of a wish by either party to end the alliance should be agreed at the outset, since this will increase the feeling of security by both parties that an end to the alliance does not represent a potential catastrophe.

WHAT HAPPENS TO COOPERATIONS IN THE LONG RUN?

Bleeke and Ernst, in a 1995 article in the *Harvard Business Review*, claim that there are six possible outcomes to alliances, including the dissolution of the alliances and the swallowing of one partner by the other. Only one solution was that the alliance continue successfully, largely unchanged over an indefinite time period. It is certainly true to say that the initial situation of two firms running an enterprise may well lead to the ultimate outcome of the simpler type, in which only one firm runs the alliance. However, this is not necessarily the case.

One key factor in the life of an alliance seems to be that, if it ceases to evolve, it starts to decay. Faulkner's research (1994) showed the factors shown in Figure 14.6 as the key ones to ensure alliance evolution.

The reality of a successful alliance is that it not only trades competences but also demonstrates synergies. Whereas the resource dependency perspective identifies a key part of a company's motivation for forming an alliance, the successful evolution of that alliance depends upon the realization of synergies between the companies, and the establishment of a level competitive advantage for the partners, that each could not as easily realize alone.

Important conditions for evolution include:
- Perception of balanced benefits from the alliance by both partners.
- The development of strong bonding factors.
- The regular development of new projects between the partners.
- The adoption of a philosophy of constant learning by the partners.

The comparison of an alliance with a marriage is a very relevant one. Western marriages could be regarded as unstable as they currently have a high failure rate. In fact, they have many of the qualities of strategic alliances. The partners retain separate identities but collaborate over a whole range of activities. Stability is threatened if one partner becomes excessively dependent on the other, or if the benefits are perceived to be all one way. But nonetheless, successful marriages are stable, and for the same reason as successful alliances. They depend upon trust, commitment, mutual learning, flexibility and a feeling by both partners that they are stronger together than

Figure 14.6
The significant evolution
variables.

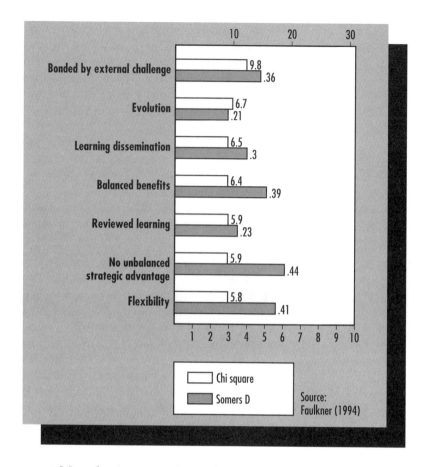

apart. Many businesses point to the need to negotiate decisions in alliances as a weakness, in contrast to companies, where hierarchies make decisions. This is to confuse stability with clarity of decision making, and would lead to the suggestion that dictatorships are more stable than democracies.

In this analogy, it is commitment to the belief that the alliance represents the best available arrangement that is the foundation of its stability. The need for resolution of the inevitable tensions in such an arrangement can as easily be presented as a strength, rather than as an inherent problem. It leads to the need to debate, to see and evaluate, and to reconcile contrasting viewpoints.

SUMMARY

Strategic alliances and other forms of cooperative strategy are now widely recognized as appropriate interorganizational forms to meet certain environmental and internal firm conditions. The alliances have distinctive characteristics such as speed of creation, flexibility, opportunities for specialization, access to additional resources, and risk limitation which make them attractive when compared to the alternatives of internal development, acquisition, or market purchases. This is particularly the case in volatile, uncertain environments, where the need to negotiate some resource security and to develop a rapid, global presence has become of paramount importance to the survival of the firm, and the development of competitive advantage in a world increasingly dominated by multinationals. Cooperative strategy is, therefore, not an alternative to competitive strategy, but is a means of achieving sustainable competitive advantage, the better to pursue competitive strategy in relation to rivals outside the alliance. It is an important way in which the corporate centre can resource its SBUs with competences otherwise difficult to obtain.

chapter

Controlling the Corporation

$\mathbf{A}$ corporate centre that has carried out its primary tasks of selecting which business areas to operate in and has resourced the various businesses in the corporation appropriately, then faces its third primary task: how to **control** the enterprise. This involves the coordination and configuration of the corporation, by which we mean organizing who does what and where, and then ensuring that it all happens efficiently.

The most commonly recommended structure of the multi-business corporation has changed in recent decades from the form of a holding company with the centre allocating resources but having little involvement in the businesses, to the M-form, or multi-divisional structure, in which the corporate centre takes strategic decisions, and the strategic business units take operational ones. In this way, the perpetual issue of centralization versus decentralization is resolved, at least in principle, although the debate continues to rage as contingent circumstances determine differing interpretations of this simple formula.

250

Figure 15.1
There are three major model organizational styles that operate effectively.

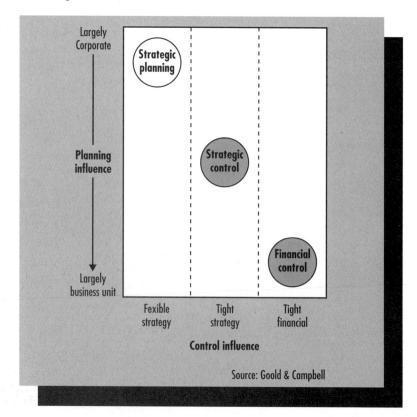

Largely Corporate

Strategic planning

Planning influence

Strategic control

Financial control

Largely business unit

Fexible strategy

Tight strategy

Tight financial

Control influence

Source: Goold & Campbell

In the real world of actual company structures, company forms are generally complex and unique to each corporation, at least in their detail. The balance between centralization and decentralization is constantly shifting to meet varying specific circumstances and changes in the internal power balance. Research by Goold and Campbell (1987) helps to crystallize certain predominant forms.

To attempt to discover the most appropriate structure for the multi-business corporation, the researchers investigated 16 major UK-based companies. They discovered that there was no single right way to organize in the views of the companies, but three distinct organizational paradigms emerged when the involvement of the centre and the SBUs was analysed from the viewpoint of strategic planning and operational control. The three different styles were named **strategic planning**, **strategic control** and **financial control** (as shown in Figure 15.1), and each was regarded as the most appropriate style in certain sets of internal and external circumstances.

THE STRATEGIC PLANNING STYLE

The strategic planning style was generally used in corporations that operate in one industry, *e.g.*, BP in the oil industry. The company has a core business philosophy, and the corporate centre is experienced in the industry and works with middle management to develop strategy. Typically, the corporation is closely integrated with few bought-in services, and has a culture of strong leadership from the top. A matrix structure is likely to operate, as the corporation will have a large number of staff departments at the centre able to provide specialist expertise to the business units. This style is very flexible in its mode of operation, but often fraught with internal politics, since clear performance measures related to individuals are difficult to apply in objective terms. The outline top management organization chart is likely to resemble that depicted in Figure 15.2.

251

Figure 15.2
Typical organizations of the strategic planning style.

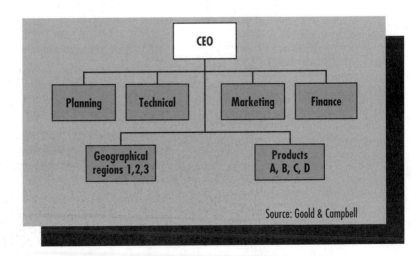

Source: Goold & Campbell

Figure 15.3
The strategic planning style.

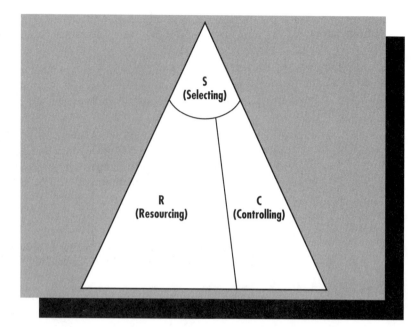

The strategic planning style is seen as most appropriate for businesses where there are close links between product groups, and where the investment decisions tend to involve large sums of money in relation to the size of the company, and to have long pay-back periods. Effective power comes very much from the top, and this is appropriate, since top management have often spent many years in the industry, and worked their way up. The corporate centre typically has large staff departments which ensure that the corporation operates as a seamless whole.

If we think of the corporate triangle in which the three primary corporate tasks of selecting, resourcing and controlling are depicted, the strategic planning style might be illustrated as in Figure 15.3.

The selecting function is fairly small, as the corporation's growth mode is organic development, and the issue of acquiring other companies or branching out into other industries is rarely high on the corporate agenda. Resourcing, in the form of internal investment and the provision of central services, is strong, as is central control.

THE FINANCIAL CONTROL STYLE

In contrast to strategic planning, the financial control style involves very little operational interaction between the corporate centre and the SBUs. The portfolio of businesses may have no connection between the businesses in a market or product sense. Indeed, this is perceived to be of little importance, since the existence of potential synergies between them is generally not seen as an important issue. However, they may all have been bought to a common formula, *e.g.*, in a mature industry, with undervalued assets suffering from undisciplined management.

Figure 15.4
Typical organization of the
financial control style.

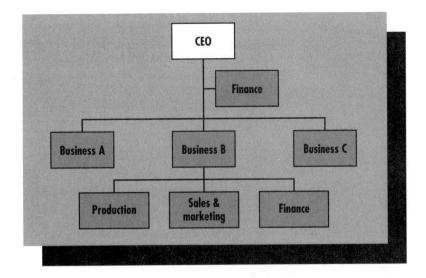

The corporate centre is peopled by financial controllers, investment appraisers and deal makers. They see their role as exerting tight financial control on the SBUs, and working with the portfolio, by buying and selling companies to maximize shareholder value. The Hanson Group is a good example of the financial control style. In this style, the SBU general managers are chosen because they are highly motivated by the opportunity for recognized successful performance and the consequent rewards. They develop their own strategies and carry them out. If they are successful, they are well rewarded; if not, they tend to move on, or the business unit may even be sold. Investment decisions tend to be relatively small with short pay-back periods, so it is rare for a high technology company requiring large amounts of R&D expenditure to fit comfortably into a financial control group. That General Electric is run in a financial control style is perhaps one of its limitations, as it makes difficult long-term decisions involving large amounts of R&D with uncertain results.

An essential feature of this organizational style is that the SBUs are easy to decouple in the event of a business sale. However, because of the difficulty of realizing many of the scale and scope economies that arise in large integrated companies, such a style is unlikely to cause a successful international major corporation in mainstream industry markets to evolve. The thinking of such a corporation is likely to be short-termist, and cost leadership is likely to be a dominant strategy. Its typical organization structure involves a very lean head office with staff positions limited to financial officers, as illustrated in Figure 15.4.

In contrast to the strategic planning style, the corporate triangle of financial control companies would show a dominant selection process, followed by the control function, especially financial control. Resourcing, particularly the development of cross-corporation competences, would feature far less, as shown in Figure 15.5. Each SBU has a full set of functional departments to make divestment easier.

253

Figure 15.5
The financial control style.

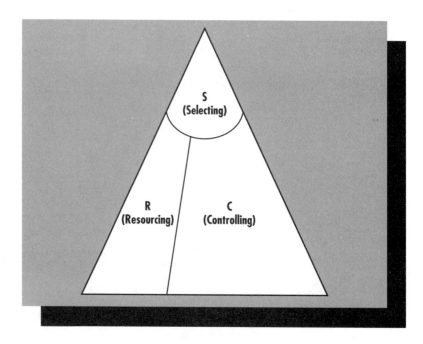

THE STRATEGIC CONTROL STYLE

This style is midway between the strategic planning and the financial control styles. For this reason it is less stable but possibly also more flexible and more likely to be adopted in the more varied systems required by the increasingly turbulent economic situations of the global economy. It is close to the paradigm of the M-form organization, in which the centre is responsible for strategy and overall resource allocation, and the divisions for operational matters.

The strategic control style is normally used where the portfolio of SBUs can be grouped into divisions under some classification, *e.g.*, retail division, electronics division, or perhaps financial services division. It might be thought that divisions should be configured where groups of SBUs exhibit similar core competences, but this is not necessarily the case in the evidence provided by the research.

The strategic role is adopted by both the centre and the SBUs, with the centre exercising its corporate strategy role and thereby setting parameters for the determination of competitive strategy for the divisions and SBUs. The organizational structure of the strategic control style is as shown in Figure 15.6, with both finance and planning appearing as staff departments at the centre, and other staff roles being carried out at either divisional or SBU level.

Synergies in this organizational form are sought at divisional level, but much less at corporate level, due to the relatively autonomous power of the divisional barons.

Although this is a most popular organizational form for the multi-business corporation, it has problems with focus, as it is difficult

Figure 15.6
Typical organization for the
strategic control style.

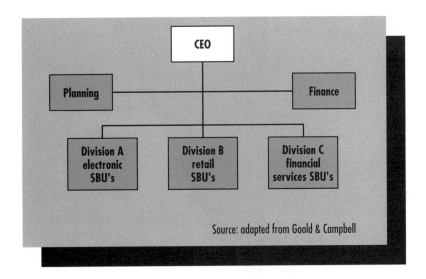

Source: adapted from Goold & Campbell

to prescribe where the power lies, and where the added value is expected to come from. Adopting this form can bring about a situation where the corporate CEO has been reduced to a holding company role whilst the divisional heads exercise all the real power in running the corporation. Contrastingly, a situation may arise with a powerful corporate CEO with divisional heads acting as little more than highly paid messengers for him.

As a result, the risk is always high that strategic control style companies will break up. Their divisions may seek separate stock exchange quotations as it is demonstrated to the satisfaction of the shareholders that insufficient value is added by the centre to justify its cost. This has happened in the UK in a number of major corporations, notably RACAL, ICI and Courtaulds.

In terms of the corporate triangle, the strategic control style is the most balanced. The selecting function is well developed, as a significant part of the growth of corporations of this style tends to come from the recognition of new opportunities in new areas, and acquisitions feature strongly in corporate strategy. However, resourcing and control at divisional level in particular are also key tasks for the strategic control corporation (Figure 15.7).

A major advantage of the strategic control style, however, is that it is ideally configured to form parts of Handy's (1989) federated enterprises of the future. Under this concept, parts of companies, *e.g.*, divisions, or even SBUs of strategic control companies, from a number of multi-business corporations create alliances or federated enterprises to meet a market need, in the expectation that when that market need ceases to exist, a part can easily uncouple and recouple with others in a new configuration. Such a concept potentially overcomes many of the inflexibility disadvantages found in the integrated traditional multinational organization.

Figure 15.7
The strategic control style.

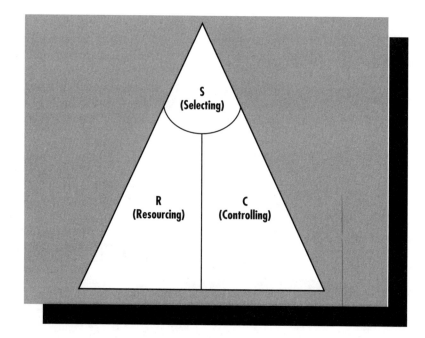

SELECTING AN APPROPRIATE STYLE

The adoption of one or other of the three primary forms of multi-business organization styles is, in Goold and Campbell's view, dependent upon two primary forces: an environmental force and a personal force.

In certain circumstances the strategic planning style is appropriate, *e.g.*, the core business is in one industry, and clear synergies exist from running an integrated corporation. Furthermore, being a winner in this industry involves using judgement to make large scale investment decisions which are fraught with considerable uncertainty. The people running such a corporation need therefore to be very experienced in the industry in question and temperamentally the chief executive needs to be a person willing and keen to get involved in the business and not just its balance sheet, profit-and-loss account and share price.

In companies operating the financial control style, the personality of the chief executive and his inner team is perhaps even more important. The chief executive needs to have an accountant's frame of mind and to be a deal-maker and good negotiator. It is perhaps best if he does not become too attached to any of the businesses he buys, as this will inhibit his enthusiasm for selling them, should this be the best course of action to maximize shareholder value. In fact, both Lord Hanson and Lord White were reported as visiting their individual companies only most reluctantly, for just this reason.

As a result of the corporate heads' personalities and views of their role, the SBU portfolios of such companies are likely to be extremely varied by product and industry, but to have the common characteristics of little synergy between them, and to be immediately available for divestment should a buyer come along at the right price.

For the strategic control style, the circumstances are less clear. The top executives need to be of both a financial and a strategic frame of mind, and corporate skills are needed at both the centre and the divisional level. The portfolio also needs to have some internal logic, in that divisions should ideally contain SBUs with some synergies between them, or share similar core competences.

The Goold and Campbell analysis of alternative styles for running a corporation is valuable, since it focuses on three clear, separate paradigms, and thereby emphasizes some of the key factors influencing organizational choice. The paradigms are rarely met in a pure form, and most multi-business organizations exhibit characteristics of one but with aspects of another. In fact, the researchers were able to fill in the other boxes in their planning control matrix, but chose to focus on the three styles described, as they most fully differentiated themselves from each other, and embodied clear philosophies and their organizational implications.

OUTCOME AND BEHAVIOUR CONTROL

Control relates not merely to systems but also in a significant way to the monitoring philosophies adopted in a company.

Lorsch and Allen (1973) suggest that:

...the internal characteristics of an effective organization are contingent upon the work it must perform in dealing with its environment.

This is basic contingency theory and is fundamentally supportive of Chandler's contention (1962) that a firm's organizational structure should be selected in order the best to carry out the corporation's chosen strategy. It is nowadays recognized that there is a degree of iteration in this process, in that corporations already have organizational structures, and the strategies they are able to carry out are to some degree also dependent upon the limitations imposed by those structures. Notwithstanding this caveat, few would dispute that the organization needs to be so adjusted to be capable of carrying out the chosen strategy most effectively. If this is so, the corporate management planner needs to develop a control philosophy as well as a structural style.

In addition to selecting a style as suggested above, the corporate centre needs to so configure and coordinate the organization as to reduce agency problems to a minimum. By an agency problem, we mean the tendency of managers to be motivated by factors other than the ultimate optimization of the performance of the corporation. They may be motivated to maximize SBU performance, sometimes to the detriment of corporate performance or even more narrowly to maximize personal satisfactions at the expense of both SBU and corporation.

In order to do this, the corporate centre needs to adopt a philosophy that will become central to the corporation: of monitoring and controlling its personnel either by outcome or by behaviour. Whichever of these methods is adopted, the life of the corporation for its executives will be very different.

Outcome control involves measuring an executive by what he or she achieves, without being too closely concerned with the time or method spent achieving it. Thus, in a university, outcome control of a tutor's performance at teaching would be measured to a large degree by the performance of his or her students in examinations and other tests of knowledge and ability.

Behaviour control is quite different. In this form of monitoring, a tutor's performance would be evaluated by having an inspector sit in at classes periodically with a check-list of factors to look for in the tutor's behaviour. In this case, the tutor could be graded highly, even if the relevant students failed their exams.

Organizations dedicated to outcome control are relatively uninterested in the number of hours an executive is present in the office, and adopt an incentive system biased strongly towards the achievement of measurable results or outcomes. Under a behavioural control system the executive's manner, political skills, actual decision processes and ability to gain a reputation as a good company man are the keys to success. Under such a system, an executive may reach high rank with only minimal achievement if his face fits. Behaviour control is more likely to be adopted in strategic planning style companies, where the link between decisions and actual corporate performance is difficult to determine – in part because so many people have a hand in all major decisions. Outcome control, on the other hand, is more closely associated with financial control style companies, where actual financial results determine people's fate.

All companies, of course, employ both control methods to some degree, and outcome control is more likely to be adopted in direct relation to seniority. Few would judge the chief executive on the hours he keeps if company results are exceptionally good. Behaviour control is, however, almost universally exercised on the shop floor. Nonetheless, the culture and style of an organization is strongly influenced by whether corporate controllers have a bias in system selection and maintenance towards outcome or behaviour control. In efficiency and motivational terms

> ...outcome control is preferable when output and effort correlate closely without being distorted by exogenous factors. Behaviour control is preferable either when there is much uncertainty or many uncontrollable events so that output and effort are poorly correlated, or when senior management understands which behavioural items most affect outcomes and so can program management tasks. As a consequence behaviour control requires an operating expertise that is found when the resource is fairly specific. (Collis and Montgomery, 1995)

Figure 15.8
Different forms of control
philosophy.

DIFFERENT FORMS OF CONTROL PHILOSOPHY		
	Outcome	Behaviour
Organization structure	Semi-autonomous SBUs	Integrated organization often functional
Rewards & incentives	Bonuses a large part of total pay and individually assessed	Low bonuses, long-term career progression based on qualitative criteria
Resourcing allocation	Tight capital control	Detailed financial plans
Personnel	Hire & fire: little internal job rotation	Internally developed career plans
Culture	The rugged individualist	A common corporate culture emphasising firm identity
Corporate office	Tiny & focused on financial appraisal and control	Experienced corporate management
Management information systems	Aggregated financial reporting the only standardized systems	Many common systems to standardize behaviour

The two different forms of control lead to very different systems for some of the main organizational variables (Figure 15.8).

AN ORGANIZATIONAL ECONOMICS INSIGHT

Ultimately an organizational style must be adopted for a corporation in which all the organization variables, *e.g.*, structure, systems, rewards, culture, and so forth, are congruent. Analyses like those of Goold and Campbell, and Collis and Montgomery, help to develop consistent philosophy, systems and supporting structures, related to the environmental contingencies in order to carry out a determined generic strategy.

Organizational economics can give helpful further insights. This discipline defines the organization of the corporation as a set of three fundamental factors (Jensen, 1983):

■ Information structure.
■ Allocation of decision rights.
■ Incentive and measurement schemes.

The information structure indicates who knows what about the corporation's current situation, and at what level of detail. The allocation of decision rights indicates who, at each level, is involved in the making of each decision inside the corporation. This paints a picture of both the formal and informal allocation of authority and power in the corporation. The incentive and measurement schemes describe the reward and punishment mechanisms that exist in order to motivate behaviour. They are also formal and informal, including both financial rewards and peer group respect.

The Mckinsey 7 S and other organizational frameworks merely suggest reader friendly ways of thinking of these three factors. Thus, aligning a multi-business organizational structure and its attendant systems is no more than an exercise in aligning an information structure, the systems of decision rights, and incentives and measurement schemes in such a way as to minimize the costs and maximize the effectiveness of running the corporation. To the extent that the wrong decisions are taken in carrying out this alignment, costs are incurred through:

- Information transfer losses.
- Agency costs associated with inferior incentives.
- Cooperative decision making between units that have a misallocation of resources.
- Imperfect decision making.

The task facing organizational decision makers at a corporate level is no less daunting than that described above. Although in our current state of corporate data development, we have no means of measuring the degree of the extra governance costs incurred by mistakes made in this exercise, such costs *are* incurred, and may crucially affect the profitability of the corporation.

SUMMARY

Corporate strategy is about adding value to whatever the individual businesses in the corporation can achieve by themselves. This is done, in the main, by the corporation carrying out its three major tasks:

1. Selecting businesses to be in which match external opportunities to internal competences.
2. Resourcing them appropriately, including going out and acquiring new competences.
3. Controlling the corporation to the greatest level of efficiency and effectiveness possible.

Selection is largely an analytical process, allied to one of judgement, when the future possibilities are to be considered.

Resourcing is a major ongoing task. It involves a careful audit of SBUs' existing core competences, followed by an assessment of the level of those competences needed to succeed in the selected product/market segments. This will lead to the corporate centre ensuring that the optimal level of economies of scope and scale are achieved, that the appropriate level of risk is adopted, that any synergies between the SBUs are realized, and that extra central services are provided. It may also involve action to increase the resource base through merger, acquisition or the various forms of joint development with other companies.

The controlling function involves setting up and running a management system that will ensure that the resources are used to optimal effect. Whilst the multi-divisional form of corporate organizational structure has been widely adopted by major corporations, there are many variants of this form developed to meet different circumstances and company philosophies. The three identified styles of strategic planning, strategic control and financial control are three of these variants.

Thus, if a strategic planning style is adopted, there would be expected to be an emphasis on selecting product/markets within the home industry. Emphasis would be placed on the achievement of synergies within the corporation, provision of central services and growth by internal development. Control would be strongly behaviour based, with a strong corporate culture developed over the years.

If the strategic control style were adopted, the selection function would stretch to a far wider range of product markets, but would be related to a small number of specific corporate divisions. Resourcing would be far more varied. Merger, acquisition, joint development and internal development would all be routinely used to develop the corporation's competences. Methods of control would be more likely to be outcome based rather than behaviour based.

The financial control style would imply a refusal to provide central services or to look for synergies between SBUs. Acquisition and divestment activity would be the bedrock of growth and shareholder value enhancement, allied to whatever internal development could be achieved under tight financial constraints. Outcome control would be central to performance evaluation.

The nature of the controlling style adopted therefore determines, to some degree, the way in which the corporate centre will carry out its mission of adding value to the SBUs, whether this be through achieving scale or scope economies, diversification activity, the achievement of internal synergies, or the provision of central services.

It is not the case, however, that the controlling style adopted is deterministically a result of the specific circumstances in which the corporation finds itself. Such factors as the management philosophy of the chief executive and his team also play a prominent part. It would, for example, be difficult to imagine Lord Hanson operating in a strategic planning style. A fair degree of choice exists in controlling styles, and evolutionary forces are often constrained by strong institutional factors that operate in favour of the existing control style, whatever its merits or demerits, in any situation short of corporate crisis.

International
Corporate Strategy

A part from the actions the corporate centre may take directly, its three fundamental tasks as we have emphasized in this book are business area selection, appropriate resourcing, and control. This applies equally to international operations as it does domestically. However, the internationalization of a corporation needs separate treatment, since the configuration and coordination of activities of a corporation on a global scale provide a more daunting and certainly a more complex task than is involved in carrying out such activities on a purely national scale. Yet, the same tasks of selecting, resourcing and controlling still underly the endeavour.

A critical question is whether to operate locally or globally. One of the key issues in operating globally is how to organize one's enterprise so that it is possible to compete with local companies, who are likely to be equipped with better knowledge of the local market in both demand and supply terms, than the new foreign entrant can hope to have. International strategy must be a very important corporate subject area for all but the determinedly local niche player.

The first question that must be addressed is 'Why should the development of an international strategy be any different from the development of a domestic one?' At first sight the answer seems to be that it should not be fundamentally different. Competitive strategy is about being able to achieve the highest level of PUV at the lowest cost in relation to one's competitors in each product/market, whether the market is national or international. Similarly, corporate strategy is about having excellent core competences in relation to one's competitors', and developing them so that they become key competences in all the markets in which one chooses to compete. This must be so whether the firm is competing nationally or internationally.

The next question is whether one has the option of defining a market as national or global, and here the answer is clearly 'No'. The preferences of the customers, and the cost structures of the operating firms make this decision. If Sony is able to bring its electronic products to the UK at competitive prices, and UK customers find them acceptable as alternative sources of PUV to those of local suppliers, then the consumer electronics market has become international. This will not, of course, apply to all products. The market for corrugated cardboard is said to have a radius of about 50 miles. Corrugated cardboard is a low value commodity in which little differentiation is possible and, once 50 miles have been traveled, the local producer is able to realize lower costs than the travelling producer. The same applies to building aggregates.

There is, then, a strategic market which is defined by the relative homogeneity of consumer tastes, and by the company's possible cost structures that enable it to be a credible competitor over varying distances. As Levitt remarked in the 1960s and Ohmae and others have confirmed more recently, with the passing of each year more and more products and even services fall into the category of global competition, as tastes become increasingly similar around the world. Technologies are also becoming global, and transportation costs are becoming a smaller and smaller percentage of delivered costs.

The question of why we should regard international strategy as in any way different from national strategy reasserts itself. The answer, of course, is that the nature of strategic analysis is in no way different, although there are factors that need to be considered in formulating international strategy that are typically less important in trading within national boundaries. These factors fall into three categories:

1. Those that determine which segments to **select**, and whether or not global competition is involved.
2. Those that affect the company's ability to **resource** and deliver the product at a competitive price anywhere in the world, such as political factors, and cost structures, *i.e.*, configuration.
3. Those that are concerned with how a company should organize itself to **control** its international activities, *i.e.*, coordination.

263

SELECTING INTERNATIONAL SEGMENTS

A useful framework to help the manager decide how to approach the selection task in his international strategy is that provided by a schema relating strategic objectives to three key bases of potential competitive advantage developed by Ghoshal (1987) as shown in Figure 16.1.

This framework holds that there are three basic strategic objectives that need to be considered in a global strategy:

1. **Efficiency.** Carrying out current activities to a required quality at lowest cost. This is the most frequently emphasized objective in the literature. Indeed, it is often the only objective mentioned.
2. **Risk management.** Managing and balancing the risks inherent in operating in a number of diverse countries, *e.g.*, exchange rate risks, political risks, or raw material sourcing risks.
3. **Innovation learning and adaptation.** The opportunity to learn from the different societies and cultures in which one operates.

This organizing framework takes the three types of strategic objective identified above and relates them to what are identified as the three key sources of competitive advantage, namely:

1. **National differences.** Competitive advantage can come from exploiting differences in input and output markets in different

Figure 16.1
Global strategy, an organizing
framework.

SOURCES OF COMPETITIVE ADVANTAGE			
Strategic objectives	National differences	Scale economies	Scope economies
Achieving efficiency in current operations	Benefiting from differences in factor costs wages and cost of capital	Expanding and exploring potential scale economies in each activity	Sharing of investments and costs across products, markets and businesses
Managing risks	Managing different kinds of risks arising from market or policy-induced changes in comparative advantages of different countries	Balancing scale with strategic and operational flexibility	Portfolio diversification of risks and creation of options and side-bets
Innovation learning and adaptation	Learning from societal differences in organizational and managerial processes and systems	Benefiting from experience cost reduction and innovation	Shared learning across organizational components in different products, markets or businesses

source: Ghoshal (1986)

countries. For example, low wage countries are perhaps the most commonly cited examples of such factors, and can reasonably be said to have led to the decline and fall of the textile industry in the UK, and the sports-shoe industry in most of Europe.

2. **Scale economies.** These provide a source of competitive advantage if one firm is able to so configure its activities that each is able to operate at the optimal economic scale for minimal unit costs, while competitors fail to do this. Of course, achieving optimal scale economies globally may lead to dangerous inflexibility, creating high risk where changing exchange rates alter or destroy these potential economies after plant has been brought on-line to take advantage of them.

3. **Scope economies.** These are most easily exemplified in the use of global brand names such as Coca-Cola and McDonalds, but can be found in any area of the firm's activities where resources used to produce or market one product in one country can be reused virtually without cost to do the same for other products and in other countries. Technology, IT, and any learning or skills are further examples of areas of potential scope economies.

The organizing framework described enables the global decision taker to identify the potential sources of global competitive advantage available to his firm, and to cross-reference them to the three basic types of strategic objective – efficiency, risk and learning – with the ultimate objective of deciding where, why and how to compete internationally.

> ### RESOURCING GLOBAL PRODUCTION

Let us deal now with the factors influencing configuration. This is concerned with the issue of which parts of the value chain for a product should be produced within the company and which outsourced, and where that production should take place: in the home country, the Far East or elsewhere. The configuration profile is influenced by a number of barriers that incur costs.

Traditional Barriers

There are a number of factors that have traditionally ensured that most markets remain local. However, some of these are becoming progressively less important. Global products had traditionally been considered to have limited potential in many industries, since people in different parts of the world living in very diverse cultures were assumed to have different tastes and values, and therefore to require different products and services to satisfy them. To some extent, that is still true; more tea is sold per head in the UK than elsewhere in the world; the Far East consumes more rice than the West, and the West more potatoes than the Far East. Yet such variations are far less common in the manufactured products area. Levitt (1983) comments that:

> ...the same single standardized products – autos, steel, chemicals, petroleum, cement, agricultural commodities and equipment, industrial and commercial construction, banking, insurance, computers, semiconductors, transport, electronic instruments, pharmaceuticals, and telecommunications [are sold] largely in the same single ways everywhere.

265

This is undoubtedly true, and the list gets longer every year.

So much for the supposed demand limitations for would-be global products. What about the supply side? There are a number of traditional barriers that make would-be international traders' jobs more difficult, for example:

- Tariffs, quotas and other market-distorting devices.
- Foreign ownership rules. In many developed nations, Western companies are prohibited from setting up local companies without major shareholdings being held by locals.
- Languages and cultures. These can provide important inhibitors to, for example, a Western company marketing abroad, and require, at the very least, packaging messages in different languages.
- Transport costs. If other costs are equal, transport costs can make the product from afar uncompetitive on price, especially for low-value, high-volume products.
- Currencies. The problem of exchange rates, and of shipping into a market or manufacturing a product in a country with

different legal, and tax system can make international trade very hazardous.

The perceived globalization of markets during the 1980s and 1990s has come about through the marginalization of the importance of, or complete elimination of, many of the traditional barriers to trade. The spread of Western culture through films, videos, travel and satellite television has done much to homogenize tastes. There has even been some movement the other way, with Eastern food, so called ethnic clothes, and *objets d'art* becoming acceptable and more common in the West.

Many of the supply side costs also have become less important. Larger trading blocs and international trade agreements have emerged, *e.g.*, the EU, ASEAN, GATT and the North American FTA, to reduce the levels of tariffs and, where possible, eliminate quotas and domestic subsidies, except for agricultural ones. Fewer countries now require local majority shareholdings in joint ventures set up with foreign companies and, where they do, the foreign companies have learnt to live with this and operate in a multicultural way.

Language barriers remain to some degree. Increasingly, however, English is becoming the language of international trade and any company wishing to operate globally is virtually required to become proficient in it.

The remaining traditional barriers are transport costs and exchange rates. Transport costs are falling, but they remain an inhibitor to competitive global trade, the importance of which varies with the value and volume of the articles traded. Transport costs are virtually irrelevant to international trade in diamonds, but of considerable importance in limiting such trade as in corrugated cardboard. Exchange rates, however, will remain of considerable importance, whilst every nation maintains a unique currency and retains the right to devalue or revalue it against other currencies, when the government or the market deems this advisable. To be caught with cash or debtors in a newly devalued or depreciated currency can wipe out any profit at a stroke.

How, then, is the corporate decision to become a global enterprise to be taken? Since the global trade inhibitors listed above are now so reduced in strength, the decision must be taken as it would be for domestic products. A customer matrix and a producer matrix should be constructed for the strategic market of each product/market. It will then become apparent which markets the company has products for, and which of the markets' required key competences are close to the firm's core competences. Market size should also be assessed to ensure it is sufficiently interesting for the firm. A separate set of matrices will need to be developed for each country, since not only are the dimensions of PUV likely to be different by country, or at least to have different weightings, but perceived price is likely to be different for each country for reasons of exchange rate, local taxation and cost of living, and the impact of transport and perhaps other costs will need to be factored into the producer matrix.

Figure 16.2
Configuration check-list.

CONFIGURATION CHECK-LIST

- Identify target markets

- Analyse needs and PUV's in these markets

- Determine if these markets are international and

- How PUVs differ across countries

- Identify key competences necessary to deliver PUV to each segment

- Determine similarities of key competences across segments

- Identify international barriers to serving these markets

- Determine whether processes would be better configured and controlled centrally or locally

- Derive appropriate global-local configuration

Figure 16.2
Configuration check-list.

Configuring the Activities

The firm also needs to configure and coordinate its activities so that it comes out in a strong position on the customer and producer matrices relevant to the particular countries in which it seeks to operate. The tension in international commercial activity between the demand led needs of local tastes and the supply led requirements for global integration needs to be resolved individually, market by market (Stopford and Wells, 1972).

The check-list in Figure 16.2 identifies the thought processes necessary to solve some of the key issues identified above on the global–local questions that have to be decided if the corporation wishes to become well configured and coordinated internationally.

The configuration issue addresses the questions of where the multinational should source the factors it needs to produce its products, and which activities it should carry out itself, and which it should subcontract, or otherwise arrange with others to have produced. The latter question can be tackled by use of the make–buy–ally matrix described above, only with the option extended to cover possible global sourcing of particular activities. Help in addressing the former issue of where particular activities might be carried out can be obtained through the use of Dunning's eclectic theorem.

Dunning's Eclectic Theorem

Dunning (1984) establishes the basic reasons why multinational corporations are able to achieve competitive and comparative advantage in his eclectic approach, and why they decide to produce abroad rather than merely to export. This has three conditions attached to it: ownership, internalization and localization.

- **Ownership** factors imply that the company owns certain key advantageous competitive aspects in certain markets, *e.g.*, strong brand names, specific and unique technology or particular and relevant know-how.
- **Internalization** suggests that there are advantages to internalizing these ownership factors. Thus, it would not be wise to franchise them, as this might lead to the loss of proprietary information. It is vital to carry out one's own R&D internally, since this is the most frequent source of innovation, and innovation is the driver of future competitive advantage.
- **Localization** means that the multinational finds it an advantage to locate its factory in a particular location, *e.g.*, to take advantage of low cost labour or to get inside the EU tariff barriers. The localization criterion requires that there is at least one key immobile factor of production. The locational factor is key, since otherwise the firm would elect to export from its more familiar, and already tested, home base.

If the internalization condition is weakened, the opportunity for strategic alliances emerges. The theory of foreign direct investment, and of alternative organizational forms to develop business across frontiers, is set out effectively by Rugman (1985), who develops a rational decision tree for choosing between the various alternatives.

Dunning's schema is called eclectic because the actual circumstances which make becoming a multinational the appropriate solution are many, varied and particular to a set of circumstances. However, in Dunning's schema they will always have the three characteristics of ownership, internalization and localization. Thus, with ownership only, the company could export to a licensee, and subcontract virtually any of its activities. With internalization only, it could operate from a home base and found all its international activities on export trade, as international traders did generally prior to the nineteenth century. With ownership and internalization, the company is committed to carrying out certain key activities itself, lest it lose the advantages to a competitor. And with all three – ownership, internalization and localization – it is committed to setting up abroad in some form to meet the criteria. In other words, it has to become a genuine multinational operator.

Application of the eclectic theorem to the resourcing problem should enable the firm pursuing a global strategy to get its unit costs down sufficiently to become price competitive, and to establish a sufficiently high level of PUV to become competitive on the perceived use value axis of the customer matrix. This should aid the would-be multinational in its quest to achieve competitive advantage on an international scale.

The way for a firm without eclectic advantages to succeed in international trade is, of course, with a partner: to so configure and coordinate the joint value chain that it thereby gains competitive and comparative advantage. In Figure 14.5, the complementary value of

Figure 16.3
An adapted Porter diamond.

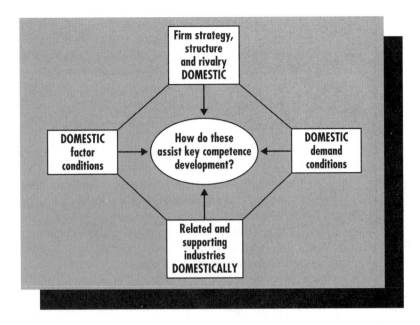

AT&T and Olivetti are shown to offer at least *prima facie* justification for a potential international strategic alliance between the companies.

The National Diamond

There are a number of influences in international trade that do not exist in a domestic market, and that will influence the position the company is able to achieve on its customer and producer matrices for foreign countries in which it wishes to operate. Porter, in *The Competitive Advantage of Nations* (1990) suggests that competitive advantage on a global scale requires more than just being a strong company. The probability of success is greatly enhanced if the company operates from a home base that is supported by a strong **national diamond**.

The national diamond is a concept intended to capture the key elements of a company's situation that influence its potential international strength (Figure 16.3).

Factor conditions refer to the availability in its domestic environment of the key factors of production required by the company. Porter emphasizes that the traditional basic factors of production, *i.e.*, land, labour and capital, are no longer sources of comparative advantage, since they are generally no longer fixed and immobile in an economy. Land itself may be fixed, but companies can buy land abroad in a world economy with decreasing capital flow restrictions. Labour, particularly skilled labour, is mobile, *e.g.*, the 'brain drain', and the exodus of Western engineers to build up the infrastructure of the Middle East oil states. Capital with an interlinked global banking system is also a global factor for the major firms.

However, within a country there are specialized advanced factors that do accord comparative and competitive advantage, some of which are less mobile than the traditional factors have become:

■ The level of managerial and technological human resources in the country, influencing its capacity for involvement in hi-tech and complex industries and products.

■ The knowledge resources in the country, exemplified by the number and quality of universities, graduates, and other knowledge based institutions, and by the sophistication of its governmental system and statistical and data collection services. The degree to which information technology is used in the country is also an important advanced factor for a would-be global company.

■ The strength of the country's currency on world markets, and the degree of development of its banking system.

■ The country's infrastructure,*i.e.,* its road and rail system, its health care, and generally the quality of life in the economy is important to the ability of a company to develop. When the infrastructure is good, it provides a sound basis for the developing company.

Post-war Japan was an unlikely candidate for international success if the traditional factors of production had still held the keys to success. It had very few natural resources, *e.g.*, minerals and oil, and its comparative advantages were difficult to identify. However, through human resources, infrastructure, financial systems and its growing knowledge base, it was able to drive itself to the forefront of global performers in the post-war world.

Demand conditions at home are also, perhaps paradoxically, an important factor in supporting the global development of a company. Thus:

■ A large and growing home demand provides a strong base for the firm, and if it proves necessary to accept lower profit margins in developing foreign sales, a strong national base makes it easier to do so. If demand has reached a plateau at home, and the industry shows signs of maturing, then this provides a strong incentive for the company to put a lot of effort behind opening up new foreign markets.

■ A strong domestic demand leads to the growth of a well-developed network of supplier industries, important to a company intent on producing complex multi-part products.

■ The effectiveness and efficiency of a company's operations are also stimulated by the existence of demanding customers in the home economy. If domestic buyers require high standards, the company will develop the systems and quality controls to provide them, and this will enhance its potential for success abroad.

■ Early demand for a product at home stimulates a manufacturing company to provide a steady stream of new products, helping the company to reach the forefront of its industry internationally, an important factor in aiding its foreign performance.

Firm strategy, structure and rivalry are also instrumental in assisting international development:

- Firms compete best where their industry structure fits their source of competitive advantage. Italian companies tend to succeed in entrepreneurial, fragmented, often family-owned industries. Their strategies are focused, niche orientated, and differentiated in industries that tend to lack obvious scale advantages.
- Strong domestic rivalry creates strong competitors able to compete in international markets through the pressure to improve and to innovate; note the strength of innovation in the electronics industry emerging from Japan.
- Many successful companies locate geographically near to close competitors, and the evident rivalry accentuates the stimulus towards excellence. The electronics dominated Route 128 in Boston exemplifies this, as does Silicon Valley in California, Silicon Glen in Scotland, and the Swindon M4 corridor in England.
- Evidence shows also that international success is stimulated by the rate of new business formation in the home country. It is possible that this is not a causal link, but both factors result from the existence of a dynamic home economy in which embryonic and growth industries predominate over mature and declining ones.

Related and supporting industries at home are also important to a company's potential international success:

- Strong supplier industries benefit the downstream industries. Illustrations of such situations are the *Keiretsu* supplier groups in Japan and the *Chaebols* in Korea, where the suppliers provide the brand-name producers with guaranteed, high quality supplies and components at an agreed price and just-in-time, to ensure super-efficient logistics, and hence reduced inventory costs.
- The existence of related industries also provides opportunities for beneficial value chain reconfiguration. The UK's traditional strength in engines has led to the beneficial development of the lubricants sector. Germany's strength in chemicals has supported the development of its printing-ink industry. Switzerland's strength in pharmaceuticals had led to it also becoming strong in food flavourings.
- This synergy between industries within countries and their inherent competitiveness, has also led to the development of clusters of world-class industries in particular countries, *e.g.*, electronics in Japan, printing in Germany, ceramic tiles, shoes and fashion clothing in Italy, automobiles in the US, and engineering in Sweden.

Whereas it is possible for a company operating within a weak national diamond to achieve international competitive advantage,

271

the task is far more difficult than for a company operating within a strong diamond.

We can relate Porter's diamond to our producer matrix (Chapter 3). If, as Porter argues, the four elements of the diamond help firms achieve success in competing globally, then, using our approach, these elements should assist the development of key competences (Figure 16.3). We can see that favourable factor conditions can make a direct contribution to competence development by providing the right cost and quality of skills and resources. Similarly, high performing related and supplying industries provide a richer pool of resources for the corporation to draw upon; relevant knowledge can be more readily transferred into the corporation. So, factor conditions and related and supporting industries can provide some of the means for competence development.

On the other hand, demanding customers and strong domestic competition provide the stimulus or motivation for competence development. A vigorous and sophisticated home demand, competitively served, will stimulate suppliers to outperform each other in terms of PUV and price. These competitive stimuli will help to ensure that motivator dimensions of value will become hygiene dimensions in this market first. Similarly, learning and scale advantages will accrue to firms in this market ahead of less stimulated markets. The combination of a strong stimulus to develop key competences coupled with the means to effect these developments results in these favourably situated firms taking a lead in a globalizing market.

CONTROLLING TO ACHIEVE COMPETITIVE ADVANTAGE INTERNATIONALLY

It is not just the configuration of the value chain that is the key to international competitiveness; it is also the way in which it is coordinated and controlled. This issue underlies a key part of the firm's global producer matrix and addresses the question of how to run a global enterprise.

Four possible configurations for dealing with the wider world are illustrated in the matrix shown in Figure 16.4. The differentiating axes measure firms vertically on the basis of the percentage of home-based production that is exported, and horizontally on the percentage of total sales that are produced abroad.

The medium-sized firm in the bottom left-hand box does not think of itself as an international company. It exports opportunistically. Domestic customers are its lifeblood, but it will sell abroad if approached by an international customer and, in times of recession, when overcapacity looms, it may actively solicit international sales to fill its factory. Generally, however, the export percentage of home-based production is low, as is its foreign production, if any, as a percentage of total sales.

Figure 16.4
Possible configurations for
dealing with the wider world.

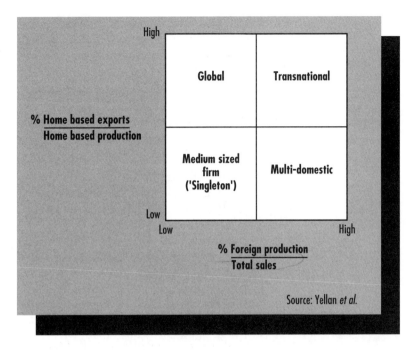

The global firm in the top right-hand box is similar to that implied in the Porter diamond described above. As Yetton, Davis and Craig (1995) put it:

> Porter's primary concern with the capacity of the US to compete with Japan leads to a preoccupation with the globally exporting firm, which is the principal form by which Japanese manufacturing firms have competed internationally. He focuses not on the complexity of international operations, but on the characteristics of the home base market as a platform for a successful export strategy. Consequently the 'Global' MNC is his primary interest.

In this model, the global corporation treats overseas operations as delivery pipelines to a unified global market. Most strategic decisions are centralized at the home country base, and there is even tight operational control from the centre. There is likely to be very little adaptation of products to meet local needs.

The classic global organization model was one of the earliest international corporate forms. It built global scale facilities to produce standard products, and shipped them worldwide. This model is based on the centralization of assets, with overseas demand operations used to achieve global scale in home based production.

The global corporation may have an international division in order to increase its foreign sales, but the international division is very much the poor relation of the domestic divisions, which are probably further subdivided into product group divisions. The company ships from its home base whenever possible, with very little regard for the differing tastes and preferences of the countries to

273

which it is exporting. This form of organization was typical of the Japanese exporting companies of the 1970s, and is still common in many current US corporations. The Spalding Sport Group is an example of this mode.

THE TRANSNATIONAL ENTERPRISE

Bartlett (1986) in *Competition in Global Industries* (Porter (ed.), 1986) and with Ghoshal (1989) in *Managing Across Borders* suggests, in the concept of the **transnational** enterprise, a modern form for the multinational corporation quite similar to a strategic alliance. It is located in the top right-hand box of the matrix. with a high percentage of home-based exports, but also a high percentage of foreign production. It is, however, not strongly directed from the home-base country. As Bartlett and Ghoshal (1989) put it:

> *Managers are being forced to shift their thinking from the traditional task of controlling a hierarchy to managing a network.*

The transnational organization seeks to overcome the weaknesses of more traditional models. To be globally competitive it must be locally responsive, see learning as a key requirement for success, and achieve optimal global scale and scope efficiencies. This can be done only by adopting new attitudes: knowledge must pass in all directions as appropriate; the firm should be truly global in mind-set and not be, say, a Japanese or US-based company with foreign subsidiaries. It may have three or more head offices (like NEC), as suggested by Nonaka (1989).

In Bartlett and Ghoshal's words, the transnational form recognizes three flows that have to be integrated:

> *First, the company has to coordinate the flow of parts, components, and finished goods. Second ,it must manage the flow of funds, skills, and other scarce resources among units. Third, it must link the flow of intelligence, ideas, and knowledge that are central to its innovation and learning capabilities.*

The transnational is, to date, more an aspirational form than an existing one although some organizations, *e.g.*, ABB or NEC are often quoted as examples. It is, however, the model upon which optimal coordination processes should be based to achieve global competitive advantage.

The transnational is characterized by the fact that it is a truly global enterprise, neither owned in one country, nor controlled from one unified corporate headquarters. To operate effectively it needs to control, globally, three distinct flows:
1. The flow of parts, components and goods.
2. The flow of funds, skills and scarce resources.
3. The flow of intelligence, ideas and knowledge, leading to innovation.

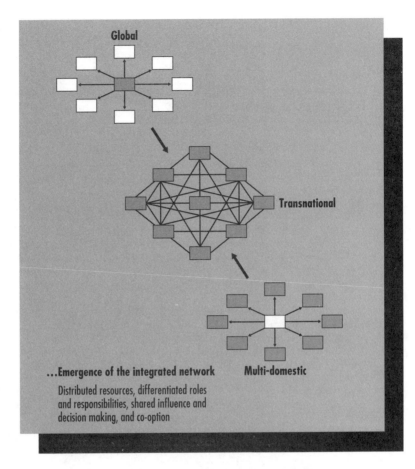

Figure 16.5
The transnational enterprise.

Global

Transnational

...Emergence of the integrated network   **Multi-domestic**

Distributed resources, differentiated roles
and responsibilities, shared influence and
decision making, and co-option

275

*Increasingly, the management of complexity, diversity, and change
is the central issue facing all companies.*
– Bartlett and Ghoshal (1989)

Figure 16.5 illustrates the position of the transnational. Thus, formal
organization charts are only one aspect of the glue that binds the
organization together. It is held together more strongly by the
managerial decision making process, which depends on the information flows. Bartlett and Ghoshal believe it is not a new organizational form that is needed to meet the needs of the future, but a new
philosophy that will achieve global competitive advantage, local
differentiation and global learning, by transforming the anatomy,
physiology and the psychology of the global enterprise.

Clearly, the transnational is a new and very much more sophisticated concept than earlier organizational forms of the international
enterprise. With its emphasis on a network philosophy and the
absence of domination by a home country based head office, the
philosophy can embrace equally well the enterprise based on a
network of alliances as it can the integrated corporation. It can be
seen for example in Fujitsu's approach to the development of the
global Fujitsu family of companies.

CAP GEMINI SOGETI: AN EXAMPLE OF A TRANSNATIONAL ORGANIZATION

Cap Gemini Sogeti (CGS) has grown since 1975 into Europe's No. 1 computer services and consulting company. It has developed by organic growth, by acquisition, and by alliance, and has an organizational structure that reflects the nature of its history, its varied requirements and tensions, and its aim to be a modern transnational company.

CGS grew from a merger of Cap, a computer services group, and Sogeti, a business management and information processing company. This brought it operations in the UK, the Netherlands, Switzerland and Germany, with a head office in France. It then acquired a large number of small groups in Europe, and some in the US. This expanded its role to IT consulting, customized software, and education and training. The acquisition of SESA in 1987 broadened its culture from its origins in computer 'body-shopping'. Its current mission is to assist clients to get the highest possible benefit from the opportunities afforded by state of the art information technology.

CGS is strongly decentralized, and when any of its branches reaches 150 personnel, it splits it in two. In response to the varieties of local demand, CGS has grown from a focused business to one offering a full range of computer services. These services are divided into four distinct businesses:

1. Facilities management, spearheaded by its acquisition, Hoskins, based in the UK.
2. Systems integration, which develops packages of hardware and software to meet the client's needs, e.g., it will automate a factory, or computerize an invoicing process.
3. IT consultancy, which was the original base of CGS.
4. Management consultancy, which is led by Gemini, created as a professionally-

independent group by bringing together three leading consultancy firms: the MAC Group, United Research and Gamma International. Gemini has been structured to be legally, organizationally, and culturally separate from CGS, although obviously part of the 'family'.

CGS has developed information-pooling systems so that innovative solutions developed in one country or business are rapidly communicated to the others. These include electronic bulletin boards, and extensive electronic- and voice-mail facilities, in addition to the informal networks developed through the enabling culture by committed professionals, working in frequently-reforming project teams.

A major part of CGS's growth strategy is to be present in more international markets. It has created an international support division to facilitate this process and to strengthen existing international operations.

In 1991 CGS developed an alliance with Mercedes Benz, in which the German company took a 34% holding in CGS for US$585 million, and includes a joint venture with Debis Systemhaus, Daimler's software company.

In 1992, CGS established a Benelux presence through an alliance with Volmac, and the creation of Cap Volmac, with 4,000 staff and annual turnover of about US$500 million.

For the fast-growing transnational, the challenges are to integrate the wide variety of organizations into a group, acknowledging a complex web of ownership relationships, whilst benefiting from the strengths of a 'family' of semi-autonomous professionals. The establishment of a common culture, the creation of effective cross-selling activities, and the leverage of the wide range of expertise to meet transnational needs all represent tasks of considerable magnitude and complexity.

Interestingly, a similar philosophy is emerging amongst strategic theorists in Japan. Nonaka and Yamanouchi (1989) in *Managing Innovation as a Self-Renewing Process* see information as the key to success. Information is of two types: syntactic, *i.e.*, bare data, and semantic, *i.e.*, information with meaning and concepts. The creation of meaning, *i.e.*, semantic information, is an inductive process and, to have a good chance of success, it needs to have considerable redundancy of information. Deductive management using syntactic information needs no redundancy of information, but it is basically uncreative.

> *Globalization comes about through the interaction of articulated globalized knowledge and tacit localized knowledge, partly through the hybridisation of personnel and consequent internalization of learning.* — Nonaka (1989)

Nonaka (1989) calls this **compressive management**, an interesting echo of Ansoff's (1990) **accordion management**, similarly devised to deal with the uncertainties of the modern turbulent environment.

This process can also lead quite acceptably to hybridization of the company's headquarters, with perhaps one headquarters in Japan, another in the US and maybe a third in Europe. As Contractor and Lorange (1988) point out:

> *One model of the MNC sees it as a closed, internalized, administrative system that straddles national boundaries. An alternative paradigm is to view the international firm as a member of various open and shifting coalitions, each with a specific strategic purpose.*

There is considerable congruity between the philosophical standpoints of Bartlett and Ghoshal, Contractor and Lorange, and of Nonaka in their rejection for the future of the rigid hierarchy of the traditional MNC, strongly controlled from its home base, even when allowing for local product variation. A world of sometimes shifting but continually renewing strategic alliances and even more informal networks fits well within this philosophy.

The **multi-domestic form** lies in the bottom right-hand box of the matrix. This form is sensitive to local needs, but may not always achieve possible production scale economies. Although the same company name may be used in all countries in which the firm operates, this may be all that is in common between the operations in those countries. The products are fashioned to meet local demand and to meet local tastes.

Although there is a risk that scale economies may not always be achieved, the multidomestic can provide an alternative effective form to the transnational if it concentrates on other scale and scope economies that are available to the large corporation. This involves the corporate centre playing a very positive value-adding role to ensure that best practice in one country is successfully transferred to the other countries in which the corporation operates.

To compete successfully in a multinational organizational form, the multi-domestic must, of course, excel in responding sensitively to local PUV needs. In addition, it operates best where the centre

277

is able to establish a degree of friendly competition between country units, where benchmarking is rigorously employed, and where process learning in one country is spread rapidly to the others.

Innovation must be similarly spread around the group with vigour, and Brownie points established for executives concerned to think beyond the confines of their own country SBU for the good of the corporation. The successful modern multi-domestic also has a centre which carries out its selection task carefully, only entering markets where there is a clear demand for its standard products. In the words of Yetton *et al.* (1995):

> *Successful multi-domestic corporations decouple the local, constrained product responsiveness from the global, integrated process and production platforms and manage them separately. In addition they minimize the risk by entering only friendly rather than relatively hostile markets, and outsourcing the local responsibilities to their local management.*

…which may be an acquisition by take-over or a joint venture partner.

Multi-domestic forms that sacrifice production economies of scale yet do not achieve economies of scope or of learning, innovation and process are, however, an endangered species. The Phillips Group was an example of such a company prior to its reorganization in 1986. Management at the centre regarded overseas operations as a portfolio of independent businesses, and the corporate centre did not add value as it was in the unique position to do.

SUMMARY

A corporation will adopt an international strategy if it believes that it can achieve a competitive position on the customer matrix and the producer matrix with any of its businesses in the country it decides to target. Use of the strategic objective/competitive advantage organizing framework will assist it to take strategic decisions on where to compete, *i.e.*, the selecting task. However, in order to arrive at such a conclusion in this area, the corporation will also need to consider more factors than it otherwise would if it restricted its aspirations to the domestic market, although it will still need to carry out the tasks of selecting, resourcing and controlling.

In relation to basic costs or potential costs, it will need to consider transport costs, including insurance, and the costs of hedging against the movement of exchange rates. In terms of its overall strength compared with local companies and other international companies operating in the target countries, it will need to evaluate the strength of the various components of its national diamond. Do these give it an advantage or put it at a disadvantage?

It then needs to consider how to configure its activities internationally. In order to do this, Dunning's eclectic theorem will assist in determining which activities should be carried out at home, and which on foreign soil.

Finally, in coordinating and controlling activities, it will need to consider the steps necessary to become a truly global corporation, achieving optimal levels of efficiencies, knowledge transfer and local product sensitivities, particularly in terms of product adaptation, and to review the practicalities and costs involved in such organizational adaptation. In this exercise there is no simple solution, although the transnational form and the modern process-integrated multi-domestic provide alternative solutions to the fundamental problem of optimizing global integration to achieve the optimal levels of scale and scope economies coupled with sensitive local responsiveness.

chapter 17

Summary
and Conclusions

In this closing chapter we summarize the main points of our argument. This summary follows closely the order of the chapters in the book, moving from business-level issues of competitive strategy through to corporate and international strategy. We then effect a substantial shift in our focus. We address the very real and practical concerns of an individual senior executive. Specifically, we ask the question: What factors lead an individual executive to behave strategically? We feel this is an appropriate point at which to leave the reader.

Having developed concepts and techniques to help in the strategic analysis of an organization, we finally turn our attention to the very personal questions of: 'Why should I bother to get out of my comfort zone, stick my head above the parapet and start doing strategic things? What's in it for me?'

But first, we try to summarize the essence of our approach.

BUSINESS LEVEL STRATEGY

To recap, our argument at business level revolved around some basic tenets:

- Value is defined by the customer.
- Total value (TV) is a product of perceived use value and the customer's willingness to pay. So, our definition of total value is: price + consumer surplus, for each customer.
- Total value is made up of two types of perceived use value: hygiene value and motivator value.
  Hygiene value refers to standard order qualifying product or service aspects that every firm has to provide just to be a credible player in the game. Motivator values excite customers, and are the sources of differentiation.
- Total value can only be increased by increasing motivator value. There is no point in increasing the level of qualities that are not order winning, *i.e.*, hygiene factors, as the customer expects those anyway, and only notices if they are absent.
- The power relationship between the firm and the customer determines who captures the larger share of total value.
- Motivator value migrates into hygiene value through competitive imitation.
- The firm's activities can be classified into those that deliver motivator value, and those that deliver hygiene value. Activities that deliver hygiene value dimensions should be

managed for lowest costs. Activities associated with the delivery of motivator value dimensions, both now and in the future, should be managed to maximize their effectiveness.

■ Normally, only motivator activities can generate profits above average.

Hygiene activities can, at best, only pass on their costs to the customer. Therefore, if there is a continuous process of use value migration from motivator value into hygiene value, firms will eventually cease to earn above-average profits unless they are able to create new motivator values. Thus, firms need to invest continually in motivator activities. This requires them being able to anticipate future perceived use values, and to manage the relevant activities to achieve excellence in differentiation.

So, our argument is a dynamic one. The process of motivator value migration through competitive imitation is continuous. No firms can have a sustainable competitive advantage in the long term, unless it is contained in the ability to learn faster than their competitors. Processes of competitive imitation and innovation determine the relative bargaining strength of firms and hence their relative performance.

We explained the two devices that are central to our arguments about competitive strategy: the customer matrix (Chapter 2) with its axes of perceived use value and perceived price, represents the customer's view; and the producer matrix, which refers to aspects of the firm's activities which are not directly visible to the customer, *i.e.,* unit cost and key competence endowment (Chapter 3). The producer matrix can be regarded as representing the means required to deliver the ends valued by the customer. For instance, in order to offer a superior product at a low price, the firm would need to be well endowed with the relevant key competences, and it needs to have low unit costs in relation to competitor firms. Key competences provide the link between the two matrices.

When considering the competitive structure of a market segment we identified two areas of critical importance:

1. What is the nature of the effective demand in the segment? What are the needs of customers? What is the volume of demand? Is demand growing or shrinking?

2. Competence imitability. How easy is it for firms to replicate the key competences required to meet the demand?

Demand strength and competence imitability affect the relative bargaining powers of customers and individual firms, which in turn affects who captures the lion's share of total value.

We then turned our attention to issues of organization and change. We subscribed to a contingency view which was set out as follows:

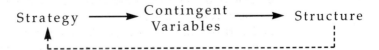

But we agree that the process is iterative and structure/culture constrains strategy. We suggested there was evidence of a new configuration of strategy and structure, the machine adhocracy. This structure enables a firm to gain the advantages of efficient product/ service delivery, at low cost and with high levels of conformance quality. This is a feature of the machine organization, without the stultifying and disabling inflexibility which so frequently accompanies the machine form. The machine adhocracy should deliver continual incremental improvements in the efficiency and effectiveness of the operating core. We described the critical role of the university, its research role, and its ability to facilitate learning within the operating core.

We explained how cultural processes can impede the process of adjustment and adaptation to a changing environment, and how an increasing lack of alignment between the organization and its environment can act as a trigger for change, forcing the top management explicitly to address the strategy and to set in motion actions to change the organization.

We argued that real strategic change can only be achieved through changes in cultural processes, and that such changes will have to be tackled on a broad front, in which the many interlocking dimensions of culture are addressed, *i.e.*, restructures, systems, symbols *etc.*.

A further implication was that, if implementation was attempted through existing structures and processes, the culture may too easily absorb, dilute and dissipate the intended strategy.

We argued that, when compared with the problems of building capabilities, draconian changes such as cuts are fairly straightforward to implement. And, of course, if cutting is easy to implement, it cannot be a source of competitive advantage, because it can be imitated.

CORPORATE LEVEL STRATEGY

We viewed corporate level strategy through our competitive strategy lens, thus addressing the question 'To what extent does being part of a corporation help a business to compete more effectively?'

The way in which the corporate centre seeks to do this is to carry out effectively three key tasks of selecting, resourcing and controlling. Selecting involves determining in which product/markets it should operate, such decisions to be based on the degree to which corporate wide and business unit competences match those required for success in particular markets. The resourcing task involves ensuring that the existing business units have appropriate means to do their job, and ensuring, through strategic alliances, mergers and acquisitions, that any perceived deficiencies in this regard are made good. Controlling involves setting up and operating a corporate structure and systems to avoid the development of internal inefficiencies in the corporation, and to ensure high levels of motivation and performance.

Above all, the corporate strategy needs to identify clearly how and where the corporate centre will add value, both by what it does well, and by how it is able to assist the business units to achieve a higher performance within the corporation than they could alone.

We explored how to identify corporate competences that will either help the SBU competences to become stronger, or deliver some value over and above the SBU competences but be of value to the corporation overall, or both. The corporate centre can provide value in its direct actions, over and above its primary tasks of selecting, resourcing, and controlling the SBUs. It can carry out activities relevant to the development of the corporation, but in addition to those concerned directly with competitive strategy.

So, the corporate centre can carry out two distinct functions: it can identify and develop the core competences that bind the business units together, and it can exercise certain competences directly itself.

The strategic-risk cube enables corporations to address the 'How?' of development. Should the firm grow incrementally, relying on its own resources, or should it form alliances or acquire? The selection task is also of concern to the corporation at the level of activities. Such questions as 'Should we do our own production, or focus solely on being a marketing company?' are not only of interest to the SBU. These issues were explored using arguments from transaction cost economics, *inter alia*.

We concluded that markets take place between companies as well as between individuals, and are to be found within companies, operating alongside hierarchically organized activities. Similarly, cooperative activities take place between companies, and within them, and even in cooperative alliances some activities are market based.

Further, the question of which activities the corporation should carry out itself, which it should buy-in, and which it should carry out with partners, addresses the fundamental corporate task in a central way. We have to address these questions before we can address the basic questions of resourcing, and control of those resources.

An acquisition strategy is generally pursued by companies in order to strengthen their chances of achieving sustainable competitive advantage, by providing them with a stronger producer matrix position in terms of both effectiveness and efficiency. When compared with the other 'How?' strategies, *i.e.*, internal development or strategic alliance, an acquisition strategy is a high risk one. To buy a company is always more expensive than to form an alliance with one, and a management selling its company has less incentive to be absolutely truthful in the negotiations than one attempting to set up an alliance. It also has less incentive to stay around and ensure the success of the joint endeavour after the deal has been concluded.

We pointed out that strategic alliances and other forms of cooperative strategy are now widely recognized as appropriate inter-organizational forms to meet certain environmental and internal firm conditions. They have distinctive characteristics, such as speed of creation, flexibility, opportunities for specialization, access to additional resources, and risk limitation that make them attractive when compared with the alternatives of internal development, acquisition, or market purchases.

The controlling function involves setting up and running a management system that will ensure resources are used to optimal effect. Whilst the multidivisional form of corporate organization structure has been widely adopted by major corporations, there are many variants on this form, developed to meet different circumstances and company philosophies. In this regard, we explored the three styles of strategic planning, strategic control and financial control.

We then shifted our focus to international issues. We suggested that the corporation will need to consider more factors than it would do if it restricted its aspirations to the domestic market, although it will still need to carry out the tasks of selecting, resourcing and controlling.

It will need to consider transport costs, including insurance, and the costs of hedging against the movement of exchange rates. In terms of its overall strength compared with local companies and other international companies operating in the target countries, it will need to evaluate the strength of the various components of its national diamond. Do these give it an advantage or put it at a disadvantage? It then needs to consider how to configure its activities internationally.

Finally, in coordinating and controlling activities, it will need to consider the steps necessary to become a truly global corporation, achieving optimal levels of efficiency, knowledge transfer and local product sensitivities, particularly in terms of product adaptation, and review the practicalities and costs involved in such organizational adaptation. In this exercise, there is no simple solution, although the transnational form and the modern process integrated multi-domestic provide alternative solutions to the fundamental problem of optimizing global integration to achieve the optimal levels of scale and scope economies coupled with sensitive local responsiveness.

We now shift our focus, and address the perspective of an individual senior executive.

BEHAVING STRATEGICALLY

Top management team (TMT) members have a responsibility for the strategic development of the organization. However, this responsibility is often not discharged as effectively as it might be, primarily because individual TMT members can lack the necessary strategic capabilities. If a TMT member feels uncomfortable in behaving in a truly strategic role, this can lead to him over-emphasizing the operational agenda. This can result in an unhelpful combination of executives, overloaded with urgent and important operational concerns, who also lack the capabilities to shed these agendas and to comfortably assume a strategic role.

Figure 17.1
A model of strategic
behaviour.

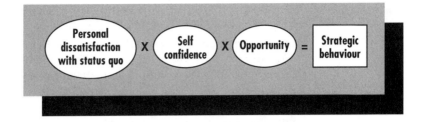

Figure 17.1 outlines a model of strategic behaviour. It is a development of the model of strategic change explained at the end of Chapter 9. However, whereas that model referred to groups and organizations, Figure 17.1 operates at the level of the individual executive. The model depicted here indicates that, before an individual executive will engage in purposeful strategic behaviour, three conditions have to be in place.

Personal Dissatisfaction

The argument is that individuals will not undertake behaviour that exposes them to personal risk unless they are sufficiently dissatisfied with their current situation. If they are quite comfortable with the way things are for them, then there is little incentive to try to change things. Personal goals and motives influence these feelings of comfort, *i.e.*, if I am driven to seek more powerful organizational positions, then I may be dissatisfied with my present circumstances.

Note that the model operates at the level of the individual. The organization may be in real difficulty, but if an individual executive is personally comfortable with his situation there is little impetus to change things. The individual manager would need to be aware of the organization's state, and the personal implications of this, before it would trigger a response.

285

Self-Confidence

In order to behave strategically, an individual needs the self-confidence to act in new ways, to experiment, and to take difficult and personally-risky decisions. Where does this confidence come from? Undoubtedly, the strongest factor is successful past experience. Individuals who have experienced significant change, who have successfully tackled difficult and challenging strategic assignments, grow in confidence. Self-confidence can be augmented through the development of strategic skills of analysis, debate, or influence, and knowledge of the situation facing the organization. The role of this book, then, is to augment the experience of senior managers, through knowledge and skill development, so that they can assume strategic roles with more confidence.

More specifically, strategic capabilities can be categorized into:
- **Content** capabilities.
- **Process** capabilities.

Content Capabilities

These refer to the skills and abilities to engage in a constructive debate about what the strategy of the organization should be. Generic capabilities would include skills in analysis and synthesis, a breadth of vision and the ability to exercise judgement and to simplify complexity. These skills can be enhanced where executives can master a range of tools, techniques and frameworks which assist strategic thinking. They should be able to frame their experiences and to be able to form novel insights into familiar industry phenomena with the appropriate use of models and metaphors.

Context specific competences include a deep insight into the industry, and an awareness of the particular trends and issues in the environment which will impact on the organization.

Process Competences

The most critical process competence is the willingness to assume a strategic role. This can be helped by developing the content competences. But, more typically, process competences address the personality and interpersonal capabilities of the executive. Process competences include: an emotional robustness and maturity; an ability to engage in constructive dialogue; to be able to manage debate that may well be personally challenging and uncomfortable; the ability to construct, communicate and enact a personal vision.

Although the process and content competences can be explored separately, the complete strategic executive clearly needs to possess both sets of competences. In practice, the two sets of competences are usually developed simultaneously.

Opportunity

An executive needs opportunities to behave strategically. Individuals buried in the ranks of middle management rarely have the chance to behave strategically. This can be an immense source of frustration, particularly where the manager feels that action needs to be taken, but feels powerless to influence events. Opportunities arise where the organization's situation combines with role discretion. Here, the extant circumstances in the organization permit those executives with the power and role discretion to undertake strategic initiatives.

Usually, the organizational situation that permits strategic behaviour is one of impending or actual crisis, but opportunities also arise in times of growth. Opportunities also arise where the individual can judge that there is a groundswell of support for change amongst his or her colleagues. The emergence of a critical mass in favour of challenging the *status quo* also boosts the self-confidence of the individual executive.

286

STRATEGIC ACTION

The model of strategic behaviour is multiplicative. This means that if any of the elements on the left of the arrow in Figure 17.1 are zero, then no distinct strategic behaviour takes place. So, for example, a manager may be personally dissatisfied with the *status quo*, and may have the opportunity in his current senior executive role to behave strategically, but lacks the confidence to take action outside of his narrow functional domain.

Alternatively, we have an individual recently returned to the company from an executive development program brimming with confidence, and desperate to flex his strategic muscles, but the opportunity never arises because his boss is fearful of change.

Similarly an executive may have the self confidence to act strategically and perceives the opportunity to do so, but if there is an insufficient level of dissatisfaction with the *status quo* and results are acceptable, complacency will rule and that opportunity will not be translated into change. This situation is very common among market leaders strong in a technology that is on the point of being replaced by a new one. IBM suffered from this syndrome when they convinced themselves that the future lay in mainframe computers largely because that was their historical area of strength.

This book has proposed a number of frameworks for ordering the messy facts and perceptions of business life in order to stimulate the insights necessary for strategic change. It has also no doubt made some simplistic behavioural observations that need to accompany the use of the frameworks if they are to be used successfully. Finally it has noted that, in the authors' experience, there are many more declarations of the intention to achieve strategic change than there are actual changes made. If this book can provide some impetus to narrowing the gap between intention and realization, it will have been well worth writing.

References

Amit, R. and Shoemaker, P .J. H. (1993) Strategic assets and organizational rents. *Strategic Management Journal*, **14**, 33–46.

Ansoff, H. I. (1965) *Corporate Strategy*, McGraw Hill, New York.

Ansoff, H. I. (1990) General management in turbulent environment. *Practising Manager*, **11** (1), 6–27.

Ash, D. (1983) Managing Strategic Change in a Hign-Technology Environment: The Case of Rank Xerox (UK). International Review of Strategic Management 4, 205–225.

Auster, E. R. (1987) International corporate linkages: dynamic forms in changing environments. *Columbia Journal of World Business*, **22** (2), 3–6.

Bain, J. (1956) *Barriers to New Competition*, Harvard University Press, Cambridge (MA).

Barney, J. B. (1991) Firm resources and sustained competitive advantage. *Journal of Management*, **17** (1), 99–120.

Bartlett, C. A. (1986) Competition in global industries, in Porter, M. (Ed.) *Competition in Global Industries*, Harvard University Press, Cambridge (MA).

Bartlett, C. A. and Ghoshal, S. (1989) *Managing Across Borders*, Hutchinson Business Books, London.

Beckhard, R. (1969) *Organization Development: Strategies and Models*, Addison-Wesley, Reading (MA).

Bleeke, J. and Ernst, D. (1995) Is your strategic alliance really a sale? *Harvard Business Review*, Jan/Feb, 97–105.

Boisot, M. (1995) Preparing for turbulence: the changing relationship between strategy and management development in the learning organization, in Garratt, R. (Ed.) *Developing Strategic Thinking*, McGraw Hill, Maidenhead.

Bowman, C. and Carter, S. (1995) Organising for competitive advantage, *European Management Journal*, **13** (4), 423–433.

Brandenburger, A. and Nalebuff, B. (1995) The right game: use game theory to shape strategy, *Harvard Business Review*, July/August, 57–71.

Buzzell, R. D. and Gale, B. T. (1987) *The PIMS Principle*, Free Press, New York.

Caves, R. E. (1980) Industrial organisation, corporate strategy and structure, *Journal of Economic Literature*, **18**, 64–92.

Caves, R. E. and Porter, M. (1977) From entry barriers to mobility barriers: conjectural decisions and contrived deterrence to new competition, *Quarterly Journal of Economics*, **91**, 241–262.

Chandler, A. D. (1962) *Strategy and Structure*, MIT Press, Cambridge (MA).

Child, J. (1972) Organization structure, environment and performance: the role of strategic choice, *Sociology*, **6**, 1–22.

Coase, R. H. (1937) The nature of the firm, *Economica*, 386–405.

Collis, D. K. and Montgomery, C. A. (1995a) Competing on resources. *Harvard Business Review*, July/August, 118–128.

Collis, D. K. and Montgomery, C. A. (1995b) *Corporate Strategy*. Notes prepared for class work at Harvard Business School.

Contractor, F. G. and Lorange, P. (Eds) (1988). *Cooperative Strategies in International Business*, Lexington Books, Boston (MA).

Cowling K *et al.* (1980) *Mergers and Economic Performance*, CUP, Cambridge.

Cyert, R. M. and March, J. G. (1959) A behavioural theory of organizational objectives, in M. Haire (Ed.), *Organization Theory*, Wiley, New York, 76–90.

Daniels, K., Johnson, G. and De Chernatony, L. (1994) Differences in management cognitions of competition, *British Journal of Management*, **5**, 21–29.

Drucker, P. F. (1980) *Managing in Turbulent Times*, Harper and Row, New York.

Dunning, J. H. (1974) *Economic Analysis and the Multinational Enterprise*, Allen and Unwin, London.

Emery, F. E. and Trist, E. L. (1965) The causal texture of organizational environments, *Human Relations*, **18**, 21–32.

Fama, E. (1980) Agency problems and the theory of the firm. *Journal of Political Economy*, **88**, 288–307.

Faulkner, D. (1994) *International Strategic Alliances*, McGraw Hill, London.

Galbraith, J. R. and Kazanjian, R. K. (1986). *Strategy Implementation: Structure, Systems and Process*, St. Paul (Minnesota).

Ghoshal, S. (1987) Global strategy: an organizing framework, *Strategic Management Journal*, **8**, 425–440.

Goold, M. and Campbell, A. (1987) *Strategies and Styles*, Blackwell, Oxford.

Goold, M. and Campbell, A. (1991) From corporate strategy to parenting advantage, *Long Range Planning*, **24** (1), 115–117.

Grant, R. M. (1991) The resource-based theory of competitive advantage: implications for strategy formulation, *California Management Review*, **33** (3), 114–135.

Hamel, G. and Prahalad, C. K. (1994) *Competing for the Future*, Harvard Business School Press, Boston (MA).

Handy, C. (1989) *The Age of Unreason*, Business Books, London.

Hannan, M.T. and Freeman, J. (1977) The population ecology of organisations, *American Journal of Sociology*, **82** (5), 929–963.

Heisenberg, W. (1971). *Physics and Beyond*, Harper and Row, London.

Jaques, E. (1951). *Changing Culture of the Factory*, Tavistoke Publications.

Jensen, M. C. (1983) Organization theory and methodology, *Accounting Review*, **56**, 319–338.

Jensen, M. C. (1989) The eclipse of the public corporation, *Harvard Business Review*, September/October, 61–74.

Jensen, M. and Roebach, R. (1983) The market for corporate control: empirical evidence, *Journal of Financial Economics*, **11**, 5–50.

Johnson, G. (1987) *Strategic Change and the Management Process*, Basil Blackwell, Oxford.

Johnson, G. and Scholes, K. (1993). *Exploring Corporate Strategy*, Prentice-Hall, London.

Levitt, T. (1969) *The Marketing Mode: Pathways to Corporate Growth*, McGraw-Hill, New York.

Lorsch, J. and Allen, S. (1973) Managing diversity and interdependence, Division of Research, Harvard Business School, Boston.

Mason, E. S. (1957) *Economic Concentration and the Monopoly Problem*, Harvard University Press, Cambridge (MA).

Metcalfe, J. L. (1974) Systems models, economic models and the causal texture of organizational environments: an approach to macro-organization theory, *Human Relations*, **27** (7), 639–663.

Milgrom, P. and Roberts, J. (1992) *Economics, Organization and Management*, Prentice-Hall, Englewood Cliffs (NJ).

Miles, R. E. and Snow, C. C. (1986) Organizations: new concepts for new forms, *California Management Review*, **28** (3), 62–73.

Miller, D. (1986) Configurations of strategy amd structure: towards a synthesis, *Strategic Management Journal*, **7**, 233–249.

Miller, D. (1990) Organizational configurations: cohesion, change, and prediction, *Human Relations*, **43** (8), 771–789.

Miller, D. and Friesen, P. H. (1980) Momentum and revolution in organizational adaptation, *Academy of Management Journal*, **7**, 233–249.

Mintzberg, H. (1973) *The Nature of Managerial Work*, Harper and Row, New York.

289

Mintzberg, H. (1979) *The Structuring of Organizations*, Prentice Hall, Englewood Cliffs (NJ).

Mintzberg, H. (1983) *Structures in Fives: Designing Effective Organizations*, Prentice Hall, New Jersey.

Mintzberg, H. (1989) *On Management*, Free Press, New York.

Mintzberg, H. and Waters, J. A. (1982) Tracking strategies in an entrepreneurial firm, *Academy of Management Journal*, **25** (3), 465–499.

Nonaka, I. (1989) Toward middle-up-down management: accelerating information. Paper presented at Oxford International Strategy Colloquium, May 4.

Nonaka, I. and Yamanouchi, T. (1989) Managing innovation as a self-renewing process. *Journal of Business Venturing*, **4**(5), 299–315.

Nelson, R. R. and Winter, S. G. (1982) *An Evolutionary Theory of Economic Change*, The Belknap Press, Cambridge (MA).

Ohmae, K. (1985) *Triad Power: The Coming Shape of Global Competition*, Free Press, New York.

Ohmae, K. (1989) The global logic of strategic alliances, *Harvard Business Review*, March/April, 143–154.

Pellegrinelli, S. and Bowman, C. (1993) Implementing strategy through project. *Long-Range Planning*, **27**(4), 125–132.

Peteraf, M.A. (1993) The cornerstone of competitive advantage: a resource-based view, *Strategic Management Journal*, **14**, 179–191.

Peters, T. J. and Waterman, R. H. (1982) *In Search of Excellence*, Harper and Row, New York.

Peters, T. J. (1988) *Thriving on Chaos: Handbook for a Management Revolution*, MacMillan, London.

Pfeffer, J. and Salancik, G. R. (1978) *The External Control of Organizations: A Resource Dependence Perspective*, Haper and Row, New York.

Polanyi, M. (1958) *Personal Knowledge: Towards a Post-Critical Philosophy*, Routledge and Kegan Paul, London.

Polanyi, M. (1966) *The Tacit Dimension*, Doubleday & Co., New York.

Porter, M. (1987) From competitive advantage to corporate strategy, *Harvard Business Review*, May/June, 43–59.

Porter, M. E. (1980) *Competitive Strategy: Techniques for Analysing Industries and Competitors*, Free Press, New York.

Porter, M. E. (1985) *Competitive Advantage: Creating and Sustaining Superior Performance*, Free Press, New York.

Porter, M. E. (1991) *The Competitive Advantage of Nations*, Free Press, New York.

Prahalad, C. K. and Hamel, G. (1990) The core competence of the corporation. *Harvard Business Review*, May/June, 79–91.

Ruelle, D. (1991) *Chance and Chaos*, Penguin Books, London.

Rugman, A. M. (1985) *International Business: The Firm and the Environment*, McGraw Hill, New York.

Rumelt, R. (1984) Toward a strategic theory of the firm, in Lamb, R. (Ed.), *Competitive Strategic Management*, Ballinger, Cambridge (MA), 137–158.

Rumelt, R. (1987) Theory, strategy and entrepreneurship, in Teece, D. J. (Ed.), *The Competitive Challenge*, Ballinger Publishing Company, Cambridge (MA), 137–158.

Rumelt, R. (1996) Paper presented to the Conference on Firm Capabilities and Business Strategy, London School of Economics, January 10.

Scherer, F. M. (1980) *Industrial Market and Economic Performance*, Rand McNally, Chicago.

Simon, H. A. (1957) *Administrative Behavior*, MacMillan, New York.

Smircich, L. and Stubbart, C. (1985) Strategic management in the enacted world, *Academy of Management Review*, **10** (4), 724–736.

Stacey, R. (1993) Strategy as emerging from chaos, *Long Range Planning*, **26** (1), 10–17.

Stopford, J. M. and Wells, L. T. (1972) *Managing the Multinational Enterprise: Organization of the Firm and Ownership of the Subsidiaries*, Longman, Harlow.

Terreberry, S. (1968) The evolution of organizational environments, *Administrative Science Quarterly*, **12**, 590–613.

Tirole, J. (1988) *The Theory of Industrial Organization*, MIT Press, Cambridge (MA).

Tushman, M. and Lomanelli, E. (1985) Organizational evolution: a metamorphosis model of convergence and reorientation. *Research in Organizational Behaviour*, **7**, 131–222.

Wernerfelt, B. (1984) A resource-based view of the firm, *Strategic Management Journal*, **5**, 171–180.

Wernerfelt, B. and Montgomery, C. A. (1986) What is an attractive industry? *Management Science*, **32**, 1223–1229.

Williamson, O. E. (1975) *Markets and Hierarchies: Analysis and Antitrust Implications*, Free Press, New York.

Williamson, O. E. (1985) *Economic Institutions of Capitalism*, Free Press, New York.

Yetton, P., Davis, J. and Craif, J. (1995) Redefining the multidomestic: a new ideal type MNC. Working Paper 95–106, AGSM, New South Wales, Sydney.

Subject Index

292

293

Name Index

Amit, R. and P. J. H. Shoemaker 33
Ansoff, H. I. 201, 276
Asch, D. 156
Auster, E. R. 97

Bain, J. 31, 81
Barney, J. B. 3, 31
Bartlett, C. A. 274
Bartlett, C. A. and S. Ghoshal 274, 275, 277
Beckhard, R. 177
Bleeke, J. and D. Ernst 247
Boisot, M. 98
Bowman, C. and S. Carter 131
Brandenburger, A. and B. Nalebuff 24, 31, 115
Buzzell, R. D. and B. T. Gale 32, 89, 187

Caves, R. E. 3
Caves, R. E. and M. Porter 3
Chandler, A. D. 218, 257
Child, J. 209
Coase, R. H. 208
Collis, D. K. and C. A. Montgomery 179, 191, 258, 259
Contractor, F. G. and P. Lorange 276, 277
Cowling, K. 225
Cyert, R. M. and J. G. March 96

Daniels, K., G. Johnson and L. De Chernatony 92
Drucker, P. F. 96, 97
Dunning, J. H. 267, 268

Emery, F. E. and E. L. Trist 95

Fama, E. 222
Faulkner, D. 244, 246, 247

Galbraith, J. R. and R. K. Kazanjian 116
Ghoshal, S. 263
Goold, M. and Campbell, A. 180, 251, 256, 257, 259
Grant, R. M. 32, 45, 47

Hamel, G. and C. K. Prahalad 73
Handy, C. 255
Hannan, M.T. and J. Freeman 214
Heisenberg, W. 98

Jaques, E. 139
Jensen, M. C. 222, 259
Jensen, M. and R. Roebach 220
Johnson, G. 148, 157
Johnson, G. and K. Scholes 205

Levitt, T. 235 263, 265
Lorsch, J. and S. Allen 257

Mason, E. S. 32, 81
Metcalfe, J. L. 96
Milgrom, P. and J. Roberts 225
Miles, R. E. and C. C. Snow 116
Miller, D. 122, 129, 144
Miller, D. and P. H. Friesen 156
Mintzberg, H. 8, 99, 116-117, 118, 121, 122, 126, 129, 131, 132, 136, 137, 144
Mintzberg, H. and Waters, J. A. 156

Nonaka I. 274, 276, 277
Nonaka I. and Yamanouchi, W. 276
Nelson, R. R. and S. G. Winter 52

Ohmae, K. 235, 263

Pellegrinelli, S. and C. Bowman 172
Peteraf, M.A. 31
Peters, T. J. and R. H. Waterman 73, 144
Peters, T. J. 130
Pfeffer, J. and G. R. Salancik 236
Polanyi, M. 52
Porter, M. 3, 31, 32, 39, 81, 83, 84, 129, 131, 187, 188, 193, 221, 222, 226, 238, 269 272–274
Prahalad, C. K. and G. Hamel 32

Ruelle, D. 98
Rugman, A. M. 268
Rumelt, R. 32, 69, 70, 81, 225, 226

Scherer, F. M. 32, 81
Simon, H. A. 34
Smircich, L. and Stubbart, C. 150
Stacey, R. 98
Stopford, J. M. and L. T. Wells 267

Terreberry, S. 95, 96
Tirole, J. 32
Tushmann, M. 156

Wernerfelt, B. 3, 32
Wernerfelt, B. and C. A. Montgomery 225
Williamson, O. E. 34, 208

Yetton, P., J. Davis and J. Craig 273, 278

295

Company Index